ISBN: 9781313052450

Published by:
HardPress Publishing
8345 NW 66TH ST #2561
MIAMI FL 33166-2626

Email: info@hardpress.net
Web: http://www.hardpress.net

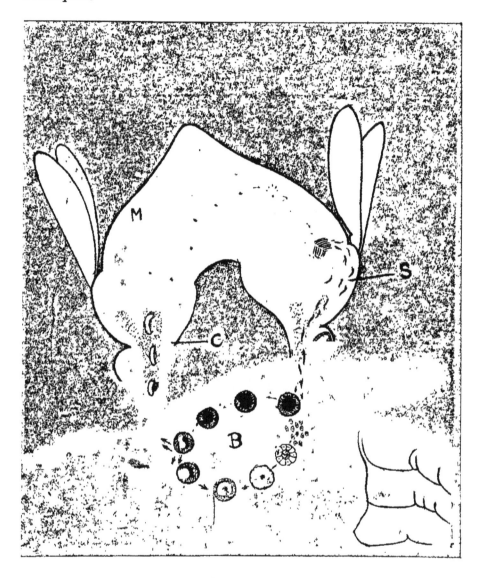

Diagram showing the two ways in which the malaria parasite multiplies.—B shows the asexual cycle in the blood-corpuscles of man. On the left side are shown crescents (at C) being sucked by a mosquito. These develop into male and female (at M) in the mosquito's stomach (shaded black). The fertilised female encysts on the stomach wall, and from her burst forth a family of young parasites (at S) which settle in the mosquito's salivary gland (shown by the large arrow). If the mosquito now bites someone else these young parasites injected with the saliva infect the blood corpuscles of the person bitten. Here they grow, and while some pursue the cycle B, some may become crescents and be sucked up by another mosquito, to go through the sexual cycle in its body.—(From *Indian Insect Life* by kind permission of Mr. Maxwell Lefroy.)

TROPICAL HYGIENE

FOR RESIDENTS IN TROPICAL AND SUB-TROPICAL CLIMATES

BY

THE HON'BLE

SURGEON-GENERAL SIR PARDEY LUKIS

K.C.S.I., V.D

Hon. Surgeon to His Majesty the King-Emperor ; Knight of Grace of the Order of St. John ; Director-General of the Indian Medical Service ; Fellow of the Calcutta University

AND

LT.-COLONEL R. J. BLACKHAM, C.I.E., R.A.M.C

Hon. Surgeon to His Excellency the Viceroy ; Knight of Grace of the Order of St. John ; Barrister-at-Law ; Kaiser-i-Hind Medallist

THIRD EDITION
(Revised and Enlarged)

CALCUTTA AND SIMLA :—THACKER, SPINK AND CO

LONDON :—W. THACKER AND CO., 2, CREED LANE

1915

LL.

CALCUTTA :

PRINTED BY THACKER, SPINK AND CO

PREFACE TO THE THIRD EDITION.

Owing to the very favourable reception which has been accorded to this book, and to the fact that the Indian Council of the St. John Ambulance Association have distributed a considerable number of copies to officers of the Territorial units now serving in India, the second edition has been exhausted in less than a year. The present edition has been carefully revised, enlarged, and brought up-to-date. Amongst the various additions, we may mention a full description of " Hookworm Disease and its Prevention," a dissertation on " Goats' Milk and Malta Fever " as well as two entirely new Chapters, one dealing with the Sanitation of Camps and the other with Hydrophobia in the Tropics. The authors sincerely hope that, like its predecessors, this edition may be found useful not only to students of Elementary Hygiene but to junior practitioners and students of Medicine.

CONTENTS.

TROPICAL HYGIENE.

CHAPTER I.

THE COMMUNICABLE DISEASES OF THE TROPICS.

" When man learnt how to protect himself from wild beasts he made the first step in civilisation. To-day man is learning how to protect himself against microbes—it is a step of equal importance. A day will come when in Berlin, in London, and in Paris a man will not die of Diphtheria, of Typhoid, of Scarlet Fever, of Cholera, of Tuberculosis, any more than he does in these cities to-day from the venom of snakes or the teeth of wolves."—Frankland's " Pasteur," p. 129.

SANITATION has been defined as a science which has for its object to make growth more perfect, decay less rapid, life more vigorous, and death more remote.

The climate of India, during the hot weather months and the rainy season, undoubtedly causes discomfort to Europeans, but, with ordinary care, there is no reason why they should not enjoy as good health in India as they could reasonably expect to secure in England ; on the other hand, many a valuable life has been thrown away owing to the neglect of a few simple precautions, the necessity for which is only learned by bitter experience.

The object of this book is to point out the chief dangers to which residents in India are exposed, and the best way of avoiding them. In India, even more than elsewhere, it is especially true that " prevention is better than cure." It is comparatively easy to prevent disease, but it is by no means so easy to cure it, once it has supervened.

At one time it was thought that the prevention of disease was merely a matter for the doctors and did not concern the layman, but this view is surely not tenable in these days when it is recognised that the preservation of health is a personal and not a purely medical matter. It is the duty of the priest to preach the doctrine of his special faith, but the salvation of the individual must depend on his personal exertions. Moreover, it is clearly the duty of the individual not only to take care of his own health, but to see that his neighbours also look after theirs. In this relation, a general officer with wide Indian experience, Sir R. C. Hart, v.c., very truly says " even an elementary knowledge of sanitation saves many lives and much suffering. People contract sickness, frequently with fatal results, as a consequence of the ignorance and carelessness of their neighbours : it is therefore the duty of every individual in the community to pay strict attention to the simple rules of health."

This is specially necessary in the tropics, where houses are frequently crowded together in a way almost unknown in the West, with the result that if one person is seized with an infectious disease, it is likely to be communicated rapidly to his neighbours. The crowding together of houses is also apt to lead to a general deterioration of the health of the inhabitants, and thus render them more liable to contract disease.

The causes of sickness in the tropics may be divided up under five heads :—

(1) Infection by various microbes and parasites.
(2) Improper exposure to the sun's rays.
(3) Chill.
(4) Indiscretions in eating and drinking.
(5) Excessive and violent exercise.

Of these five causes, the first is by far the most important, for, as Sir Patrick Manson has recently shown, more than nine-tenths of all tropical diseases are the result of infection by microbes and parasites. These cause what are known as the *communicable diseases*, *i.e.*, diseases which can be communicated or conveyed by one person to another.

The germs of disease may be introduced into the human body in various ways, the chief of which are :—

(1) By *contagion*, *i.e.*, by direct contact with an infected person.

(2) By *inhalation*, as from the breath of patients suffering from tuberculosis, whooping-cough or diphtheria.

(3) As the result of *inoculation* by biting insects, such as mosquitoes, midges, fleas, etc.

(4) By the *ingestion* of food or water contaminated by (a) flies, (b) dust, (c) discharges from the sick, (d) dirty hands.

In all communicable diseases, therefore, it must be remembered that the actual exciting cause is always the introduction into the human body of some germ or microbe in one or other of the ways just mentioned. But the mere introduction into the body of germs is not sufficient to set up disease. The reader is doubtless aware that, in the production of disease, two factors require consideration :—

(1) The introduction of the germ.

(2) The power of the human body to destroy it.

Germs exist everywhere around us, and all of us take numbers of them into our bodies every day, but, normally, these germs are quickly destroyed, chiefly by the white corpuscles of the blood, and no

evil results accrue. But if there be any lowering of
the vitality of the individual, these germs are
enabled to obtain a footing in the body where they
grow and multiply with marvellous rapidity and
disease is the result. This may be put into simple
language by saying that persons who are run
down in health are very liable to " catch " any
disease that may be prevalent at the time.

Anything therefore which causes deterioration in
health is said to be a " predisposing cause " of
communicable diseases. These predisposing causes
are :—

(1) Impure air.
(2) Impure water.
(3) Uncleanliness of the household.
(4) Pollution of the soil round the house.
(5) Errors in diet.
(6) Fatigue and exposure.

All these predisposing causes will be referred to
in detail in subsequent chapters, and we will now
consider the most important communicable tropical
diseases. These are malaria, cholera, dysentery,
small-pox, plague, and tuberculosis.

Malaria is such an all-important disease in the
tropics generally, and in India in particular, that a
chapter is devoted to it alone.

In the following brief notes our object is to bring
out the means of prevention. With treatment and
details of diagnosis the student has no concern.
These are matters for the consideration of the
medical attendants.

CHOLERA.

Cholera is one of the most dreaded of tropical
ailments, but its incidence in India varies greatly,
as may be gathered from the fact that in the year

1906 it accounted for more deaths than small-pox, plague, dysentery, and diarrhœa collectively, whilst in 1907, plague in its turn produced a bigger death-roll than cholera, small-pox, dysentery and diarrhœa put together.

There is nothing mysterious about cholera. It is easily recognised by the fact that the patient passes copious colourless stools which look like the water in which rice has been boiled. It is an infectious disease, the outcome of filth and filthy habits, and easily preventable by a due recognition of this fact. The disease is caused by a minute germ which is taken into the system usually in water, but often in contaminated milk or other food. Hitherto it has been supposed that it not only lives but multiplies with amazing rapidity in water, especially if it be muddy, but recent researches by Greig go to prove that the life of the cholera microbe outside the body is of comparatively short duration, and that, on the other hand, as in the case of enteric fever, apparently healthy people may discharge the germ from their bowels for long periods after their recovery from the disease. The habit of the natives of India of frequenting tanks and river banks in order to obtain water for washing their person after going to stool is responsible for the contamination of water with the microbes, and the subsequent dissemination of the disease. The germs may pass directly into food through careless handling of plates and dishes by native servants with unwashed hands. They may also be conveyed by flies. In all tropical communities where a safe water-supply has been provided and efficiently guarded against pollution, the disease has been practically stamped out, but recent observations have shown the importance of protection of food-supplies from contamination.

To recapitulate, therefore, the essential measures for protection against this, the most dreaded and the most easily preventable of all tropical diseases, are :—

(1) Pure water.
(2) Clean food.
(3) Efficient conservancy and disinfection of the stools.
(4) Personal cleanliness.
(5) Isolation of the sick.
(6) Careful disinfection of all clothing or other articles which have come into contact with a sick person.
(7) Banishment of flies.
(8) Clean houses and clean surroundings.

The provision of a pure water-supply and its protection from pollution form the subject of the fourth chapter, but it is necessary here to draw attention to the value of Permanganate of Potash as a means of rendering safe all suspicious sources of water-supply, especially wells. Practical experience in recent cholera epidemics has confirmed the value of this method, and the rule to be adopted is to add sufficient permanganate to make the water in the well distinctly red, so that it does not recover its normal colour for eight hours. If this is done in the evening, the water is ready for use the next morning.

As regards the protection of food, there are four points that require careful attention at all times, but especially during a cholera epidemic—

(1) Make your servants thoroughly wash and disinfect their hands with Condy's fluid before allowing them to touch your plates and dishes. This is particularly important in connection with what has been pointed out above, as regards the carrying of the disease by apparently healthy persons.
(2) Pay especial attention to the cleanliness of your pantry and prevent the *masalchie*

from cleaning the plates, etc., with the horrible swab tied on to a stick which is in use in so many households.

(3) Cover all food, milk, etc., so as to prevent flies from settling on it.

(4) Regard with suspicion all watercress, salads, and raw fruits, especially cucumbers, strawberries, and melons, which are grown on manured ground.

The comma bacillus has one remarkable peculiarity, which is of great importance. Notwithstanding the fact that it will grow and multiply very rapidly in muddy water, it dies almost immediately in any fluid that has an acid reaction.

Normally the contents of the human stomach are acid on account of the presence of the gastric juice. It follows therefore that, even if cholera germs are introduced into the stomach of a perfectly healthy person, they are usually killed right off. If however that person be suffering from dyspepsia and his stomach is full of alkaline mucus instead of acid gastric juice, or if he be suffering from diarrhœa and the cholera germs are hurried on into the intestine before the gastric juice has a chance of acting upon them, they are not killed, but grow and multiply, and an attack of cholera is the result. From our knowledge of this property of the cholera germ we are able to deduce *three very important rules* which should *always be observed when cholera is prevalent.*

(1) Never eat rich or indigestible food, which may set up dyspepsia, and avoid all unripe or over-ripe fruit which is likely to cause diarrhœa.

(2) Never allow diarrhœa to run on unchecked.

(3) Never take purgatives, especially salines such as Sulphate of Magnesia, Seidlitz Powders or Eno's Fruit Salt.

When a case of cholera occurs in a house, the following precautions are necessary :—

(1) Isolate the patient, and set apart particular utensils for his special use.

(2) Carefully disinfect all clothing or other articles and utensils which have come in contact with the sick person.

(3) Carefully wash and disinfect your own hands after touching the patient, especially before meals, and never partake of any food in the sick room.

(4) Prevent flies from settling upon either the patient or any of the discharges from his body, or soiled linen.

(5) Carefully disinfect all stools and vomit, and then dispose of them either by burning or by burying them in some suitable spot where they cannot contaminate the water-supply. They must never be disposed of by throwing them on the ground, where they will quickly dry and pass into the air as infected dust.

DYSENTERY AND DIARRHŒA.

It is now well recognised that there are many types of diarrhœa, and *at least* two different kinds of dysentery, but two points require to be emphasised which are very little understood by the laity, namely, that dysentery is an infectious disease and that diarrhœa, if allowed to run on, may develop into cholera.

Diarrhœa.—The chief predisposing causes of diarrhœa are :—

(1) Chills.
(2) Overcrowding.
(3) Dirty surroundings.
(4) Bad and ill-cooked food.

The disease may be caused directly by foul water. This is due to the presence in the intestines of all animals of germs which have the power of setting up irritation of the bowels, the chief symptoms of which are diarrhœa and colic.

Water from the vicinity of a burial-ground and which contains a large amount of vegetable or mineral material is always harmful, and "brackish" water, that is water containing salt, is also very likely to cause diarrhœa.

Besides predisposing to the condition, ill-cooked and badly-masticated food, or unripe or decaying fruit, may be the direct causes of an outbreak of diarrhœa.

Flies play a most important part in the transmission of this and other diseases, as will be shown in Chapter IX.

Dysentery.—Dysentery is a highly dangerous disease caused by microscopic parasites. It is recognised by the fact that the patient passes, with great straining, stools consisting chiefly of blood and slime.

It is now well known that there are two distinct varieties of the disease. One is due to a minute animal, whereas the other is due to bacteria or vegetable fungi.

Both varieties of the disease are characterised by the presence of ulcers or sores in the intestine.

The type due to bacteria is usually acute in character and is the form which is rapidly fatal.

The form due to the minute animal usually takes on a chronic character. It is, moreover, the kind of dysentery which is followed by most dangerous consequences. The Amœba, as the minute animal is called, finds its way to the liver and causes destruction of portions of it ; pus or matter forms, and what is known as abscess of the liver results ; a condition which is highly dangerous to life.

In order to escape from dysentery, it is necessary to observe the following rules :—

(1) Avoid chills and especially avoid wearing wet clothes.

(2) Always wear a cholera belt at night especially when sleeping under a punkah.

(3) Avoid overcrowding, *i.e.*, breathe pure air.

(4) Eat only well-cooked and sound food.

(5) Avoid salt meat, tinned foods, coarse atta, and raw corn.

(6) Drink only pure water. If in doubt as to its purity, boil it.

(7) Disinfect everything that passes from a sick person and either bury or burn it. Never throw dysenteric stools on to the ground.

(8) Disinfect by boiling all bedding and clothing which has been used by a patient.

(9) Never eat in the room with a person suffering from this disease.

(10) Always wash the hands after attending to your patient, especially before eating.

(11) Thoroughly lime-wash or " leep " with cowdung any room in which a person has been sick or died of this disease.

(12) Keep your house and its surroundings clean and free from flies.

If you observe these rules, you or yours will never suffer from dysentery.

PLAGUE.

This disease occupies so prominent a position in the public mind and so many erroneous impressions prevail with regard to it that it requires special consideration.

Bubonic plague was epidemic throughout Europe during the Middle Ages. In England during the fourteenth century it appeared as the Black Death,. and in the seventeenth century as the Great Plague of London, while numerous other lesser visitations have been recorded.

It seems to have been almost always present in Persia and Syria, whilst at the present time it is spread over the entire surface of the globe.

The disease from time to time completely disappears from a district which it has decimated to reappear again after a considerable interval. This has happened not only in India, but in Persia,. Syria, China, and even in Europe.

It is a disease characterised by :—

(1) High Fever.
(2) Delirium.
(3) Great Depression.
(4) Collapse.

If the patient lives, bleeding may occur underneath the skin, forming the so-called plague rashes.

In about 80 per cent. of cases enlarged glands appear, on the second or third day, in the armpit or groin. These constitute the buboes from which the disease derives its name.

In a small percentage of cases the lungs are affected and the disease is almost indistinguishable from ordinary pneumonia. In a still smaller percentage the disease takes the form of acute blood-poisoning.

The disease is caused by a bacillus, *i.e.*, a minute fungus, discovered by a Japanese doctor in 1894. It is an extremely delicate organism, and can have no existence in nature outside an animal body.

It is an old observation that plague epidemic amongst human beings is invariably preceded by a serious mortality amongst the rats. After the discovery of the plague bacillus the rat disease was soon shown to be true plague.

The relationship between the rat and plague has recently been carefully studied in various parts of the world, especially by the present Plague Commission at Bombay and in two villages in the Punjab.

What has been the result of this study ?

The conclusions arrived at are admirably summed up by Major Lamb, I.M.S., a member of the Advisory Committee for Plague Investigation in India, in a paper read before the Bombay Medical Congress in 1909, as follows :—

(1) Bubonic plague in man is entirely dependent on the disease in the rat.

(2) The infection is conveyed from rat to rat and from rat to man solely by means of the rat-flea.

(3) A case of bubonic plague in man is not in itself infectious.

(4) Insanitary conditions have no relation to the occurrence of plague, except in so far as they favour infestation by rats.

(5) Plague is usually conveyed from place to place by imported rat-fleas, which are carried by people on their persons or in their baggage. The human agent himself frequently escapes infection.

When a human being contracts plague, what usually happens is this. The rats in the house first contract the disease. Then, when they begin to die of it, the remainder, as is their custom, at once desert the infected house, but they leave behind them their nests which are full of rat-fleas. These fleas contain plague bacilli owing to their having sucked the blood of infected rats. Presently they become hungry, and finding no rats to feed on, they sally out and bite the inhabitants of the house, and thus infect them with plague.

From the above we learn two very important lessons. The first is that a plague patient is not infectious and that there is no need for being afraid of going near him. The second is that the whole question of the prevention of plague is one of domestic hygiene. What is required is to teach the public that they should not allow in their houses collections of rubbish behind which rats can build their nests—neither should they throw about in the vicinity of their houses remnants of food which will attract rats. In fact, every precaution should be taken to prevent the rat from becoming a domestic animal. The rat is not, as a rule, a domestic animal in the houses of Europeans, but there is one custom which undoubtedly encourages it to become so. We refer to the habit of many ladies of keeping the horses' grain in the verandah in order to prevent the syces from stealing it. If plague is prevalent, we strongly advise ladies to abandon this custom—it is far better that the syces should steal a few handfuls of grain rather than that you and your household should run the risk of plague. You must also be very careful to see that the houses of your servants do not become rat-infested, because there is always the danger that a plague-infested rat from one of your servant's houses may wander into your bungalow to die. If this happens, the rat-fleas will desert the rat's body as soon as it becomes cold, and then you may be bitten by them and so fall a victim to the disease. Many a mysterious attack is due to this cause. One of the writers knows of a case which occurred only a few months ago in which a European lady suddenly developed plague and, on searching for the cause, they found that a rat had died of plague in one of the drawers of her dressing table.

Two other points require consideration :

(I) Plague is usually conveyed from place to place by rat-fleas which are carried in the clothes or in the baggage of persons coming from infected localities.

The question therefore is—how is this danger to be avoided ? Luckily this question has been settled by the recent investigations of Captain Cunningham, I.M.S., who has shown that no expensive or elaborate method of disinfection is necessary. All that is required is to expose the clothing and baggage for a certain length of time to direct sunlight, which will effectually kill all the fleas.

Captain Cunningham has drawn up the following rules, which we recommend to the reader's careful consideration :—

(1) The ground which is to be used should be so chosen that the sun will be able to shine on it for the whole day.

(2) It should be flat and devoid of grass or stones or anything which would afford shelter to the fleas.

(3) It should be covered with a layer of fine sand, 3 inches deep.

(4) The surface temperature of the sand must be 120°F.

(5) The clothes should be spread on the ground in a single layer and should be left in the sun for one hour. Padded clothing and rezai should be turned over once or twice during the exposure.

(6) No clothes should be placed within 3 feet of the edge of the sand.

(7) The whole area should be fenced in to prevent animals from straying over it.

(II) When plague breaks out in a village at the commencement of the plague season, it usually "burns itself out," and does not act as a focus of infection, when the epidemic season commences in the following year. If however a village is only attacked late in the plague season, the disease does not exhaust itself but remains dormant during the off-season, and that village will certainly start a new epidemic the following year. It is extremely important therefore to notify these " late-infected " villages, in order that a vigorous anti-plague policy may be undertaken during the healthy period, and the lay public can often afford useful aid to the authorities by giving them information as regards such villages.

It is obvious therefore that the question of plague prevention is a very simple one. Our failure to cope with the disease is not due to want of knowledge on our part, but to the ignorance and obstruction of the masses. Education is the only remedy for this, and we hope that this little work may do something to improve matters in this direction.

ENTERIC OR TYPHOID FEVER.

Enteric fever must be regarded as one of the most formidable diseases with which we have to contend in India, not only on account of the amount of sickness and number of deaths for which it is responsible, but because of the expensive sanitary measures which are considered necessary to prevent its spread. It is a disease characterised by continuous fever lasting for about 3 weeks, and usually accompanied by persistent diarrhœa, the stools somewhat resembling pea-soup.

To appreciate the importance which the military authorities attach to the subject, one has only to observe the efforts put forth by those responsible for the health of our Army in India to stamp out the disease in the cantonments of European troops.

Dr. Woods Hutchinson, in his admirable book on Preventable Diseases, says :—" The cause of enteric fever is simplicity itself, merely eating or drinking the excreta of someone else. ' Eating dirt ' is the popular phrase : simple, but of deadly effectiveness and disgracefully common."

At one time it was thought to affect only Europeans, but thanks to the labours of Major Rogers, I.M.S., we now know that it is exceedingly common among natives of India, except in Eastern Bengal and Assam where there is a heavy and continuous rainfall.

A writer in the *Transvaal Medical Journal* believes that the disease is very common amongst not only Indians but all dwellers in tropical countries, and states that Kaffirs suffer from it more frequently than is supposed, and tend to scatter infection broadcast.

Major Leonard Rogers points out that whilst enteric fever is not uncommon in Indian children and poor Europeans in Calcutta reared under the same conditions as Bengalis, it is comparatively rare in Indian regiments and in Indian jails.

This he explains by the fact that the disease usually occurs before the age of twenty-five in this country. Personally, we are of the opinion that the disease as it occurs in the sowar and sepoy is mild in type and has frequently been overlooked.

Enough, however, has been said to show that enteric fever is a very real danger to Indians.

The disease is caused by a minute bacillus, which very closely resembles a microbe found in the intestines of man and animals in countless myriads.

Roberts, in his book on *Enteric Fever in India,* inclines to the theory that this harmless parasitic fungus may develop in the intestinal canal into true typhoid or enteric organisms, and Caldwell enthusiastically supports the view.

The microbe is conveyed by :—

(1) Water or food (especially milk) which have been contaminated by either the stools, urine, or saliva of typhoid patients.

(2) Dust.

(3) Infected clothes.

(4) Apparently healthy persons who are " typhoid " or " enteric carriers."

1. *Water.*—The spread of the disease by this means is detailed in Chapter 4.

2. *Food.*—The microbes of enteric are usually conveyed to food or milk by flies which were shown in the Spanish-American War to fly straight from the enteric latrines to food-supply. This point is again referred to in Chapter 5.

3. *Dust.*—Dust becomes infected from uncovered dejecta or soiled clothing. It is again referred to in detail in Chapter 3.

4. *Infected clothing.*—The dangers of infected clothing are given in Chapter 6.

5. *Typhoid or Enteric Fever Carriers.*—Up till comparatively recently the reasons why typhoid and dysentery should dog the footsteps of armies in the field and cause countless outbreaks of enteric fever, under conditions where the water-supply was good and food pollution out of the question, had remained inscrutable. In the year 1906, however, it was shown that a female baker, herself apparently healthy, had infected every new employee at the bakery which she owned, whilst an apparently healthy female engaged in the milk trade had been the cause of another outbreak of enteric.

These cases were rapidly followed by others in which it was shown that individuals who have had enteric fever, dysentery, and cholera, frequently harbour the microbes of the malady in their gall-bladders for many years after recovery.

They become what are called " carriers " of the disease. The bacteria pass from their gall-bladders to their intestines and are passed in countless myriads at irregular intervals, so that it is difficult for even expert bacteriologists to discover them.

Under conditions of life where the water carriage system of sewage disposal is adopted, these persons are harmless, *unless they have to do with food-supplies.*

T H   2

Here in India, however, such persons are a constant source of danger as their dejectà are too often exposed to the action of flies and the Indian sun. Entangled on the legs of flies or in the form of dust, the microbes of disease from the bowels of these carriers gain access to water and food-supplies with the result that inexplicable outbreaks of the disease occur.

The fact that the dejecta of apparently healthy persons are often the source of the most potent danger must be grasped by every Anglo-Indian and Indian, as for this reason prompt and efficient disposal of refuse of men and animals is the very first essential of Indian sanitation.

As regards enteric fever, moreover, it is important to recognise the fact that it is not only the stools which convey infection—the urine and expectoration are equally dangerous.

The disease may be avoided by the same precautionary measures which we have laid down for dysentery, but there is an additional measure which is worthy of the greatest consideration by Anglo-Indians in particular. This measure is anti-typhoid inoculation.

The advantages of the method are concisely stated in the following leaflet, compiled by one of the writers (Lieut.-Colonel Blackham), and issued by the Lieutenant -General commanding the 1st (Peshawar) Division a short time ago.

" In relation to the prevention of enteric fever, inoculation is a measure of first importance.

The following statistics show the results of inoculation amongst 16 British corps of all arms :—

	Inoculated.	Non-inoculated.
Strength	5,473	6,510
Cases of Enteric Fever	21	187
Deaths	2	26
Number of cases per 1,000	3·8	28·3

The figures show the inoculated man has a much better chance of escaping enteric altogether than the non-inoculated, and if he does get the disease, he has a 7 to 1 best chance of getting well than the man who has declined it.

The case of the 17th Lancers at Meerut is a very striking one.

The regiment encountered an enteric epidemic shortly after its arrival in India. There were 60 cases of enteric altogether.

. Of these cases, 58 had not been inoculated, whilst the remaining two had not had their second dose of the vaccine. The men who had been fully inoculated escaped the disease altogether.

To come closer home, most cases which have occurred in this division for some months past have occurred in uninoculated individuals.

These facts are entirely unanswerable, and the officer or non-commissioned officer who does not use every means in his power to persuade his men to adopt this mode of prevention takes on himself a very serious responsibility.

The protection afforded against typhoid lasts for at least two years, but the resistance of the blood to the enteric organism remains as high as four times the normal for as long as six years.

It is not intended that the method will absolutely protect against enteric as vaccination will against small-pox, because enteric and small-pox are different types of disease.

One attack of small-pox is practically an absolute protection against another, but one attack of enteric, although it renders a second attack uncommon, is by no means an *absolute* protection. Anti-typhoid vaccine may be compared to quinine. Would any individual be justified in withholding quinine from the inhabitants of a malarial country? Similarly, as in this country every article of food and drink, and every particle of dust inhaled, is a potential source of enteric, the individual who withholds the weight of his council and advice in securing the wide adoption of a method of prevention which has the approval of every scientific mind in Europe and Asia must have feelings which no one will envy him when he hears that one of his comrades— perhaps his dearest friend—has gone to hospital with enteric fever."

The fluid used for the purpose of inoculation is nothing more than a culture of the enteric bacillus killed by heat, with a. disinfectant added, which renders all possibility of an .occasional microbe escaping death absolutely out of the question.

It is no more dangerous than any other stewed vegetable material, and as it is absolutely sterile and injected with every conceivable care, it gives less trouble even than ordinary vaccination.

One last word only is necessary before we conclude our remarks on this important disease, and that is that the young Indian civilian must realise that no process of hardening against enteric germs takes place from continuous disregard of precautions. An individual predisposed to the disease and imbibing the specific germ will certainly not escape. More especially is this the case if he has been exposed to the enervating influence of great climatic heat or exhausting exertion under a tropical sun.

We wish therefore to impress strongly upon our readers the vital importance of anti-typhoid inoculation. Prevention is always better than cure, and we all know from sad experience the difficulties of treating this disease, once it has obtained a hold.

TUBERCULOSIS.

During the past few years so much attention has been paid to so-called tropical diseases that the rapid extension of some of the diseases of cool climates in tropical countries has been overlooked. This remark applies particularly to tuberculosis, which will ere long become an even more serious problem in this country than that presented at the present moment by plague.

In the British Islands tuberculosis claims 75,000 victims every year, but modern methods are every year reducing both the sickness and the death-rate from this fell disease, which has been so aptly termed the "Great White Plague." In India, on the other hand, it is advancing by leaps and bounds, and the mortality from tubercular diseases in large Indian cities like Calcutta and Bombay is now considerably higher than that in Glasgow, Birmingham, or Manchester.

The disease was for a long time, like cholera, a mysterious malady, but, thanks to the researches of Professor Koch, we now know that there is nothing remarkable about it. It is caused like cholera and most other diseases by a minute fungus—the tubercle bacillus.

The tubercle bacillus can be found everywhere where dust and dirt have accumulated. There are two chief types, one derived from human beings and the other from cattle, but the differences between them are not of any great importance, and we now know that all forms of this bacillus—whether derived from man or cattle—are capable of setting up the disease in human beings.

The two main sources of these bacilli which destroy the human race are milk and butter and the sputum of consumptive patients. These facts are established beyond all possibility of criticism. Many samples of milk contain tubercle bacilli in considerable numbers. Dr. Newsholme, Principal Medical Officer of the Local Government Board, estimates that 20 per cent. of the mixed milk supplied to towns in the United Kingdom contains living tubercle bacilli. In other words, every fifth glass of milk sold at present is capable of producing tuberculosis in its consumer. In America, too, tubercle bacilli have been found in 11 per cent. of all samples of butter, whilst Dr. Turner, the Health Officer of Bombay, has recently proved that 15 per cent. of the samples of milk sold in that city contain these organisms.

It is obvious, therefore, that a pure milk supply is one of the most important safeguards against tuberculosis. The ideal measure would be to establish herds of cattle free from tuberculosis and to prohibit the sale of milk from tuberculous cows. This, however, is an impossible task, and fortunately the attempt is not necessary.

Mr. Nathan Strauss, the American Philanthropist, has dealt with this difficulty and has shown that milk may be rendered absolutely safe if it is pasteurised for 20 minutes at 140°F. This precaution we wish to bring most prominently to the notice of those who are feeding their children upon cow's milk.

The other great source of tubercle bacilli is from the expectoration of consumptive patients, and that this is a very serious danger is shown by the recent observations of Dr. Turner in Bombay. He collected some hundreds of samples of sputum from the roadside, and he found that one in every ten of these contained tubercle bacilli. This will surely bring home to all the importance of doing everything possible to prevent and discourage promiscuous expectoration which is such a common habit in this country.

In the case of sick persons, their expectoration should be received into a covered vessel containing a disinfectant, and should be systematically disposed of by burning and never buried or thrown on the ground.

It must be remembered that the consumptive is not himself a direct source of danger. If you put a consumptive, who is careful of his sputum and cleanly in his habits, in a well-lighted, well ventilated room, there will be very little danger of any other member of the household contracting the disease. It is not necessary therefore to isolate every consumptive. On the other hand, if he be allowed to spit wherever he likes, and if he be crowded up with others in dark ill-ventilated rooms, then one after another the different members of the family will infallibly fall victims to the malady.

Fortunately for us the bacillus of tuberculosis is an exceedingly delicate organism—sunlight destroys it rapidly, and it is nearly always killed by complete drying. Hence it is exceedingly probable that in most cases consumption is conveyed from patient to patient by moist sputum or by sputum not long exposed to air and light.

It is those brought very close to the consumptive and living the same life as the consumptive, inhabiting the same rooms, sleeping in the same bed, using the same vessels for eating and drinking, handling the same articles and the same tools, who are most liable to infection. Notwithstanding this, we have to face the appalling fact that in the British Isles alone 75,000 people die every year because they have swallowed or inhaled living tubercle bacilli produced in the lungs of consumptive persons living or working near them, and that each of these 75,000 people certainly induces the disease in one or more other persons before he dies, thus preparing a new set of victims for the following year's sacrifice.

Lastly, bear in mind that flies are now known to be carriers of this disease. It is very important therefore that they should not be allowed to settle on tubercular sputum, which should be kept always in covered vessels.

Remember also what is set forth in the earlier portion of this chapter as regards the two factors in the causation of disease, and do everything to promote the general health of the members of your household, so as to enable them to resist the tubercle bacilli should they ever be attacked by them.

The necessary precautions therefore may be summed up as follows :—

(1) Fresh air and avoidance of overcrowding, especially in bedrooms.
(2) Good food.
(3) Disinfection and destruction of sputum.
(4) Banishment of flies.
(5) Pasteurisation or boiling of milk.

SMALL-POX.

Small-pox takes the first place amongst epidemic diseases in the tenacity and malignity with which it has pursued the human race over all the world, and the tale of the destructive ravages of this pestilence in early times and of the suffering which resulted from it fills the mind with horror.

When the disease first appeared in India it must have extirpated whole races of men. Indeed, we have only to call attention to the chief characteristics of the disease, namely, that it seizes on almost all who for the first time come within its range, that it is eminently contagious from person to person, and that among unprotected natives 50 per cent. is a low estimate of the case mortality, for the reader to realise, in the words of Sir John Simon, that its effects must have been comparable to that obliteration of vegetable life which ensues when the army of locusts, descending on pastures and vineyards, converts into the likeness of a desert what just before was all freshness and fertility.

In Calcutta, in 1850, the deaths from small-pox constituted 47 per cent. of the total number of deaths; in Lahore, in 1865, 7,000 people died of the disease in two months; whilst in India as a whole, in 1869, over the comparatively limited area in which death registration was attempted, nearly 200,000 deaths from small-pox were recorded, and having regard to the known neglect of registration at that time, we are justified in assuming that at least double that number actually occurred.

Enough has been said to convey an idea of the dreadful scourge with which the people of India were afflicted for many centuries.

So dreaded and so inevitable did the disease appear to the Oriental mind that small-pox inoculation was introduced so far back that its origin is obscured in the twilight of early Indian history with the idea of "buying it cheaply," that is contracting for an inevitable attack by voluntarily having one which would be so mild that life would be hardly endangered.

The disadvantages of this practice are well stated as follows :—

(1) Persons undergoing the operation have to subject themselves to a preparatory course of treatment and to various arduous restrictions for many days after the operation. Even in England, where it may be supposed that great skill and care were used, the preparatory treatment lasted a month, and medical attendance was required for five or six weeks after the operation.

(2) There is always a risk, which often is great, that the inoculated person may die as the result of the operation.

(3) When the disease is produced in a severe form, all the suffering which attends an ordinary attack of small-pox has to be endured, and disfigurement and even lameness, deafness, or blindness may ensue.

(4) The disease set up by the inoculation, in however mild a form, is as contagious as ordinary

small-pox, so that every unprotected person in the neighbourhood of an inoculated patient may catch the disease, and an epidemic of small-pox may be started.

(5) The operation, being apparently very easy to carry out, is one in which nearly all countries where it was introduced has been largely employed by quacks and other ignorant people as a means of making money. Such people take no care in regard to the kind of inoculating matter used or in regard to the precautions against the infection of other people, and there is much evidence that under those circumstances the prevalence of and mortality from small-pox have often been greatly increased.

The hopes of the great benefits which this measure would confer upon mankind were doomed to disappointment, but fortunately for the human race it was to be supplanted by a method of protection, namely, *vaccination*, which has been described by Sir John Simon as "the greatest physical good ever given by science to the world." The general employment of this method was due to the genius of an English surgeon Jenner, who for this reason is justly honoured in history as one of the greatest benefactors of mankind.

The term vaccination means the intentional inoculation with the matter of *vaccinia* or cow-pox, and, contrasting the results of small-pox inoculation with those of this newer method of protection, we may say that while the former practice produces in the individual operated upon an attack of human small-pox which is dangerous not only to the inoculated person but also (from its contagiousness) to everyone around him, the latter practice produces a mild local disease which effectually protects the vaccinated individual against human small-pox, and is, moreover, entirely without danger to him, and (not being contagious) entirely without danger

to others. Again, while small-pox inoculation
tends—at any rate in crowded communities—to
increase the prevalence of the disease, vaccination
reduces the prevalence and mortality of small-pox
in a remarkable manner. Obviously, therefore,
vaccination is the better practice, and it is not
surprising that from the time when the famous
work of Jenner brought to every civilised country
a knowledge and appreciation of "the greatest
sanitary fact the world has ever known," it has in
those countries entirely supplanted the practice of
small-pox inoculation.

Vaccination possesses, therefore, none of the disadvantages of inoculation and many advantages
not possessed by that measure and has slowly
taken the place of the older practice almost
throughout the country, but there are some areas
even in British territory where inoculation is still
carried on.

The results already effected by vaccination in
this country are such as justly afford reason for
enthusiasm and pride ; much still remains to be
done before we shall be within measurable distance
of completing the emancipation of the people
from the horrors of small-pox. " A discriminating
person will realize that, especially in a country
like India, there is a great danger that the declin-
ing prevalence of an epidemic disease may bring
about forgetfulness of the means by which such
success has been attained. In one or two European
countries such forgetfulness has led to serious
neglect of vaccination, with the result that in those
countries small-pox—at one time controlled—has
again caused disastrous epidemics."

CHAPTER II.

MALARIA, YELLOW FEVER, KALA-AZAR, AND SAND-FLY FEVER.

" The mortality from malaria is a mere trifle compared with the ravages fever commits in sapping the strength and vigour of the people, fever destroys the life of the country—the deaths must be multiplied by 50 or 60 to give the attacks."—Florence Nightingale's *" Life and Death in India."*

WE used to hear much of climate as an obstacle to civilization and barrier to settlement. Now for climate we read " malaria."

Fortunately for the inhabitants of the United Kingdom their well-drained soil and climatic conditions at present preserve them from ague or malaria : although in earlier days it was common enough in the Fen country. In other regions of the earth, over extensive areas, it attacks millions of people and does enormous damage not only by the great death-roll directly due to the disease itself, but by the lowering of vitality induced by repeated attacks. In ancient days malaria was one of the most prominent diseases amongst the Romans, and probably did much to sap the vigour and physique of that dominant race and to lead to the fall of that mighty Empire.

As is so aptly pointed out by the author of " The Dawn of the Health Age," malaria is still the scourge of modern Italy : hundreds of thousands of the inhabitants of the U. S. of America are affected by it : it has earned for West Africa the appellation of the " White Man's Grave ; " and thousands of the natives of India die annually directly from its ravages.

Yet this is a disease for which, in the shape of quinine, we have had a specific remedy for the past 270 years.

For most ordinary attacks of malaria, quinine is an absolute specific, but notwithstanding the fact that this remedy has been in constant use for nearly three centuries, the disease has continued to ravage, without abatement, the populaces of whole continents. It is obvious therefore that, although quinine has been of very great and undeniable use to the individual, it has been of little or none to the race. We bring this prominently to the notice of the reader in order to impress upon him once again the fact that, in every case, prevention is better than cure, and that in the medicine of the future what we shall have to do is to ascertain the true causes of disease and then prevent its occurrence—not merely to tinker with it and endeavour to patch up the victims of its attack.

Let us now consider therefore the problem of the prevention of malaria. In order to do this, we must trace out, in brief outline, how the cause of this disease was discovered.

The name of the disease—Malaria—*i.e.*, " bad air "—shows that it was originally believed to be due to atmospheric conditions, and for centuries it was taught that it was caused by " miasma " or vapours arising from stagnant marshes, but what puzzled the physicians in those days was the ordered sequence of events in each attack, which consists of a cold stage, a hot stage, and a stage of excessive perspiration followed by relief from all symptoms and a period of complete freedom from fever.

The explanation of this sequence was given when Dr. Laveran discovered that malaria is due to a minute parasite existing in the blood and undergoing a series of changes corresponding in its time-period to the different stages of an attack of "ague." These parasites live and grow inside the red blood corpuscles. At a certain stage they divide up into a number of spores—the corpuscles then burst and the spores with the poison produced by them are discharged into the blood and this it is which causes the malarial attack. The spores thus set free then enter fresh blood corpuscles and start a new cycle, the consummation of which is a fresh outbreak and a fresh attack, and so the cycle continues to be repeated.

This discovery of Laveran's adequately explained the phenomena of a malarial attack, but there still remained the puzzle to solve how the malarial parasite got into the blood corpuscles and what was the connection between malaria and marshes.

The honour of supplying this portion of the history in quite recent years is shared by two British observers—Sir Patrick Manson and Sir Ronald Ross—and we now know that the cycle we have already described does not constitute the complete life-history of the malaria parasite. The observations of Ross have proved that a certain portion of the life of the malarial parasite is passed in the stomach of a particular kind of mosquito, called Anopheles, which breeds in the marshes and small ponds and puddles near malarious districts.

We are now able to understand that malaria, like plague, although it is not directly contagious, is essentially a communicable disease, but that the intermediary in this case is the anopheles mosquito instead of the rat flea.

While therefore no one can have malaria unless bitten by an infected anopheles mosquito, on the other hand, no anopheles can communicate malaria unless it has been infected by a human being suffering from malaria. Hence the problem of the prevention of malaria is a twofold one. First, we must prevent the mosquito from sucking the blood of a person sick with malaria, and, secondly, we must prevent this same mosquito, if she has become infected, from biting a healthy person. This problem is again twofold. We can either prevent the mosquito from reaching a person suffering from malaria, or we can destroy with quinine the parasite in the blood of the infected person.

The campaign against malaria may therefore be conducted on the following lines :—

1. We may attack the mosquitoes themselves in all stages of their development.
2. We may defend ourselves against them.
3. We may attack the parasite of malaria.
4. We may defend ourselves against it.
5. We may attack the allies and reinforce the enemies of the malarial parasite.

The Campaign against Malaria.

1. *The attack on Mosquitoes.*—A campaign against mosquitoes may consist of—

(*a*) An advance in force, or Government action, in the form of drainage and the organization of mosquito brigades.

(*b*) Guerilla warfare, or personal efforts.

Let us consider these separately.

(*a*) *Advance in force.*—What we may call frontal attacks, or measures undertaken by Government, fall under two headings :—

1. *Permanent measures* which consist in engineering efforts to deal once and for all with the breeding grounds by draining land, filling up pools and ponds, rectification of water-courses, etc.

2. *Annual measures* which consist in the action which is necessary year by year in dealing with small pools, rain puddles, collections of water in gurrahs, fire buckets, and such like, by what are called " mosquito brigades."

(a) 1. *Permanent measures.*—This variety is of
course the kind to be hoped for and desired, but
such measures involve enormous expenditure as
may be gathered from the following table by Chris-
topher and James which gives some idea of the
cost involved in places where such measures have
been attended with a large amount of success.

Place.	Population.	Cost per Head.	REMARKS.
Ismailia ..	6,000 to 7,000	6·5 frcs. initial	Exclusive of qui-nine.
Klang and Port Swettenham.	4,000	£2-10 initial ..	Exclusive of qui-nine.
Panama ..	40,000	£10 per head annually.	Inclusive of medical and sanitary ex-penditure.

Heavy expenditure of this nature may be possible
over a limited area, but where a vast tract of territory has to be dealt with, as in India, it is often difficult, if not impossible, to obtain the sinews of war—
i.e., the money—for a campaign of such magnitude.

It must, however, be realized by Indians that
the very first essential of anti-malarial work is free
drainage, and as this is naturally attained, more
particularly in isolated mountain elevations, such
situations are usually free from fever, although
these maladies are not uncommon in warm mountain valleys, thus showing that to some extent
at least it is only in proportion as mountains are
better drained than the plains that they are more
free from breeding grounds of anophelines. We
know that the Himalayan Terai is one of the most
malarious tracts in India.

An admirable summary of permanent measure
for the prevention of malaria will be found in
Colonel Hehir's *Prophylaxis of Malaria in India*,
a book which the authors recommend to all

sanitary officials. They feel that a description of these permanent measures would be out of place in the present brochure : they pass on therefore to those annual measures which are best conducted by " mosquito brigades."

(a) 2. *Annual attacks.*—Annual attacks on all collections of water which may prove possible breeding-grounds are of great value in some districts, but have their limitations in many parts of India.

These measures should be directed against :—

1. Water Channels.
2. Tanks and Pools.
3. Borrow Pits.
4. Garden Cisterns.
5. Discussed Wells.
6. Brick Factories.
7. Grass Farms.

These operations are best conducted by what are called *mosquito brigades.*

The work of these brigades is applicable to a great variety of places in this country—towns, collections of villages, cantonments, jails and all large industrial works and factories : one would emphasize the necessity of their employment wherever large gangs of labourers are employed on famine relief works, making of railway embankments, roads, canal works, tea gardens, extensive building operations, etc. In these latter cases, half a dozen of the coolies under one head-man could be taught their duties in a few days. A few gangs of such men working efficiently can prevent much of the malaria amongst thousands of labourers.

A mosquito brigade consists of from 10 to 20 or more workers under the direction of a skilled super-intendent, the duties of the workers being—(1) to visit regularly once a week the compound of every house and destroy every pool of water which can harbour mosquito larvæ ; (2) to cover with a layer of kerosene oil and pesterine every collection of water which is too large to be destroyed ; (3) to remove all broken tins, pots, bottles, etc., which can contain water and harbour larvæ ; (4) to instruct the inhabitants in the recognition of mosquito larvæ and in the method of destroying them; (5) to see that bye-laws requiring that all fixed receptacle of water, cesspools, etc., should be made mosquito-proof, is carried out, and to·bring to the notice of the superintendent any house-holder in whose premises mosquito larvæ are frequently found ; (6) during the rains to drain off quickly all superficial collections of water which can last long enough to become breeding-grounds of mosquitos ; (7) to endeavour to kill adult mosquitos in houses, out-houses, and stables by fumigation with sulphur and other means ; (8) to make observations of the seasonal prevalence of mosquitos on their habits, and on every matter regarding which increased knowledge might aid in the extermination of these insects.

In towns which extend over a wide area, it is necessary, of course, to employ a number of brigades, the town being sub-divided into areas of such size that every house and every possible breeding-place of mosquitos can be visited once a week by a member of the brigades.

Pesterine is strongly recommended by Dr. Bentley of Bombay : it is crude petroleum purchasable from Messrs. Graham & Co., Bombay, in 4-gallon tins at Re. 1-4-0 per tin. In bulk it costs about Rs. 40 a ton. As a larvicide its action is much slower than kerosene oil. One great advantage of it is that its colour tells us whether it has been properly applied. It is best used with equal parts of kerosene oil, and should be applied by means of an ordinary garden spray. In this way the liquid may, when necessary, be caused to find its way among grass and weeds which otherwise break the continuity of the film and allow larvæ and pubæ to escape destruction.

The proportion in which it should be used is a three-gallon tin to every 10,000 square yards.

In the case of canals where the flow is cut off periodically the oiling should be done after each flow of water.

(b) *Guerilla warfare.*—A guerilla warfare of personal efforts can be carried on by everyone. It simply consists of *personally* seeing to the destruction of isolated bands of the enemy which may invade one's house and compound.

These efforts, remember, are very important and indeed essential. Without them all the labour of Government may be brought to nought, for just as the efforts of Government to prevent the spread of plague are made of no avail owing to the fact that Indians encourage the rat as a domestic animal, so large sums of money may be fruitlessly expended in draining marshy areas simply because the villagers allow mosquitos to breed in *gurrahs* and empty tins and jam-pots lying about in their compounds. It is therefore the bounden duty of everyone to do their utmost to banish mosquitos from their house and compound. The marvellous success which has attended the efforts of the Americans to stamp out Yellow Fever in the West Indies is a useful object-lesson as regards the value of guerilla warfare and individual efforts.

Yellow Fever is a disease which, like Malaria, is conveyed from man to man by a species of mosquito.

But these mosquito campaigns have always been instituted on account of either Malaria or Yellow Fever. There is consequently an impression, even among medical men, that unless Malaria or Yellow Fever actually exists in a community, there is no necessity to try to reduce mosquitos. They say " there are no Anopheles here. Why bother about the ordinary domestic mosquitos that do no harm ? "

This is a fatal mistake, we shall be able to prove to the reader.

In the first place it is necessary to explain what is meant by the term " domestic mosquitos."

Now mosquitos are classified in accordance with the habits of the different species.

The type of mosquito that inhabits houses in towns and villages is different from the type that lives in marshes and forests and on the banks of rivers. In the same places, of course, both kinds of mosquito are found together—for example, in the houses of villages on the borders of swamps or ricefields, or in towns where there is much irrigation, but in the ordinary cantonment or civil lines,. the domestic species are always more common than the sylvan. The reason for this is that mosquitos will not, as a rule, fly far from their breeding-places : the sylvan or marsh mosquitos will remain near the forest or swamp—the domestic mosquito will not go far from the compound round the bungalow.

There are *two varieties of domestic mosquito*—

1. The ordinary grey. mosquito, or *Culex*, which haunts rooms in the evening or at night, and which in the early morning can always be seen resting on the mosquito curtains tired and gorged with its nocturnal meal of blood.

2. The speckled or " tiger " mosquito, the scientific name of which is *Stegomyia*. This is the brightly coloured, black and white striped mosquito which bites in the daytime, especially just after the dawn. It haunts dark coloured clothes and shady verandahs.

Of the *Sylvan* or *marsh mosquitos*, there is *only one kind* that need concern us here. This is the dapple winged mosquito, or *Anopheles*, which we have already told the reader is the carrier of Malaria.

It may be recognised in two ways (a) by its spotted wings, and (b) by the fact that, whereas the culex stands on the wall or mosquito curtain with its body parallel to the surface, the Anopheles holds its body straight out almost perpendicular to the wall. Neither of the domestic species convey Malaria, but we now know that the Culex conveys that very unpleasant disease known as Dengue or Breakbone fever, whilst the Stegomyia has been proved in the West Indies to be the carrier of Yellow Fever.

The readers may possibly say " What does that matter ? " Yellow Fever doesn't exist in India." Quite so—but, in these days of rapid travel and communication are you prepared to say that it never will be introduced ? And you may take our word for it that if ever it is introduced, it will certainly spread with alarming rapidity unless we can reduce the number of Stegomyia mosquitos in the country before it comes. If say in 1894 anyone had prophesied the awful ravages which plague would make in India during the next fifteen years, he would probably have been laughed at. But think what a difference it might have made if the peril had been realised and if we had only known then what we do now about the rat-flea.

In the case of Yellow Fever we are better off, because we know before the disease reaches the country that the carrier of this disease is the common speckled domestic mosquito.

What we particularly want you to realise is that the danger of the introduction of this disease into India is not by any means so remote as one might imagine. The reason why India has escaped for so long is that there is no direct route between India and the West Indies, but the great Panama Canal is now completed and when vessels come direct to India from infected ports, the greatest care will be necessary to prevent the introduction of Yellow Fever into India. The Government is fully alive to this danger and elaborate precautions are now being taken to keep the disease out of the country: meanwhile it is the duty of all of you to wage war against domestic mosquitos, so that, if ever Yellow Fever obtains a footing it may die out from want of carriers of the disease.

But, in addition to this danger, which is surely important enough, the domestic mosquitos are disgusting insects that pass their lives, in their larval stage, in drains, cesspools, blocked up water channels, gutters, and such like collections of filthy water and the newly-hatched flying insects feed on the floating matter found in such water. Then they proceed to suck the blood of the first human being they can find, thrusting their infected proboscis through his skin.

Can you say therefore that the domestic mosquitos do no harm ? Now, having shown the necessity for destroying domestic mosquitos, the question arises " How is this destruction to be accomplished ?" This is the plan of campaign which we recommend—

(1) Make a regular weekly inspection of the compound and destroy (by filling up or draining it) every pool of water that can harbour mosquito larvæ.

(2) When dealing with a collection of water, such as a tank, which is too large to be destroyed, two methods may be employed. The first is that of covering the whole surface of the water with a thin layer of kerosene oil or Pesterine, as already described. The second is the adoption of what is now known as ' water-tidiness,' *i.e.*, by seeing that the banks of all tanks are properly sloped and cleared of jungle, and that all

weeds are removed from the surface of the water. In this way the mosquito larvæ are deprived of protection against their natural enemies, referred to in paragraph 5 below.

(3) Pay particular attention to your bath-rooms. They should be well lighted and airy and you should never allow gurrahs full of water to remain in them, or bath water to accumulate in catchpits outside. Never keep large tubs, with shrubs in them, near the bungalow.

(4) Remove all broken tins, pots, bottles, etc., which may contain water and so harbour mosquito larvæ. In this connection, pay especial attention to the servants' quarters and the kitchen.

(5) See that all fixed receptacles of water—such as water butts, cesspools, etc., are made mosquito-proof by covering them with cheese cloth or some similar material, or fine gauze.

(6) Remove all thick curtains from living rooms, especially during the hot weather, and shake out and place in the sun at least once a week all clothes hung on pegs.

(7) Lastly, endeavour to destroy all adult mosquitos that may lurk in nooks and crannies in your rooms. This may be accomplished by fumigation with various substances, such as sulphur or the ordinary bazaar drug called " *loban.*" In using either of these substances, you must carefully seal up the room exactly as you would do when disinfecting it after illness.

In America great success has been attained by fumigation with a mixture of 3 parts of powdered pyrethrum with one of saltpetre. This is spread in a layer ½ inch thick on an iron plate and then lighted in several places. The amount you require to use is 8 ounces of the mixture for 1,000 cubic feet of air space. For a large room you will probably require to use more than one plate.

2. *The defence against mosquitos and sand-flies.*— That is to say, how can we protect ourselves from being bitten ?

The means we can adopt are—

   (1) Mosquito-proof houses.
   (2) Mosquito nets.
   (3) Mosquito-proof clothes.
   (4) Applications which prevent mosquitos from biting.
   (5) Avoidance of certain colours.

(1) *Mosquito-proof houses.*—These are largely used in America and Italy and even in some parts of India. They are so costly as to be quite out of the question for general use.

Failing actual mosquito-proof houses, much can still be done. For instance, all windows may be protected by gauze or mulmul and door chicks should be kept carefully closed *all* day. They should, however, be rolled up for a short time in the evening and then let down again and strict orders should be given to the sweeper not to roll them up when he comes into the house at dawn. You will understand the reason for this, if you will consider for a moment the mosquitos' habits. They love the rest all day in some cool dark nook in the bungalow, but as evening sets in you will hear them beginning to sing and this is the time when they like to go outside in search of water. Now is your opportunity, roll up the chicks and let them out, and it is often a good thing to hasten their departure by lighting an incense stick (which is easily procurable in the bazaar). If you do this, in a short time all the mosquitos will have departed, and you may prevent them from returning by letting down the chicks before the smell of the incense has passed off. Another point to remember is that mosquitos always fly low in the air and that if you have upper rooms in your house you should, on that account, always sleep in them instead of the ground floor.

(2) *Mosquito nets.*—These must be our chief defensive weapons, and very powerful ones they are. Remember that they act in two ways :—

(*a*) by protecting individuals from being bitten by infected mosquitos, and thus contracting malaria ;

(*b*) by preventing patients suffering from malaria from becoming a source of infection to others.

The following rules must, however, be used if a mosquito net is to be of any real use :—

(*i*) The bed must be broad enough to leave a considerable space between the sleeper and the net, otherwise exposed portions of the sleeper's limbs will come in contact with the net, and the mosquito, even though it cannot get inside, will push its proboscis through the openings in the mesh and so get its fill of blood. If the bed is not wide enough then the lower feet of the net should be lined with calico.

(*ii*) The net should always be let down in the afternoon and carefully inspected for mosquitos and sand-flies.

(*iii*) The sides and end of the nets must always be inside the poles and the lower border carefully tucked under the mattress ; not left hanging on the ground. (See Fig. 1.)

(*iv*) Always examine your mosquito net carefully before going to sleep, to make sure that none are inside it.

(3) *Mosquito-proof clothing.*—Thin cotton clothing must not be used, as mosquitos bite through it. The feet and hand should be kept covered, if

possible after sundown, and the ankles by drawers and thick socks and by using boots instead of the more comfortable shoes.

FIG. I.—A MOSQUITO NET PROPERLY APPLIED.

(4) *Agents that prevent mosquitos from biting.*— Essential oils, such as citronella and lemon grass oil, essence of cinnamon, or eucalyptus are agents in common use. But remember these applications cease to protect as soon as the volatile part of the oil ha' evaporated. While, therefore, they are protective foi the first half hour, they are of no use afterwards. They merely lull to false security with the result that one dozes off and then is badly bitten during sleep.

(5) *Avoidance of certain colours.*—Blue, dark red, brown and black are much more attractive to mosquitos than white, grey, green, yellow and violet. The former colours should, therefore, be avoided. Indeed, in malarial regions, it is safest to wear nothing but white.

3. *The attack on the Malarial Parasite.*—For this we have a powerful agent at our disposal in quinine, which will not only cure malaria but will prevent it.

The best way of using this drug for purposes of prevention is to take 5 grains every evening or with your " chota hazri " cup of tea during the malarial season. If you do this, any malarial parasites with which you may be inoculated by infected mosquitos will be killed off as soon as they enter your body.

The chief point to remember is that when quinine is used to prevent malaria it must be taken regularly. If it is taken irregularly, especially in small doses, it seems to do more harm than good. It is this irregular use of quinine that has led to its falling into disrepute, whereas it is not the fault of the drug but of the manner in which it has been taken.

Another reason, as we shall show presently, is that it is often used for fevers which are not malarial in their nature.

4. *The attack on the allies.*—All persons infected with the malarial parasite are the allies of the disease and essential to its spread, so we must avoid them, but unfortunately the measures we can adopt against them are not numerous. Isolation of those infected with malaria is to some extent carried out in most hospitals in India. As a general measure of protection it is, however, impracticable, but much good may be attained by keeping malarial patients under mosquito curtains. The childern of the poorer classes who are the most prolific sources of malaria cannot be isolated. There is

one thing that everyone can do, and that is to endeavour by the regular administration of quinine to limit the number of such cases amongst his personal servants, for if one or more of these are infected their proximity renders us liable to infection through the mosquitos they infect. In a general way it may be said that when malarial fever occurs in Europeans, the latter have acquired it from mosquitos that have previously bitten an infected Indian who is more often than not one of their own servants or a child in the compound.

5. *The reinforcement of the mosquitos' enemies.*— The natural enemies of mosquito-larvæ are fish, frogs, dragon fly larvæ and the larvæ of water beetles.

It is essential, therefore, that the edges of all pools, tanks and streams should be properly sloped and kept clean of weeds, behind which the mosquito larvæ seek refuge from their natural enemies ; also that tanks be stocked with suitable fish. To those wishing for further information on this subject we recommend the perusal of a pamphlet on " Indian Fish of proved utility as mosquito-destroyers," by Sewell and Chaudhurie, published by the Superintendent of the Indian Museum, Calcutta, at the nominal price of 8 annas.

The enemies of the adult mosquito are bats, lizards and spiders, so that the ordinary dislike for spiders is ill founded.

We have been brought up from our earlier days to think of the horrid cruel spider and the poor little harmless fly, but science teaches us that we should encourage spiders in our houses, as these insects are the genuine friends of man whilst the poor little flies are our ruthless enemies.

The fact has long been known to the villagers in some parts of Mexico who deliberately introduce a special variety of spider into their houses with a view to ridding them of flies. A French writer tells us that the results are marvellously good and the importation of the *mosquero*, as the special variety of Mexican spider is called, may well be an Indian sanitary measure in the future.

Far more powerful foes of the disease, however, than any of these physical enemies, are a good water-supply, good drainage, good paving, good conservancy, good building organization and an organized sanitary service to see carried out and maintained systematically and continuously the necessary sanitary routine : everything, in fact, that tends to raise the general standard of health and so render individuals less liable to fall victims to the disease.

The chief allies of malaria in this country are—neglect of ordinary sanitary precautions and especially puddles and pools in and around dwellings, and empty vessels containing water in which the mosquitos breed.

Malaria disappears before good sanitation as we know from English experience and even from our knowledge of some districts of India.

" Peshawar Fever " was at one time known and dreaded from one end of India to the other. It was a form of malaria with choleraic symptoms and very fatal, but it has now practically disappeared from the Peshawar Valley.

We have got rid of one form of malaria why should we not seriously try to get rid of it altogether ?

KALA AZAR.

For many years it was believed that a disease associated with great enlargement of the spleen, progressive weakness and anæmia and a perceptible darkening of the complexion, was the result of repeated attacks of malaria, and it was called " chronic malarial cachexia." This disease is specially common in Assam and the Dooars where it is known as " Kala Azar," and where it is the cause of much sickness and mortality amongst the coolies on the tea plantations. We now know that it is caused by the totally different parasite to the one which causes malaria ; also that quinine is practically useless ; and that the agent which conveys infection from one human being to another is not a mosquito but is possibly the bed-bug. General sanitation, therefore, and the systematic destruction of bugs, are the only weapons which, in the present state of our knowledge, can be regarded as being of any avail. It is interesting, however, to remark that on the Mediterranean littoral a disease of very similar nature has been described as occurring chiefly in children. This disease, which also occurs in dogs, is conveyed from dog to man through the dog-flea, and Professor Laveran regards it as being the same disease as Indian Kala Azar. So far, however, observers in India have been unable to discover the disease in Indian dogs, and, with one exception, all attempts to inoculate them with the disease have failed.

SAND-FLY FEVER.

The sand-fly is one of the pests of the Indian plains and new comers to districts where it abounds suffer from short febrile illnesses of from three to seven days' duration, especially during the summer months when the fly is most in evidence.

Since it has been shown that sudden outbreaks of a short fever, unlike ague, prevail every spring, summer and autumn in various parts of India, and that these attacks only occur where sand-flies abound, it is pretty clear that many of the short febrile ailments, hitherto diagnosed as influenza, dengue or ague, or attributed to " touch of the sun," " chill," " intemperance," " over-eating," " water-drinking," " lack of food," " constipation," " diarrhœa," " excessive exertion," " want of exercise," or what not, are really caused by the invisible virus carried by the sand-fly.

An account of the various insects known in India as the sand-fly is given in Chapter IX.

The ordinary method of prevention is the use of a mosquito net made of the material known in Indian bazars as *ab-i-rawan*, or if this is not procurable, common *mulmul* : the insect passes through ordinary mosquito netting. On a hot night however it is almost impossible to sleep under a mosquito-curtain made of " mulmul," which keeps out all the air. It is interesting therefore to learn that in a recent outbreak of " sand-fly fever " at Kamptee, the medical officer discovered that he could keep off the sand-flies by sprinkling a little powdered camphor on his bed, and that he could then dispense with a mosquito-curtain altogether. We recommend a trial of this method.

Quinine is useless either as a preventive or in the treatment of an attack.

It is possible that a large amount of the so-called malaria of Indian Troops and the Indian Jails is really sand-fly fever.

The insect has been found to propagate itself in the dejecta of lizards and wood-lice and is only prevalent where walls and roofs are badly constructed and in bad repair thus favouring the development of the indirect hosts of the insect.

The chief methods of prevention in addition to a fine mesh mosquito net are :—

1. Good walls to houses.
2. Painting or distempering intsead of whitewashing walls.
3. Good floors and disuse of matting.
4. Removal of old walls and ruins.
5. Formalin spray.
6. Removal of all old wood work, and painting and varnishing of all doors, etc., yearly.

CHAPTER III.

AIR AND VENTILATION IN HOT COUNTRIES.

Our individual moral responsibilities with regard to the air which we breathe are great. Our first duty is not to befoul the air any more than we can help ; to keep all about us clean and pure inside our houses, and our rooms free from dust ; and not to allow accumulations of refuse outside.—(Newman's Health of the State, p. 63.)

" THE mistake of most modern ventilation is that there is not enough of it," writes Dr. Ransom in a learned treatise on the treatment of pulmonary disease.

If the principle be conceded that persons with diseased lungs cannot have too much fresh air, surely the necessity for an abundant supply for healthy individuals must be sufficiently obvious.

It is well known that the blood is the medium by which various food materials and oxygen are carried to the tissues and organs of the body for their growth and nourishment.

The food is obtained from the digestive system, while the oxygen is absorbed from the air we breathe. The tissues not only absorb nourishment from the blood but also pour into it their own waste products and this waste material is largely disposed of in the lungs.

The lungs, therefore, are a sort of exchange where oxygen is absorbed and waste products added to the air.

In the first chapter we pointed out the two great dangers that occur as the result of a deficient supply of fresh air :

 (*a*) the risk of contracting tuberculosis, as the result of direct infection ;

(b) the increased danger of " catching " any disease that might be going about, owing to lowering of the power of resistance ;

and it will be remembered that " impure air " was the first of the six predisposing causes, which deprive your body of the power of resisting disease.

If the air breathed in is impure, the lungs are unable to obtain a sufficient amount of oxygen. This causes what is known as " oxygen starvation," and the nourishment of the whole body is lowered.

It is obvious therefore that fresh air and efficient ventilation are not only important in the sick room, they are equally necessary for healthy individuals if those individuals wish to remain in perfect health.

It is on this simple principle of physiology that all need of fresh air and, therefore, of ventilation is based.

To understand the subject it is necessary to know—

1. The constituents of the atmosphere.
2. The chief sources of its impurity.
3. The amount of air space necessary.
4. Nature's agents for purifying the air.
5. Our artificial means of supplying the individual with fresh air.
6. The dangers of impure air.

We will consider these seriatim.

1. THE CONSTITUENTS OF THE AIR :—

Fresh air consists of a mixture of gases, some water and a certain amount of solid matter in very fine sub-division. The chief constituent, from the point of importance, is oxygen, but, from the point of quantity, nitrogen.

Oxygen is a colourless, tasteless gas, which burns up any material exposed to it, whilst nitrogen has no specific properties as a portion of the atmosphere, and merely serves to dilute the potent oxygen.

TH   4

In addition to these two constituents, the air contains, in varying amounts, a third gas—Carbonic Acid—which differs from the other two in being poisonous if breathed in large quantities.

Except in rare instances, however, it is not found in the air in sufficient quantity to produce by itself serious results.

2. THE CHIEF SOURCES OF IMPURITY OF THE AIR :—

(a) Products of respiration.
(b) Products of combustion.
(c) Products of decomposition.
(d) Dust.
(e) Bacteria.

(a) *Products of Respiration.*—Respiration adds to air the following :—

1. Carbonic acid.
2. Water.
3. Dead tissues.
4. Germs or bacteria.

The proportion of the last two added to the air varies greatly, but the quantities of carbonic acid added is comparatively constant. In round numbers 4 per cent. of oxygen is abstracted from the air in the lungs, whilst 4 per cent. of carbonic acid is added to it.

Expired air is usually saturated with watery vapour, but the exact amount of water added varies with the degree of saturation which obtains in the air breathed.

As a rough average it may be stated that about ten ounces of watery vapour are given off by the human lungs in 24 hours.

In health expired air contains few microbes but much organic matter. This organic matter diffuses sluggishly through the air of a room and is destroyed slowly by fresh air. It promotes the growth of microbes, and milk, meat or other foods in contact with it rapidly become tainted.

The average adult gives off about half a cubic foot of carbonic acid per hour and oxen or horses about three times that amount. In other words, if we had a box about twelve inches long, twelve inches broad and six inches high, a man would fill it with pure carbonic acid in an hour.

It will readily be grasped from these figures how indescribably foul the air of Indian huts can become when half a dozen human beings and several animals are herded together in one small unventilated room.

(b) *Products of combustion.*—The chief products of combustion which concern us are carbonic acid and carbon monoxide.

It is desirable that every one should appreciate the difference between these two gases. When one looks at a fire burning in an *angethi,* one is unconsciously witnessing the process of a chemical combination. The carbon of the wood, coal, or charcoal is uniting with the oxygen of the air, to form one of two chemicals, either carbonic acid, which is comparatively harmless compound, and which we consume in large quantities in ærated waters, or carbon monoxide, an active narcotic poison.

It is this latter gas which is the source of danger when an *angethi* is burning in a closed apartment. Cases of death due to charcoal fumes are not infrequent in bazars, so that the poisonous gases given off by any kind of stove and especially by a charcoal *angethi* should be known to intelligent Indians.

Indeed, Europeans are often very careless and ignorant in this respect, and amongst troops under canvas in cold weather accidents frequently happen due to ignorance of this simple sanitary fact.

Oil, candles and gas used for lighting are powerful sources of pollution.

(c) *Products of decomposition.*—The chief practical point in this connection is that, decomposing vegetation produces poisonous and inflammable gases, so that the heaps of rotten leaves, etc., which are generally to be found outside a bedroom in India are things to be avoided.

Sulphuretted hydrogen, the gas which gives to rotten eggs their characteristic odour, may occur in marshes, in and near excavations, in collections of refuse or decaying vegetable matter and other waste heaps.

The inhalation of this gas is followed by more poisonous results than is commonly supposed. An atmosphere containing one part in seventy thousand parts of air is dangerous to human life, whilst air containing one to two parts per thousand kills in a few minutes. When only minute quantities are present, giddiness, headache, and general depression are produced.

(d) *Dust.*—This is a source of impurity of the greatest importance to us in India where many infectious diseases are conveyed by this means. The following ingredients may be found by microscopical examination of ordinary bazar dust :—

1. · Bits of charcoal.
2. Bits of cotton and other fabrics.
3. Bits of skin.
4. Bits of insects.
5. Bits of hay and straw.
6. Dried sputum.
7. Dried bits of excrement.
8. Germs anchored on to all these various particles of matter.

The harmless-looking motes which we see dancing in the sunshine are, therefore, very frequently as dangerous as cordite, and constitute, not only an undesirable but a positively disgusting mixture.

Rooms should, therefore, be constructed to facilitate the removal of dust.

The Indian servants' idea of dusting is to flick a *jharan* at an article in the hope that he will hit some of the dust and that when he has displaced it into the air it won't fall again into the same spot and offend his master or mistress's eye. That he should aim at removing it from the room never occurs to him. The sweeper's method is to keep one small twig broom, which is his badge of office, and to use it for every purpose.

He sweeps up the drive, the kitchen, the stable, and the best dhurrie with the self-same article. It would be difficult to imagine a more disgusting practice, and we suggest that for indoor use the " Knight of the Broom " should be supplied with a special brush of English pattern and a dustpan. The apparatus is not costly, and we feel sure that a little more attention to details of this nature might make life easier and healthier in this country. Again, a few lessons in the use of a damp cloth for dusting or in the value of wet sawdust or used tea leaves before sweeping out rooms might be a useful addition to the elementary education of Indian scholars.

(*e*) *Bacteria in air.*—Bacteria in air vary in number and species according to certain external conditions, such as the pollution of the air, the dampness of surrounding surfaces, gravity, and various seasonal and climatic conditions.

(i) *The pollution of the air.*—It was Tyndall who in 1878 first pointed out that dust might carry microbes, and that, other things being equal, dusty air contained more bacteria than dust-free air. Since that time Haldane and others have confirmed this by examination of the air of workshops, school-rooms, etc. In open fields free from habitations few bacteria are present, and the same is true of mountain and sea air : in towns or crowded rooms the reverse is the case. Miquel found an average of 455 bacteria per cubic metre in a French park, but an average of 3,910 in the chief street of Paris, and 79,000 in a hospital ward. A polluted or dusty atmosphere generally contains many bacteria, and much carbonic acid, but there seems to be no direct relation between them. An atmosphere may be offensive and yet comparatively free from bacteria, as in sewer gas, certain offensive trades, railway tunnels, etc. The presence or absence of an offensive odour, therefore, must not be regarded as a criterion of the purity of the atmosphere.

(ii) *The dampness of surrounding surfaces.*—Air over sandy soil contains more bacteria as a rule than that over damp clay soils. Rain and snow also diminish the number of organisms in the air. It has also been proved that air saturated with moisture is almost germ free. Hence the comparative absence of bacteria in expired air in ordinary quiet respiration, though in the act of coughing, sneezing, or shouting, organisms may be present in the expired air. Haldane, Andrewes, and others have shown that the same principle applies in a sewer, the air of which frequently contains fewer organisms than that of outside air. This is also the explanation of the retention of bacteria in sputum (the tubercle bacillus), or excreta (the typhoid bacillus), so long as these materials remain moist.

(iii) *The influence of gravity.*—The influence of gravity operates upon microscopic cells in the same way as upon other matter. Hence, fewer bacteria are found at high altitudes or on the tops of lofty buildings. For instance, it has been found that, at the top of the Clock Tower of the Houses of Parliament in London, there was only about one-third of the number of bacteria found at ground-level.

(iv) *Seasonal and meteorological conditions* also exert an influence upon the number of bacteria found in the air.   The seasonal maximum in the open air seems to occur about midsummer, and the minimum about the middle of winter, but in hospital wards and houses the reverse occurs, owing no doubt to ventilation.   Air currents and wind, of course, exert a marked influence, as also do rain and snow.   Direct sunlight possesses great bacteria-destroying powers and thus reduces the number of air organisms.

Unlike the organic matter and carbonic acid, the number of microbes in the air of *crowded rooms* is dependent rather upon habitual ventilation and cleanliness than upon the conditions at the time of observation.   They are not due, as we have seen, to respiration or as a rule to want of cleanliness of persons or clothing, but are derived from the walls, ceiling, and floor of the room itself, especially if these are porous and absorbent, and if made to vibrate and thus create dust.   As to the nature of microbes found in the air, little that is final can be said.   Their variety is considerable, and for the most part they are harmless to man but they may include putrefactive, suppurative, and intestinal organisms, and the specific germs of disease. Under exceptional conditions bacilli of tubercle, typhoid fever and other diseases have been isolated from air, and Gordon has detected an " air-fungus " and a " skin microbe," indicative of filth and human pollution.

Spores of moulds, though much more bulky than most other air-borne organisms, are less readily deposited.   Other low forms of organisms and pollen may also be found, and may be the source of certain forms of disease such as hay fever.— (Whitelegge.)

3.   THE AMOUNT OF AIR SPACE NECESSARY :—

This will depend on whether the room is to be used as a working place (as in a factory), or as a dwelling place only.

At least 1,000 cubic feet of air space should be allowed for each person occupying the room, *i.e.*, a space 10 feet long, 10 feet wide and 10 feet high. The cubic capacity of a room is got by multiplying together the length, breadth and the height of the room. In calculating the cubic space of a room, deduct the cubic space occupied by furniture and do not forget to make some allowance for the number of lamps generally used. The more lamps used, the larger must be the cubic space allowed for each person ordinarily occupying the room, and it may be taken as a rough average, that every kerosene oil lamp burning in a room pollutes the air to the same extent as seven adults.

In buildings which are only *occasionally* used and not continuously inhabited (such as religious meeting places, theatres, schoolrooms and other places of the kind) it is generally quite impossible to allow enough cubic space for the large number of persons assembling there. To make up for this ventilation should be as free as possible. In hospitals a much larger cubic space and the freest ventilation are particularly necessary. In workshops, printing premises, shops and offices particular attention must be given to providing as much cubic space and as free ventilation as possible.

The superficial area should be 100 feet (*i.e.*, a space of floor 10 feet long by 10 feet wide) *for each person*. And there must also be a height of 10 feet at least between the floor and the ceiling. In this way the 1,000 cubic feet required is obtained. (In India, the height from floor to roof should be 15 feet or more for coolness, but this extra height must not lead to any reduction in the amount of floor space). This 1,000 cubic feet is the very least space that should be recommended, especially in India. But this is by itself not enough, for in order to keep the air sufficiently pure for health, this 1,000 cubic feet space of air must be changed thrice *every hour*. In this way 3,000 cubic feet of air will be given to a person every hour.

For instance, if six people are living in a room, then the size would require to be 30 feet long, 20 feet broad, and 15 feet high, and the air must be changed thrice every hour so that it may continue to be healthy to breathe. This would mean building very big houses and would be too expensive for most people.

How is the difficulty to be got over ? By changing the air oftener than thrice every hour. For a room containing 500 cubic feet of space for each person living in it, it would therefore be necessary to renew the air six times every hour. In cold climates, such as that of England, or of India in the cold season, this is difficult to do as it is found that if the air is changed more than thrice an hour the room becomes too cold and draughty and people are apt " to catch cold " and get ill. One way to get over this difficulty is to heat the air before allowing it to enter the room. This is done by making the air as it enters the room pass over pipes containing hot water, or by some similar plan. In this way the air is heated without being made impure by the gases given out by fires, stoves, etc. We shall presently see how this is to be arranged for in India. (See Ventilation.)

4. NATURE'S AGENTS FOR PURIFYING THE AIR :—

They are—

(*a*) Rain.
(*b*) The action of sunlight.
(*c*) The action of plants.
(*d*) Winds.
(*e*) Diffusion of gases and differences of temperature.

(*a*) *Rain* is simply a mechanical purifier : it washes the air. As it falls, it removes all suspended organic impurities, and absorbs some of the harmful gases.

(b) *The action of the sun.*—Sunlight has the power of killing germs in the air and will be further referred to later.

(c) *The action of plants.*—Plants absorb carbonic acid from the air and give off oxygen. No better illustration of the ceaseless cycle of matter can be conceived than the consideration of the course and transmutation of this carbonic acid gas given off by the lungs. Though we exhale it as a waste product every time we breathe, though it is thrown off in enormous volumes by gas jets, fires and furnaces, it never accumulates in the free air of heaven around us, for the economy of Nature tolerates no waste—no accumulation of effete matters. This gas which is so inimical to animal life is ordained to be indispensable to vegetable life. We *exhale* it, and plants *inhale* it, so that every tree which is left to grow in the crowded Indian city—and every plant in the village garden, transmutes it by the heat of the sun into blossom and leaf and stem, imprisoning the carbon and setting the oxygen free. The coal which we now burn so generally in India was made up long ages ago, of plants and trees fed by the nourishing heat of the sun, from the carbonic acid in the air, and both the heat and carbonic acid are returned to us as we sit in front of the blazing fire. And so, although we cannot re-breathe this gas without injury, we can use it as a food in our vegetables and transmute the heat pent up in the leaves and roots into the warmth of our bodies, the strength and activity of our limbs and even the very thoughts which flash through our brains.

(d) *Winds.*—The winds tend to distribute the air, and thus by mixing the gases produce uniformity of composition.

It is due to unequal heating of the air that we have winds. Imagine a portion of the Earth at which the air has been very strongly heated, for example at the Equator where the sun is hotter than elsewhere. This hot air being lighter rises up and colder air rushes in to take its place and mix with it. The cold air rushing in is the wind.

Winds are splendid means of ventilation. They sweep impurities out of the streets, houses, and every place where they can enter. A strong wind has often caused an epidemic of disease to cease suddenly by means of sweeping away the stagnant air containing millions of germs of disease; and also by causing better ventilation of houses and streets, etc.

When the wind passes freely *through* a room from one side to the other—the process is called *ventilation by perflation* or "flowing through." This is the best means of ventilation. Our houses should have windows and doors nearly facing one another so that the air may enter by those at one side of the room and escape by those at the opposite side.

When screens, purdahs, or furniture block up the windows the wind, of course, cannot cleanse the air of the rooms properly. Perflation cannot, however, alone be exclusively relied on as the winds change, often from day to day, or cease altogether for days at a time.

(e) *Diffusion of gases and differences of temper-ature.*—If we place two gases in a jar, without shaking them up, we shall find that they slowly mix with one another or diffuse, until a uniform mixture of the two gases results.

Differences of temperature assist the mixture of gases. Air moves from a hot to a cool place, so that the daily changes of temperature cause varying degrees of air movement. In a room in which several people are sitting the heat given out by

their breaths and bodies, heats the air and it ex-
pands, gets lighter, and rises to the roof. Colder
air then flows in to take the place of the hot air.
As the air becomes heated and therefore lighter, the
colder and heavier air tries to mix with it and flows
into the room in order to do so. The hotter the
air in a room becomes and the colder the air outside, the quicker does the mixing of the gases occur.
This explains why it is that when the window of a
very hot room is opened on a cold night the outside
air rushes so quickly into the room.

The nearer the temperature of the outside air is
to that of the inside air, the less the mixing that
occurs and therefore the worse the ventilation.
This is a most important point to remember especially as regards ventilation in India.

(f) *Aspiration.*—This is another natural means
of ventilation. This occurs when the wind blowing
over a hollow tube (such as the chimney of a room)
sucks the air out of the tube. More air from
below flows up to take the place of the air which
has been sucked out and so a constant movement
of air passes from the room up the chimney.
Winds act as great ventilating agents by sucking
up the air from rooms and so removing it. In the
same way when a fire is burning in the fireplace of
a room it helps greatly to ventilate the apartment.
The fire heats the air round about it and in the
chimney, the heated air rises up the chimney and
colder air flows into the room to take its place,
thus setting up a current of air and changing the
air of the room. Similar results may be attained by placing lamps or gaslights near ventilation
outlets.

5. ARTIFICIAL MEANS OF SUPPLYING THE INDI-
    VIDUAL WITH PURE AIR :—

Ventilation is the removal of impurities which
collect in the air of inhabited rooms by means of

fresh air from outside the room. Ventilation may be *natural* or *artificial*. *Natural ventilation* is at work when we open windows to let in fresh air and allow the foul air at the same time to escape. *Artificial ventilation* consists of some special method of changing the air in a room, such as pumping apparatus for sucking bad air out of a room or by driving in fresh air by machinery, such as fans. It is important to bear in mind that in all systems of ventilation, however simple or however complicated, we must have an *inlet* by which the fresh air is supplied and an outlet by which the foul air escapes.

The points to remember in connexion with *inlets* are :—

(*a*) They should be above the level of the heads of the people living in the room. This prevents draughts, etc., from the air in cold weather. For this reason it is best to place them eight feet or so above the level of the floor. If *heated air* is being used the inlets should be near the floor.

(*b*) The flow of air through the inlet should be directed *upwards* to the roof. This can be done by the means of a sloping piece of wood.

(*c*) Several small inlets are better than one or two large ones. This tends to break up the cold air

FIG. 2.

Tobin's Tube Ventilators.

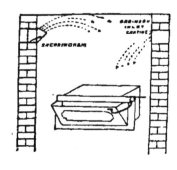

FIG. 3.

Sheringhum Valve Ventilators.

entering the room and not only prevents draughts
but cleanses more effectually the air of the room.
Inlets for each person, in India should measure
48 square inches. Bricks perforated with small
holes make excellent inlets, but the openings on
the outerside of the brick must be smaller than
those of the inner (or room) side.

The points to remember in connexion with *outlets*
are :—

(*a*) They should be in or near the roof as heated
air tends to rise.

(*b*) Lamps or gaslights should be placed near
the outlets to increase the escape of the heated air,
and in order that the smoke and burnt gases from
the lights may escape by the outlets and not get
into the air of the room.

(*c*) A ventilation shaft or a chimney must have a
cowl to keep out rain and prevent down draughts.

(*d*) Both inlets and outlets should be kept clean
and *not blocked up in any way*, and the size of the
outlets should correspond to that of the inlet.

When we come to apply these principles to
Indian houses we may enunciate the following
rules :—

1. Do not close up all windows and doors even
in the coldest weather. Windows in India are
often provided with *jhilmils*. When these are
opened, air passes freely into
the room. If there are glass
or wooden doors *also* these
should be closed as seldom
as possible. Close the
j h i l m i l s instead. Small
windows near the roof, the
so-called clerestory windows,
are excellent ventilators and
can be kept open at night
without any appreciable
draught.

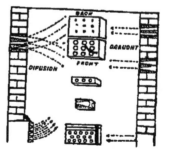

FIG. 4.
Ellison's Air Inlets.

2. *Keep windows and doors open as much as possible, day and night.*—If a window has glass-sashes which can be moved upwards and downwards, open the lower one about 4 to 6 inches at the foot and close this open space with a wooden board. The air will enter at the space where the two sashes meet and the air coming into the room will enter as shown by the arrow in the diagram. (Fig. 5.)

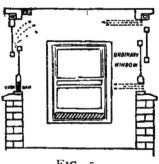

Fig. 5.

Hinches Bird's Window Inlets.

3. In cold weather a fire is an excellent ventilation shaft. *Never close a chimney up in cold or in hot weather* for at all times it acts as a ventilator ; more so of course when a fire is burning, or when a window is blowing over its top. Try to get several openings made (and *kept* clean and *open*) near the roof for the escape of foul air. A space for ventilation along the topmost ridge of the roof is a very good plan. Or a space may be left between the top of the walls and the roof.

4. In most Indian houses occupied by the well-to-do there are so many doors and windows that there is no risk of bad ventilation if they are left open. If these doors and windows are covered with *chics* or *jhilmils* to keep out glare, heat, flies, etc., the ventilation will generally be quite good. The huts of the poorer classes in India are generally very badly ventilated. There are no outlets for smoke or foul air, and if there are, they are usually tightly closed up.

5. Remember that cold air does not harm as long as we are warmly enough clothed.

6. In the hot weather, at night, doors and windows should all be left open. In the day time air finds its way in through the *chics* covering the

doors. Where punkahs (or electric fans) are used, these do not increase the purity of the air. They only move the air in the room and do not draw in the air to any extent from the outside or drive air out of the room.

In hot weather there is little difference between the temperature of the air inside and outside of the house, and so there is little or no exchange of air going on. It is thus all the more necessary that the rooms should be as large as possible and that the doors and windows be left as much open as possible. The difficulty is that by doing so the hot air enters and makes the rooms very hot. To prevent this while the weather is very hot, khus-khus tatties can be used in places where the air is dry enough and where hot winds are the rule. But in moderately hot weather doors and windows should be left open, night and day, as much as possible. The heat will do far less harm than breathing poisonous air.

The best plan for fairly well-to-do people living in a hot climate is to use a thermantidote, which sends a stream of fresh cooled air into the house, and thus cools and ventilates the rooms. The thermantidote must, however, be used so that no draught or current of air from it is felt. Where possible it ought to be placed *in a room opening out of the room in use* and the cool air should thus be allowed to mix gradually with that of the room which is being occupied. To sit in the current of air caused by the thermantidote is to run risk of a chill and chills in the Tropics often lead to fever, dysentery, etc.

Staircases in houses should be well ventilated by a large rainproof opening in the roof as they often feed the rooms with air and also receive foul air from them.

Cookhouses should be well ventilated and be provided with chimneys or vent holes for smoke ;

otherwise food becomes tainted and unwholesome from the bad air.

"During sickness good ventilation is more important than ever. Indians frequently close all doors and windows tightly in the sick room. This is the worst thing that can be done as the patient is not only being poisoned by his own breath but by the breath of those waiting on him, and there is no condition in which a man requires good fresh air so much as when he is ill. In time of sickness very few relatives or friends should be allowed to visit and attend the sick man. We have often seen patients in a small room—containing about 500 cubic feet of air altogether—with as many as 10 or 12 relatives and friends crowded together for several hours. Nothing could be more harmful to the patient who is slowly poisoned by the organic matter and gases given off by his friends' clothes and bodies. No more than one, or at most two people, should be allowed in the room with the sick person. When a person falls ill and is likely to be ill for even a day or two, he ought to be placed in the largest room in the house. He needs all the air he can have to help him to get well again. Nowadays, consumption is treated by keeping the sick person in the open air day and night. He is protected from chill and wet very carefully and is fed in the best way for his illness. Fresh air alone cannot only prevent but also cure most early cases of consumption.

When we think of how most Indians shut up all the doors, windows and ventilation holes in their rooms, how several persons go to sleep in the same small room, and how they cover up their faces with a sheet or blanket, we cannot wonder at the feeble health so many suffer from."

Most Indian ladies *when travelling in doolies* are shut up so tightly that fresh air cannot get in. After such a journey, they often suffer from severe headache and remain ill for several days on account of the poisoned air they have had to breathe.

Another point in relation to ventilation is the keeping of pets. We have already seen that domestic animals consume large quantities of oxygen, but there are other dangers to consider.

Monkeys are very liable to consumption and parrots suffer from a peculiar disease due to a bacillus closely allied to the typhoid or enteric organism. Monkeys have been shown to have infected their masters with consumption, and considering what bacteriology tells us parrots cannot be regarded as altogether safe sharers of bed and board. Influenza is often contracted from the horse and diphtheria is certainly spread by various kinds of domestic pets, especially cats, fowls and pigeons. Lastly, it must be remembered that bedding and clothing require to get their share of fresh air and sunlight, just as much as the person who uses them.

6. THE DANGERS OF IMPURE AIR :—

To recapitulate air is, as we have seen, the medium by which many diseases are conveyed. On the other hand, a defective or impure air supply may also be a potent factor in the causation of the following ailments—

(1) Indigestion.
(2) Bronchitis.
(3) Pneumonia.
(4) Weakness and debility.
(5) Heat stroke.

This question of fresh air is one of the most important of all sanitary problems. Pure water was as much appreciated by the Grecian conquerors of India as by ourselves, but even half a century ago fresh air as a remedial measure was not only undreamt of, but the early exponents of the " fresh air " treatment had to meet with much opposition and ridicule. Even now the term "*fresh air fiend*" is constantly used in a disparaging sense.

The natives of India have not yet realized its importance, and there can be little doubt that a large proportion of the thirty-seven per thousand of the population, who die annually in India, die from spending a third of their existence in an impure atmosphere.

The fact that only half that number per thousand die annually in England is largely due to the fact that Englishmen have learned to appreciate the necessity of pure air.

Dangers of Overcrowding :—There is very great danger in living in an overcrowded room.

(*a*) *Temporary Overcrowding :*—The bad effects of this are headaches, giddiness, fainting, and even vomiting and diarrhœa. If the overcrowding is extreme death may result.

(*b*) *Constant Overcrowding :*—Where people constantly living in a bad atmosphere—that is in small overcrowded rooms—their health rapidly deteriorates. This is shown by loss of strength, sleeplessness ; loss of the desire for food ; bad digestion ; great feeling of unhappiness and of being unable to make any prolonged effort of body and mind. The sufferer becomes pale and "bloodless," partly as the result of "oxygen-starvation," but chiefly on account of chronic poisoning by the foul air taken into their lungs.

Individuals whose vitality has been lowered in this way are very liable to contract other diseases such as Consumption, Inflammation of the Lungs or Bronchial Tubes, Dysentery, Cholera, Plague, Small-pox, Typhus Fever, Measles, Diphtheria, as well as a severe inflammation of the eyes called Ophthalmia which often causes total blindness. Children are especially liable to severe illnesses as the result of bad ventilation and it was found in a certain hospital for children in Europe that one out of every three children brought there died under treatment. When the ventilation was improved, the number of deaths in that hospital was ninety per cent. less than before.

In one of the finest regiments in the British Army consumption was extremely common less than fifty years ago. The soldiers in that regiment lived in very small, badly ventilated barrack rooms. When the ventilation was improved and fewer soldiers made to live in each room, it was found that consumption rapidly disappeared.

Overcrowding is moreover bad in another way. Children see and hear many things they ought not to and if they are crowded together with grown-up people, privacy and decency are impossible.

From what has been written above it is clear how extremely dangerous it is to live in rooms too small for the number of persons living in them and into which enough fresh air cannot find its way.

CHAPTER IV.

Water and Water Supplies in the Tropics.

The rapidity with which water passes through the stomach causes it to be a very dangerous vehicle of infection. For this reason contaminated water is a more obnoxious carrier of disease than impure food. All the greater then the reason for insuring that our water-supply is above suspicion.—(Hutchinson's Food & Dietetics, p. 300.)

"A man must not throw any impure substance into water."—(Institutes of Vishnu.)

WITHOUT water there would be no life. The part which water plays in the human economy is of the first importance. It constitutes nearly two-thirds of the total weight of the body ; seventy-nine per cent. of the blood ; eighty per cent. of the brain and muscles, and ten per cent. even of bone.

As we shall show in the next chapter it forms the vast bulk of our so-called solid food, whereas whatever our tastes in liquor may be, it constitutes at least 90 per cent. of the fluid we drink.

Like pure air, pure water consists of two gases, but whereas in air the gases exist loosely mixed together in varying quantities, in water they are combined into a fixed compound containing one part of oxygen to two of hydrogen.

From a health point of view two principal questions present themselves with regard to our water-supply, *viz.* :—

1. The question of quantity.
2. The question of quality.

The amount of water or other liquids required by man, over and above what he obtains in his

food is from two to three pints in temperate
climates, but in the Tropics a very much larger
quantity is consumed by most people.

Man requires water for many purposes, and the
quantity which he uses varies with the locality.

Glasgow, for example, stands at the head of all
British towns with a daily allowance per head of
58 gallons, whilst Leicester stands at the bottom
of the list with an allowance of less than one-third
of that amount, viz., 17 gallons per day.

In places like Calcutta and Peshawar the daily
allowance per head is as much as 41½ gallons
of filtered water, but in many Indian towns,
villages and even cantonments, scarcity of water
constitutes a hardship.

Unfortunately, in water, as in many other things
in this world, appearances are deceptive.

The physical characters and palatability of a
water are no guide to its fitness for drinking purposes. Many horribly polluted waters are clear,
sparkling and pleasant to the taste. Filtration
through a few feet of some soils readily removes the
disagreeable appearance of the most filthy liquids,
but such slight filtration does not, of course, remove
their dangerous properties.

Pure water for drinking purposes is a commodity
not easy to obtain in the Tropics. This difficulty
is mainly due to the pollution to which the water
is subjected by the customs of the people, and it
is largely owing to this pollution that diseases
caused by microbes and parasites are so rife. In
warm climates, disease germs and parasites exist
in water in far greater variety and numbers than
in the temperate zone, where the conditions are
not so favourable to their growth and development. The drinking of impure and muddy water
in a cool climate is liable to produce enteric fever,
disturbance of the bowels and possibly worms,.
but the drinking of similar water in the Tropics

is not only liable to produce those diseases, but also cholera, dysentery, goitre and many other parasitic affections. In hot climates, even the external use of bad water for bathing purposes may cause Oriental Sores, Ring Worm and other maladies.

This is a terrible indictment against Indian water, but it is well merited.

Before considering how we can treat and safeguard our drinking water we must first consider the sources of supply.

All the world over, man derives his water supply directly or indirectly from the rainfall. Water as it condenses in the clouds from the gaseous state is absolutely pure, but by the time it reaches the surface of the earth in the form of rain it has become impure. Rain, as we have seen, is a purifier of the air, and in performing this service to man it becomes itself impure. It washes out of the air, various undesirable gases and obnoxious solids in the form of dust and either sinks into the soil or flows along its surface in streams.

Man obtains his supply from six sources which, according to their origin, are known as—

1. Upland surface water, *i.e.*, water running down hills in small streams to natural or artificially made lakes.
2. Rain water.
3. Ordinary surface water from cultivated land, such as land springs, streams, and ponds.
4. River water.
5. Ground water, from wells and springs.
6. Distilled water.

Comparison of waters derived from different sources :—

The Rivers Pollution Commissioners classify the qualities of these waters as follows, in respect of

wholesomeness, palatability, and general fitness
for drinking and cooking :—

(a) Wholesome
  1. Spring water.
  2. Deep well water.
  } Very palatable.

(b)· Suspicious
  3. Upland surface water.
  4. Stored Rain water.
  } Moderately palatable.

(c) Dangerous
  5. Ordinary surface water from cultivated lands.
  6. River water to which sewage gains access.
  7. Shallow well water.
  } Palatable.

In respect to softness, they grade them as
follows :—

  1. Rain water.
  2. Upland surface water.
  3. Surface water from cultivated lands.
  4. Polluted river water.
  5. Spring water.
  6. Deep well water.
  7. Shallow well water.

From the above it will be seen that the comparatively hard waters, derived from springs and deep
wells, are the safest for drinking purposes and that
the interests of the trading community are thus
evidently opposed to those of the householder.

A few details about these sources of supply are
necessary.

1. *Upland surface water* :—A great many stations
in India obtain their supply from sources of this
kind which are generally good ones as highland

districts are usually sparsely populated and the land is accordingly poorly cultivated, so that the risk of sewage contamination is slight.

2. *Rain water* :—As a source of water supply, rain largely concerns us in India, and in places where the rainfall is heavy and the springs are brackish it forms our chief standby.

Rain falling into a clean receptacle in country places supplies a pure water, for, in passing through the atmosphere, it takes up but few impurities except in large towns. When it reaches the ground or roof it comes in contact with many impurities. In India where dust storms are frequent the roofs of houses are generally polluted with vegetable matter from leaves ; the excrement of birds ; dust containing filth of various kinds and the eggs of insects. These matters give it an unpleasant taste, and in some instances cause disease. Impurities from the roof should therefore be prevented from gaining access to the tank. With this object contrivances have been made which reject the first washing off the roof before the water is permitted to flow into the storage tanks.

3. *Ordinary surface water* :—This must always be regarded as dangerous as the presence of sewage is well-nigh certain. Ponds and tanks constitute a particularly dangerous source of water supply which unfortunately is the only one obtainable in many parts of India.

4. *River waters* :—Such waters are constantly liable to pollution by men and animals. If it were not for the beneficent purifying work of oxygen, rivers in this country would soon become little more than open sewers, but, fortunately, purifying processes go on actively in river water, and, if the stream has many falls and eddies, the amount of oxygen dissolved in the water is so great that a moderate amount of contamination is soon got rid

of. Moreover, there are various green river plants continually at work giving off oxygen in a most active condition.

The oxidation process in rivers is a chemical process, started by bright sunlight. When the stream becomes thick or muddy, this process is checked or stopped, but even when this occurs, there is still a purifying action going on as a number of fish, shell-fish, crayfish, small animal-culæ, microscopic plants and bacteria live on sewage or other organic débris. Unfortunately these purifying processes in most rivers are not sufficient to cope with the quantity of dead organic material constantly poured in from source to mouth. The value of fish as purifying agents of water is undoubted.

5. *Ground water* :—The water which falls on the earth and sinks 'into the soil returns again for the use of man as (*a*) Wells, and (*b*) Springs.

(*a*) *Wells* :—Wells are divided into three varieties :—Shallow, deep and artesian. The descriptive words are not used to indicate the relative depth of the well, but to describe the water bearing stratum they tap, as is clearly shown in the accompanying illustration. (Fig. 6.) All shallow wells must be regarded as suspicious sources of supply.

No uncovered Indian well can be looked on as safe, and it is utterly wrong to regard any such supply as safe on the result of a laboratory analysis. Pollution of the worst kind may occur at any moment, so that an analysis which may have been perfectly correct at the time it was carried out, becomes utterly valueless as a sanitary guide.

Most Indian villages obtain their supply from shallow wells, the number of which in India is enormous. Many are simply holes dug in the ground : they are then spoken of as ' kutcha'

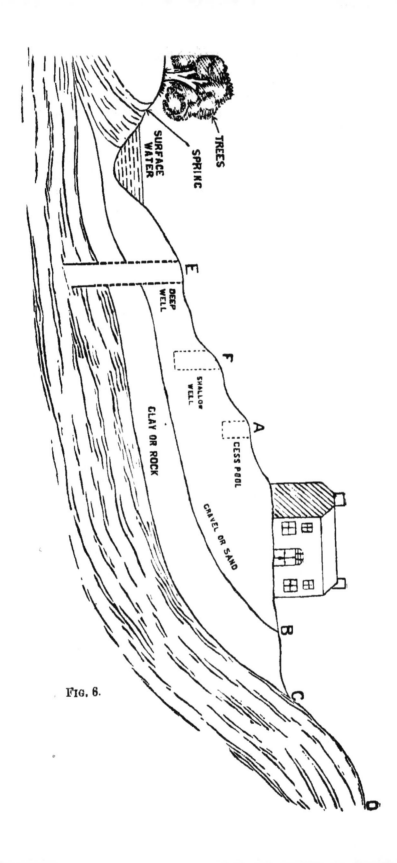

FIG. 6.

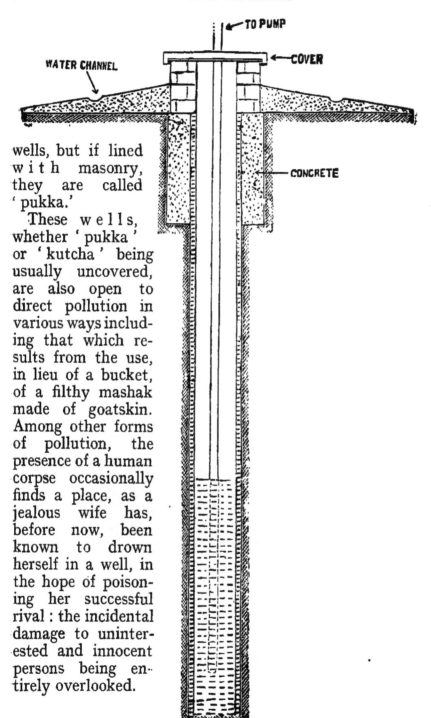

wells, but if lined with masonry, they are called 'pukka.'

These wells, whether 'pukka' or 'kutcha' being usually uncovered, are also open to direct pollution in various ways including that which results from the use, in lieu of a bucket, of a filthy mashak made of goatskin. Among other forms of pollution, the presence of a human corpse occasionally finds a place, as a jealous wife has, before now, been known to drown herself in a well, in the hope of poisoning her successful rival : the incidental damage to uninterested and innocent persons being entirely overlooked.

For a safe water supply it is essential that wells should be properly made. The well should be lined throughout or as far as possible with porous brick. The upper portion should be steined. A small brick coping with a cover should be provided, and the area surrounding the well should be concreted and provided with a water channel.

Vide Illustration from Blackham's Military Sanitation. (Fig. 7.)

Fig. 8.

BULLOCK RUN OF NATIVE WELL IN HOSPITAL COMPOUND, DELHI.
From *Caldwell's Military Hygiene*.
Plate kindly lent by Ballière, Tindall and Cox.

Pumps should be provided, as dipping of buckets provides endless facilities for contamination, and a radius of a hundred yards should be left clear around the well.

Artesian or tube wells are far better than dug wells. They consist of iron tubes hammered into

the ground until water is reached. Like shallow
wells, they must be adequately protected at the
surface to prevent pollution at that point.

The Indian *ryot* attends to the functions of
nature without the regard which the Western races
commonly pay to the question of locality and some
of his customs must be broken down if local
administrations wish to supply him with pure water.
In consequence of the customs of the inhabitants it
is not a matter of surprise that the soil in and
about the native villages is absolutely saturated
with waste organic material. The water in Indian
village wells is almost invariably even in the driest
weather, within a few feet of the surface, so that
filth deposited on the soil surrounding the well
has every possible facility for the wholesale
poisoning of native communities.

(*b*) *Springs :*—These are generally described as
land and main springs. Land springs are often
due to surface depressions touching the underground water level, generally when the underground water reaches its lowest level, such springs
run dry.

Manifestly they receive their supply from very
near the surface, and so are extremely liable to
organic pollution.

The classification of all springs as wholesome
by the Rivers Pollution Commission is therefore
misleading.

Main springs are, however, generally good, as
they act as the main outlets for geological strata,
but occasionally they, too, are doubtful sources of
supply and great care is necessary to investigate
their immediate neighbourhood for surface-derived
impurities.

6. *Distilled water :*—In rainless tracts and in
regions where the rainfall is scanty, or where
there are only salt lakes, the drinking-water is
frequently obtained by distillation. This is the

means of supply to the troops and European residents at Aden, where the wells are brackish and where rain may not occur for several years : the sea water is distilled and used for drinking purposes.

Distilled water is also largely used for drinking purposes on war ships and on other vessels. As distilled water is flat and unpalatable, æration of the water is an important process which should form part of the plant in all methods. For ordinary purposes it may be ærated by half filling an ordinary wine bottle with the water, and then, after corking it, shaking it vigorously so as to cause the air to be absorbed by the water. It is said that the oily taste of distilled water may be removed by placing a rusty nail in it.

So much for the sources of water. We must now consider how pollution may occur. This may take place—

1. At its source.
2. During storage.
3. During transit or distribution.

1. *Pollution at the Source :*—In order to prevent the fouling of the sources of supply, it is obvious that every effort must be made to prevent any form of pollution in the neighbourhood of the wells, springs, or tanks from which drinking-water is obtained. The question of the protection of " catchment areas " is one that concerns Government and Municipalities and need not be dealt with here.

In Bengal and elsewhere in India it is a common practice for the women and children of the house to bathe in the tank from which the drinking-water is taken. This is a foul and most dangerous habit and should never be allowed.

Again, people wash their bodies and spit and wash the mouth in a tank or stream used for drinking purposes. They then collect the water for their cooking and drinking supply for the day quite close to the place they have just polluted. The dangers of this practice have already been pointed out.

Pollution during Storage :—There is no doubt that much pollution of water occurs during storage. It is very little use to boil water and then leave it exposed to the contamination of insects and dust.

Drinking-water should not be stored at all during cold weather unless the procedure is absolutely unavoidable, but in the hot season some simple means of storage for the purpose of cooling becomes an imperative necessity.

The ordinary Indian *surai* certainly cools water, but it has the disadvantages of being porous and it is not always kept covered. There is no doubt that this compulsory storage of water for the purpose of cooling it during the hot weather is a fruitful source of pollution, and too much attention cannot be paid to it.

Water should be stored in *glazed chatties* or *ghurrahs* and these should always be kept perfectly clean and cool. The reason is that unglazed *chatties* take up by their pores dirt of all kinds, whilst in glazed ones these pores are filled up and so cannot absorb dangerous substances. The glazed smooth surface is also much more easily kept clean than the unglazed.

Galvanized iron or slate cisterns are the best means of storage but they are usually impracticable for Indian houses on the score of expense. What we advise is storage of all drinking-water, after boiling, in clean glass bottles with air-tight stoppers, such as those in which sterilised milk and some of the light beers are supplied. These should be placed in the ice-box till required.

In this connexion there are two points worth remembering—

(1) The water should be poured into the bottles whilst it is still boiling—this will sterilise the inside of the bottles and prevent possible contamination.

(2) The water should be cooled by placing the bottles in ice, and not by adding ice to the water at the time of drinking, especially if there be any doubt as to the purity of the ice. Remember that although boiling kills germs, freezing does not, and many an unfortunate accident has resulted from adding impure ice to water that has been carefully sterilised by boiling.

All vessels used for storing water must be kept covered, so as to prevent dirt and dust from falling into the water.

3. *Pollution during Transit.*—This is another very common source of infection.

Seeing that much water is, and must be, distributed by hand in India, this is a matter which demands constant care and supervision. In India water is very seldom brought into the house by means of pipes, as is the case in the larger towns of Europe. Even in large towns provided with modern water-works only a few of the well-to-do people can afford to introduce the water on to their premises : the vast majority are fortunate if there is a standpost in the street near the house. Our best Indian systems are therefore a street distribution and not a house distribution. In most towns the *bhisties* employ the *mashak* for the conveyance of water to the houses. This mode of transport in a leathern vessel which can never be kept clean is one which is sure to contaminate the water, however pure the source from which it is taken. If a *bhisti* lives in an infected house in which there is cholera, typhoid fever, or dysentery, his *mashak* is likely to become infected and so spread the disease to those houses that are supplied with water from the *mashak*. This mode of transport should be discontinued, but where *mashaks* are still used, no water should be drunk from them until it is first boiled. Metal vessels should

Fig. 9.

BHISTI FILLING MASHAK FROM A STAND-PIPE.

be used for storing water as they can be kept clean. The brass and copper vessels which are so prevalent in the East probably actually purify water to some small extent. Recent experiments on the effect of certain metals, such as copper and iron, on the organisms of disease point in this direction.

In most tropical countries we have to start with the idea that water is bad, and endeavour to remedy the defects of the natural supply as best we can.

It often happens in India that owing to a deficiency in the amount of pure water available, a town is provided with two supplies, a pure water for drinking, and a less pure water for washing, trade, and municipal purposes. Such is the case, to some extent, in Paris. There are circumstances, of course, in which this plan is unavoidable, but as a principle it is a bad one : it will certainly happen that impure water will be used for drinking, and in this way epidemic diseases may be spread. Moreover, if one system of pipes be used, even exceptionally, impurities from the impure supply may contaminate to an indefinite extent the pure supply. Enteric fever appears to have been caused in Paris in this way : after the impure Seine water had been cut off, the pure water has become infected by germs left in the pipes from the other supply.

Broadly speaking, there are three methods for rendering impure water innocuous :—

(1)	Physical	..	{	(a)	By distillation.
			{	(b)	By boiling.
(2)	Mechanical	..			By filtration.
(3)	Chemical	..	{	(a)	By precipitation.
			{	(b)	By use of germicides.

1. *Physical*—(a).—Distillation is, as we have seen, the chief means of supplying drinking-water at Aden, but it is not used in other parts of the Indian Empire. (b) Boiling is one of our oldest and best methods of preventing the noxious effects of bad water. Combined with some simple form of clarification or filtration, if fuel is available, it is the best method of dealing with impure water with which we are acquainted.

Boiling for five minutes will kill all germs even the deadly spores of tetanus, and we recommend this method for universal use in Indian households. The drawback to boiled water is that all the air has been driven out of it, and it is consequently flat and insipid to the taste. This difficulty can be overcome, and the water can be ærated by only half filling the storage bottle and then, after corking it, shaking it vigorously so as to cause the air to be absorbed by the water.   Or it may be ærated by passing it through a sterilised sieve.   Such a sieve can be improvised by taking a large biscuit tin and piercing the bottom with small holes.

2.   *Mechanical.*—Filtration of some kind or other is a method which has existed from time immemorial as Manu directed that water should be drunk only after filtering through cloth.   The Law of Manu recognised the necessity for purifying water, though the method advised is useless.   The Susruta also gives many good rules for the purification of water such as boiling and filtration. It is still very largely used and filtration by sand and gravel is the one use in civil communities. Filtration, even of the crudest nature, improves the potability of a water, and a simple device such as barrels fitted one inside the other with a good layer of gravel, sand, and wood ashes between them will not only clarify but actually purify water very considerably.

A few years ago there were on the market many kinds of filters, constructed of many varieties of material : including charcoal, asbestos, spongy iron and polarite which were advocated for domestic use.   They have, however, gone out of fashion, as they do not sterilise the water or render it free from bacteria.   The Pasteur-Chamberland and Berkefeld filters are the only filters much used in houses and camps now-a-days, because the Pasteur and in a lesser degree the Berkefeld really possess the property of removing bacteria from water.

(1) The disadvantages of the Pasteur filter are :— That not being a gravitation but a pressure filter, it requires a considerable head of pressure before water can be obtained in any quantity.

(2) That in consequence of the turbidity of the ordinary river water of the tropics the filter rapidly acquires on the outside of the filtering material a coating which completely blocks up its pores, stops water passing through even under pressure and renders the apparatus useless.

The same objections apply to the Berkefeld filter, with the additional one that it is more brittle than the Pasteur, and is not adapted for either rough transport or frequent cleansing. The Pasteur-Chamberland and Berkefeld filters are constructed on the same principle. The filtering material is a hollow candle composed of unglazed porcelain in the former and of a kind of earth in the latter. The Berkefeld candle is more porous than the Pasteur and therefore allows water to filter more rapidly.

The pressure difficulty is, as a rule, easily overcome, there being few places where a little ingenuity will not supply a sufficiency of pressure : and where it is not desirable to depend on this, there are numerous portable exhaust types in the market which can be adapted to every circumstance.

The readiness with which the filter candle—both Pasteur-Chamberland and Berkefeld—becomes blocked up is a much more serious affair, and leads sooner or later to the abandonment of its use. No filters of this type will be of great utility in the tropics unless, as part and parcel of their structure, there is a rough filter attached, which will first clarify the water.

Provided that water is clear, boiling is all that is necessary, but if it is muddy, it must be clarified by straining or by passing it through some simple form of filter *before* it is boiled. The reason for this is that, if even muddy water is boiled and all germs killed, the mud will act as an irritant to the bowels and will produce diarrhœa or even actual inflammation of the bowel.

This is the only use to which you should put filters. Remember that for the purpose of destroying germs in water, filters are a snare and a delusion to the unwary. The majority of filters are absolutely useless—many of them are actually dangerous, because instead of purifying the water, they contaminate it from the residue left behind by water that has previously passed through.

If such residue be not got rid of by constant cleansing and sterilisation, the germs therein will grow and multiply, and the water passing out of the filter may be infinitely more dangerous than that which went into it.

3. *Chemicals*—(a) *Mechanical.*—Alum and lime are used as mere mechanical purifiers ; they have no specific action on the water. They simply form a precipitate which falls to the bottom, carrying with it most of the microbes and the organic impurities. The following is an excellent method of clarifying water when no filtration is possible :— A lump of alum is rubbed round the inside of a barrel. Fill it with the muddy water and allow it to stand until the sediment settles, then run off the clear water and boil it. This will not affect the taste of the water. The proportion of alum should be six grains to each gallon of water.

(b) *Germicidal.*—Permanganate of potassium is chiefly used for this purpose.

The addition of permanganate to all water supplies is a valuable preventive of cholera. One to two ounces of permanganate will suffice for an ordinary well. The best plan is to place the chemical in a bucket, lower it into the well, draw up the bucket and pour into the well what has been dissolved, again lower and repeat this procedure until the whole of the permanganate has been dissolved. The treatment gives no unpleasant taste to the water ; the main objection is the colour, which is apt to offend the fastidious, prejudiced and ignorant. Practical experience in recent cholera epidemics has confirmed the value of this method. The rule now adopted is to add enough permanganate to make the water distinctly red, so that it does not recover its normal colour for eight hours. If this is done in the evening, the water is ready for use the next morning.

In conclusion, the following points with regard to water supplies should be committed to memory :—

1. With few exceptions all Indian well water is dangerous.

2. Spring water is not always safe.

3. The sparkling appearance of some springs and shallow well water is dangerously deceptive.

4. For domestic purposes, boiling is the most efficient means of sterilisation.

5. Filtration of water cannot be regarded as being entirely reliable and chemical sterilisation has hitherto proved unsatisfactory, but the treatment of wells by permanganate of potash gives excellent results when cholera is prevalent.

6. Domestic storage of water in India is most imperfect and requires more supervision.

7. Indian customs lead to gross fouling of water.

CHAPTER V.

Food in the Tropics.

Wherefore it appears to me necessary....to strive to know ......what man is in relation to the articles of food and drink—
(Hippocrates, 460 B. C.)

ALTHOUGH all of us know the necessity for food, and the unpleasantness of being hungry, and recognise that if we wish to live we must eat, there are few who really take the trouble to think why we require food. The necessity is readily recognised by the familiar illustration of comparing the human body to a steam engine. The boiler is filled with water and the various parts are properly oiled, but the steam engine does not move until a fire is lighted under the boiler. The steam is then produced, and the engine moves. But having once started the engine, we find that the coal in the furnace gets consumed and the machinery gradually stops. We must therefore replace the coal that is burnt by fresh material. In other words, fuel is required for the production of energy. So it is with the human body. Energy is produced by a process of combustion, called oxidation, which goes on continuously in the body, and food of various kinds furnishes the fuel for this purpose. We must therefore supply it in sufficient quality and quantity, or the human machine will either work badly or stop altogether.

The foodstuffs used in various parts of the world are legion, but all the important constituents of them fall under one of the following five headings :—

1. Nitrogenous compounds or proteins ; including all varieties of meat, fish, flesh, fowls, peas, beans, and also cheese.

2. Fats.

3. Carbohydrates ; or sugars, starches, and the various kinds of vegetable foods.

4. Salts.

5. Water.

In addition to these five essentials there is an important group of articles such as tea, coffee, and condiments, which are known under the comprehensive title of food accessories.

Each of these five groups has more or less specialised functions which may be stated as follows :—

1. *Nitrogenous compounds or proteins.*—The functions of nitrogenous foods are fourfold, namely :—

   (*a*) To build up the tissues, produce energy, and repair the wear and tear in the body.
   (*b*) To regulate oxidation.
   (*c*) To be used as heat producers.
   (*d*) To form fat.

2. *Fats.*—Fats are chiefly valuable as heat producers, their special functions are :—

   (*a*) the formation of fat in the body ;
   (*b*) the production of heat and energy.

3. *Starches and sugars :*—Carbohydrates act in a very similar way to fats, and to a certain extent they are interchangeable with them. Their duties are therefore—

   (*a*) The formation of fat ;
   (*b*) the production of heat and energy.

It is generally taught that in cold climates the fats should be increased, and in warm countries the carbohydrates. A well-known authority on food and dietetics disputes this statement and considers that the amount of food of all varieties should be much the same in all latitudes. We are sorry that we must disagree with so distinguished an authority on this subject, but any one with Indian experience will, we think, agree with us. It is only necessary to reflect on the avidity with which butter is consumed in England, or in the hills, and then compare this with the dislike for butter or fats of any description during the hot weather in the plains of India.

4. *Salts.*—The salts necessary for the preservation of health are many. The salts of the vegetable acids, such as are found in fruits and vegetables, are essential constituents of our dietary. When absent or deficient from the food, a state of malnutrition results. Fruits and fresh vegetables, therefore, are very important articles of diet, though of small nutritive value.

Chief amongst the *mineral* elements of the body we find common salt, which is an imperative necessity for life and health.

It is vitally necessary to the blood and tissues and also supplies the soda necessary for salivary digestion and the chlorine for the hydrochloric acid of the gastric juice. Without a sufficiency of common salt, therefore, neither the Carbohydrate nor the Nitrogenous compounds can be efficiently digested.

But here we must utter a note of warning. Remember that a sufficiency of salt is essential, but excess of it is an unmitigated evil, and there can be an no doubt that many people eat far too much of it.

We will endeavour to explain the reason for this. Salt has the peculiar property of attracting moisture and becoming saturated with it. Now, if you take more than is necessary and more than the kidneys can eliminate from the body, it is then deposited in the tissues, where it attracts moisture to itself just as it does outside the body, and so leads to water-logging and dropsical accumulations. This was well known to the ancients, and nowadays we cure dropsy by placing patients upon a salt-free diet.

If therefore there be any tendency to puffiness of the ankles, coming on in the afternoon, or if you come of a gouty family, be very careful in your consumption of salt.

The next most important group is that of the lime salts, especially the phosphates, which enter largely into the composition of the bones. If they are deficient, the bones soften and the disease known as Rickets is the result. The absence from milled rice of organic phosphates or vitamines is stated to cause beri-beri. Sulphur is present in all meat foods, and is an important ingredient in the dietary. Iron is found in small quantity in almost every tissue of the body, and it is an essential constituent of the blood.

5. *Water.*—Water to the extent of $2\frac{1}{4}$ to 4 pints daily is, as we have seen in the last chapter, an absolute necessity of life. Though not itself undergoing any chemical change, its presence is a necessary condition for the occurrence of chemical change in other bodies ; moreover, no tissue in the human body is in its normal condition without water : it is accordingly a necessary constituent of every tissue.

The atmosphere and soil are the primary sources of all food.

Air contains $\begin{cases} \text{Carbon in the form of Carbonic Acid.} \\ \text{Water.} \end{cases}$

Soil contains $\begin{cases} \text{Water.} \\ \text{Nitrogen in the form of nitrates.} \end{cases}$

Animals cannot, but plants can, make use of carbon and nitrogen in these simple forms. Plants with the heat and light of the sun, and in the presence of water, change carbonic acid$_2$ into carbohydrates. These eaten by animals are changed back again to carbonic acid and water. Plants also work up the nitrogen of nitrates in the soil with the carbon of the air into vegetable proteids. These are eaten by animals, turned into animal proteins and excreted as urea which, by the action of bacteria, is converted into ammonia, and by other bacteria into nitrates. Some of the ammonia however splits up and the free nitrogen is added to the free nitrogen in the air, and so is lost to the cycle, though some of the free nitrogen is again brought into the cycle by the action of certain bacteria which fix this free nitrogen on the roots of leguminous plants. The diagrams of the food cycle given in Fig. 10 are after Hutchison.

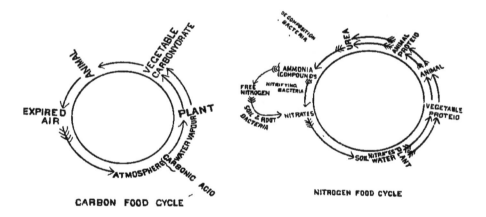

CARBON FOOD CYCLE

NITROGEN FOOD CYCLE

Fig. 10.

In addition to the five classes of alimentary principles given, there must be mentioned the group of *condiments* which give flavour to food; they stimulate secretion and digestion, but do not form tissues or evolve energy or heat.

The nutritive constituents of food, in accordance with their functions in the body, may, therefore, be classified as follows :—

Tissue Formers.	*Work and Heat Producers.*
Nitrogenous compounds or proteids.	Nitrogenous compounds or proteids.
Mineral substances.	Carbohydrates.
Water.	Fats.

Having grouped the general principles governing food values, we may now proceed to consider their practical application in the construction of dietaries.

DIETARIES.

Hutchison distinguishes four criteria of the value of a dietary ; (a) nutritive value ; (b) heat producing power ; (c) digestibility ; and (d) cheapness.

Putting on one side *air* and *water*, the necessity for which has been previously considered, it is seen that in any diet there must be (1) *a protein constituent ;*—that is, a food containing nitrogen— because nitrogenous albuminous tissues form the essential framework of the body. (2) There must also be *salts*, because these enter into the composition of all the tissues and fluids. (3) Although fat can be formed in the body from proteins, such is not its usual mode of origin, neither could the whole quantity of fat that is required be obtained from this source. Therefore, *either a fat or carbohydrate* must be present in the food. There is no doubt that fat can be formed out of carbohydrates in the body, and the fats and the carbohydrates can replace each other in the food. The chief distinction between them is that, whereas the carbohydrates are notably more digestible than the fats, a given weight of fat will produce more heat and energy than a similar amount of a carbohydrate.

So far as the body framework is concerned, it may be said, therefore, that the fleshy portions are derived from the proteins of the food ; the salts are derived from the salts of the food ; the fats are derived not only from the fats, but also from the proteins and carbohydrates of the food ; while the carbohydrates of the body are derived both from the carbohydrates and the fats of the food.

There are two chief requirements in a nutritious daily diet for a healthy man doing a moderate amount of work. First, it must contain a food which will provide sufficient energy ; and, secondly, it must provide for the up-keep and repair of the tissues of the body.

With reference to the quantities actually required by healthy men, a good standard diet adapted to English habits, and suitable for a man doing a moderate amount of muscular work, is thus constituted :—

Foundation.—1 lb. bread, ½ lb. meat, ¼ lb. fat.

Accessories.—1 lb. potatoes, ½ pint milk, ¼ lb. eggs, ⅛ lb. cheese.

In order to realise more clearly what a diet like this means, its constituents may be divided into meals, which would work out as follows :—

Breakfast..	{ Two slices of bread and butter.
	{ Two eggs.
Dinner ..	{ One large plateful of soup.
	{ A large helping of meat with some fat.
	{ One slice of bread and butter.
Tea ..	A glass of milk and two slices of bread and butter.
Supper ..	Two slices of bread and butter and 2 ozs of cheese.

When we come to consider the diet of Indians we find three meals replacing the English four.

The following are typical Indian dietaries :—

(a) *For Bengalis doing very little work :—*

EARLY MORNING MEAL : Boiled rice, three chittacks with a little dâl and vegetables : or atta (flour) 2 chittacks as a chupatti with one-twelfth of a chittack of salt, with a little ghee and vegetables.

MEAL AT MID-DAY :—

Rice	.. 5	chittacks.
Dal, fish or meat	.. 1½	chittack.
Vegetables	.. 2	chittacks.
Ghee or oil	.. ⅛	chittack.
Salt	.. ⅛	,,
Condiments	.. ½	,,

MEAL AT NIGHT : Same exactly as at mid-day meal.

(b) *For Bengalis doing hard work :—*

EARLY MORNING MEAL :—as for (a).

MID-DAY MEAL :—

Rice	... 6	chittacks.
Dal, fish or meat	.. 2	,,
Vegetables	.. 2	,,
Ghee or oil	.. ⅙	chittack.
Salt	.. ⅙	,,
Condiments	.. ½	,,

MEAL AT NIGHT : exactly as mid-day meal.

(c) *For natives of the Punjab, United Provinces of Agra and Oudh, Bihar, etc., doing light work :—*

MORNING MEAL :—

Wheat or maize flour	2	chittacks.
Rice	.. 1½	chittack.
Salt	.. 1½	,,

With a little ghee and vegetables.

MID-DAY MEAL :—

Wheat or maize flour	1½	chittack.
Rice	.. 2½	chittacks.
Dâl	.. 1½	chittack.

(or if a meat or fish eater 2 chittacks instead of dal).

Vegetables	.. 2	chittacks.
Ghee or oil	.. ⅜	chittack.
Salt	.. ⅛	,,
Condiments	.. ½	,,

MEAL AT NIGHT : exactly as mid-day meal.

(d) Natives of Punjab and Upper Provinces doing hard work :—

MORNING AND NIGHT MEALS, AS AT *(c)*.—MIDDAY MEAL : 3 chittacks of wheat-flour or 3½ of maize flour and ¼ chittack of ghee (instead of 1½ chittack as at *(c)*.) The rest exactly the same.

The diets may of course be very greatly varied by introducing other kinds of foods—eggs, milk, cheese, fowls, etc. In practice the more they can be varied the better. For variety in food gives a better appetite for it and also makes us digest it better.

The following are the scales in general use in the Bengal Jails :—

	In Lower Bengal.	In Bihar.
Burma or country rice ..	20 ounces ..	16 ounces.
Different dâls ..	6 ,, ..	6 ,,
Vegetables ..	6 ,, ..	6 ,,
Flour of wheat or Indian corn	..	10 or 12 ozs.

These amounts represent what is absolutely essential, and perhaps a better standard may be taken in the war ration of the Indian Sepoy which in the Tirah Expedition consisted of atta or rice (or if a meat or fish eater 2 chittacks instead of dâl), 2 lbs. ; ghee, 2 ounces ; dâl, 4 ounces ; salt, ¾ ounce ; also meat and condiments on payment. In some later expeditions, onions and amchur (dried mango) have been issued.

The following ration has been suggested for Aden camel-drivers :—Biscuit or rice, 1½ lb. ; dates, wet, 1 lb. ; ghee, 2 ounces ; sugar, 2 ounces ; coffee, ⅓ ounce ; salt, ½ ounce ; onions, when procurable, 2 ounces, or dâl ¾ ounces.

More than these amounts are usually consumed. Professor Chittenden, a distinguished American physiologist, considers that the current estimations of the amount of protein and total fuel-value necessary for hard work are excessive, but the recent researches do not support his view.

The body seeks to maintain a reserve supply of nitrogenous food for its cells. A man having a small reserve supply may be considered to be on a low plane of nutrition and one with a large reserve on a high plane of nutrition. Those on a high plane are better able than those on a low plane to resist such infectious diseases as beri-beri, leprosy, tuberculosis, pneumonia, typhoid fever, typhus, relapsing fever and plague. White men in the tropics, not well fed on nitrogenous food, readily fall victims to infectious diseases. They have placed themselves, from a dietetic standpoint, on a level with the natives and, like them, soon succumb to an infection that their wiser or more fortunate brothers would be able to successfully resist. Many of the natives of the tropics are in a state of chronic starvation, hence the folly of intentionally placing white men in the same condition is apparent. The comparative immunity of Englishmen to the infectious diseases that decimate the natives of India is due, in part at least, to their being better fed on nitrogenous food.

For the last four years Major McCay, Professor of Physiology at the Calcutta Medical College, has been engaged in an experimental research into this question and his final report affords abundant evidence that, other things being equal, diet is the all-important factor in determining the degree of physical development and general well-being of a people, and that with a deficient supply of nitrogenous food, moral and physical degeneration must be expected. Do not therefore be " food faddists." Remember that nuts and cheese are excellent articles of diet for squirrels and mice, but that they are not sufficient sustenance for full-grown men and women. Be careful also that your food is both sufficient in quantity, and good in quality. It is false economy to save money on your food.

For hard work all the chief constituents of the dietary may be increased, but there is evidence to show that the most valuable source of muscular energy is the sugars. For mental effort the digestibility of food is of greater concern to brain workers than chemical composition. Any reduction in the diet of a man doing hard work should affect fats and carbohydrates rather than proteins. Age and sex, of course, exert a marked influence upon dietetic requirements. The same may be said in respect of climate, season, personal idiosyncracies, and the weight of the individual.

As already mentioned, 50 to 80 ounces of water are contained in every kind of dietary, European or Indian. A man consumes daily about one-hundredth part of his weight of dry solid food and a thirtieth part of water.

Animal food is generally held to possess distinct advantages over that of vegetable origin, of which the most certain are the ready supply of blood-pigment ; the larger percentage of proteins, the greater digestibility of animal fats, and the smaller bulk required. A vegetable dietary, unless carefully selected, usually contains insufficient nitrogen, and an excess of carbohydrates. It is bulky, less digestible in the stomach, and less completely absorbed. Vegetable albuminoids are less rapidly digested than those derived from animal sources, but a well fed vegetable eater may display for a time as perfect health and energy as a meat eater. On the other hand, the argument from analogy with the herbivora, some of which are types of activity, is valueless, as man cannot digest cellulose or vegetable fibre, which is easily assimilated by the horse and other animals. The consistent vegetarian must either live on a diet deficient in protein or consume an excessive bulk of food. The adoption of the former course tends to diminish energy and tissue resistance, and the latter is likely to lead to derangement of the digestive organs.

Let us now consider briefly the chief characteristic articles of dietary :

NITROGENOUS FOODS.

Meat :—Meat may be divided into two classes— red and white. Of the *read meats,* beef, mutton, and pork are examples, whilst the flesh of fowls and turkeys constitute the *white* meats. The latter are, as a rule, more digestible than the former. They contain, however, less nitrogen, and are therefore somewhat less nutritious. Meat should always be of the best quality. The writers do not propose to deal with the question of how to distinguish good meat from bad. They wish, however, to point out here the uselessness of that much belauded article—*Soup*—which cannot be considered as being a food in any sense of the word. It is merely a stimulant and not a good one at that. You will remember that in a former chapter you were told that the blood carried nutritive materials to the tissues, and that the tissues then gave up waste products which were carried away to be excreted from the body by the lungs and kidneys.

Now when the cook makes soup, the substances which dissolve out into the water are merely those waste products—the real nourishment remains in the soup-meat which is given to the dogs—and we think you will agree with us that what are waste products in the cow are not likely to afford nourishment to the human animal. On the contrary, they are frequently harmful, because these waste products—or " *purins,* " as they are sometimes called—can only be excreted by the kidneys, thus throwing much unnecessary labour upon these already overworked organs. Soup, moreover, has a

great tendency to ferment in the stomach and
cause a very troublesome form of dyspepsia.

Fish :—Compare with butcher's meat, fish contains more water, less fat and less extractives.

An exclusive fish diet is not suitable to luxurious
races, as the digestion and appetite miss the stimulating extractives of fleshy foods.

There is a popular delusion to the effect that
fish is specially valuable as a " brain food." This
opinion is grounded on the belief that fish
is specially rich in phosphorus, and that mental
processes are dependent upon a full supply of this
substance. There is, however, no justification for
the statement either that fish is rich in phosphorus
or that phosphorus is specially good for the brain.

Lobsters and prawns are nutritious, but are apt,
when eaten freely, to cause digestive troubles or
nettle rash.

Oysters are an extravagant and over-rated food ;
they consist almost entirely of water with little
nitrogenous food matter, and a fair amount of
extractives. If a man relied on oysters to supply
his nitrogenous food, he would require *at least
ten dozen daily.* They are often grown in water to
which sewage has access and become poisonous.
Numerous deaths have occurred as the result of
eating oysters in India, and their use cannot be too
strongly condemned.

Poultry—Domestic fowls :—These are our great
standby in the hot weather, when butcher's meat
is apt to be tough and indigestible. The flesh is
almost equal to beef and mutton in nitrogenous
matters and is rich in phosphates. When derived
from young birds, it is easily digested and is well
suited for invalids. In India, however, much of
the nourishment of fowls is lost owing to the
barbarous custom of killing them by cutting
their throats and allowing them to bleed slowly to
death.

The English custom of wringing their necks is not only more humane, but it also makes the flesh much more juicy and nourishing.

Game Birds :—The flesh is more nitrogenous than that of chickens. It is tough and indigestible unless kept for a time.

Goose and Duck :—The flesh of these birds contain a large amount of fat which renders it very unsuitable for persons with a weak digestion. Ducks, moreover, are very foul feeders and they should never be eaten unless they have been carefully home-fed.

Eggs :—Eggs constitute one of the best forms of nitrogenous food. An egg consists of two parts—the white and the yellow part or yolk. The *white part* consists of what is known as albumen and a good deal of water. It is very digestible when raw or lightly cooked, but less so when the egg is hard boiled. The *yolk* contains a great deal of fatty matter and phosphates. Eggs are extremely nutritious, and are one of the best and most wholesome forms of food. They contain everything essential for the support of life except starch and sugar.

The smallness of the Indian egg is due to want of care in breeding fowls and in feeding them. They are generally allowed to pick up any food they can get. There is no reason why large fowls and large eggs should not be got here as elsewhere, and it would probably pay to go in systematically for poultry farming.

The shells of eggs are very porous, and consequently eggs decompose very quickly in warm climates. If we keep the air out by an impervious covering such as grease or the so-called liquid glass, they will keep very much longer.

Milk :—Milk is derived, in by far the greatest quantity, from the cow. The buffalo, goat and ewe yield milks largely used in India which differ more or less in their percentage composition from that of the cow, but the main characters of milk are the same in all mammals.

Physical Characters :—Good cow's milk is of a full, opaque white colour, or with very slight yellowish tinge. It has a slight and agreeable odour, and a sweet characteristic taste. Buffalo, like human milk, is bluish-white, whilst goat's milk has a peculiar odour, resembling that of the animal itself.

The milk of cows varies according to breed, the feeding, and the period after calving. The average yield of milk is 20 to 25 pints daily for the year. Buffalo milk yields much more fat than that of cows and is consequently less digestible. Most Indian cream is made from buffalo milk. Both the abundance and quality of the milk are influenced by the feeding.

The yield of milk can be increased at the expense of its quality by feeding with large quantities of watery food, or by feeding with dry food, which compels the cow to drink to excess. The best age of a milch cow is from four to seven years, and the largest yield is given after the fifth until the seventh calf. Milk should not be used until a week after calving. The milk drawn at the end of a milking (called " strippings ") is richer than that drawn at the beginning (called " fore-milk "), because a partial creaming occurs in the udder. The afternoon milk is richer in fat and in casein, or milk albumen, but less in quantity than that yielded in the morning. In autumn and early winter, milk is richer than in spring and summer.

Milk as an article of food :—Milk is most important as an article of food, because it contains all the necessary food principles in a readily digestible form. Being designed for the nutrition of the rapidly growing young animal, it contains a very large proportion of water, a relatively large proportion of fat and proteid in comparison with the carbohydrate constituent. It is not, therefore, a food suitable for the entire nutrition of the adult : but for the infant it is essential, whilst for the invalid and the elderly it is most valuable. One pint of average good milk contains about $2\frac{1}{2}$ ounces of water free food : 1lb. of meat contains about 4 ounces : but not all of this is perfectly digestible, as is the case with the whole of the solids of milk. The disadvantage of milk, however, is that a large number of adults cannot take it, because it causes flatulence and dyspepsia. It is however essential for infants, while for the invalid and the elderly it is most valuable. Flatulence and dyspepsia may be avoided by mixing the milk with Vichy Water. Another very valuable method is the addition of from two to five grains of Citrate of Soda to each ounce of milk. This prevents the formation of large lumps of curd and so makes the milk more easy of digestion, and on this account it is now largely used in the " *curd-indigestion* " of hand-fed infants. We may now add a few words about the Metchnikoff or " Sour milk " treatment. The theory on which this treatment is founded is as follows :— There are two great classes of bacilli which live in the human intestine, the one living in an alkaline and the other in an acid medium. In a normally healthy person the two fairly balance one another, but if by any chance the alkali-loving bacilli gain the upper hand, then great fermentation and putrefaction take place in the contents of the bowel and various poisonous compounds are produced which are absorbed into the blood, causing great deterioration of health. When this occurs, Metchnikoff advises the use of milk which has been made sour by the addition of the Bulgarian bacillus —an organism of the acid-loving group. In this way the natural balance is restored between the two groups and the putrefaction of the contents of the bowels comes to an end. There can be no doubt that, in carefully selected cases, this treatment is very valuable, but " sour milk " is not a universal panacea for all intestinal troubles : on the contrary it may do great harm in unsuitable cases.

It should, therefore, never be adopted except under medical advice. You must be careful also, if you do adopt it, to see that you are really using the Bulgarian bacillus ; milk rendered sour by other means is useless.

Cream is a most valuable and nutritious food, and easy of digestion in moderate quantity. Butter-milk is also a valuable food which has practically disappeared under modern systems of dairying. It contains a considerable amount of nitrogenous matter, but of course, very little fat. Skim-milk and whey are not very nourishing, but are easy of assimilation, and are agreeable articles of food for invalids.

Milk should be boiled or pasteurised before use, as many diseases, such as tuberculosis and enteric fever, are spread by contaminated milk. In order to *pasteurise* milk, the bottle containing it should be placed inside a vessel nearly full of water. The water should then be allowed to boil for half an hour. In this way the milk will be sufficiently heated to destroy all germs, but it will not be raised to the boiling point. At the end of half an hour the bottle containing the milk should be removed from the vessel and rapidly cooled.

The Local Government Board has recently issued a report on " The Value of Boiled Milk as a Food for Infants and Young Animals " at a time when some authoritative review of this controversial matter is very urgently needed. The investigations on which this report is based have been conducted for the Board by Dr. Janet Lane Clay-pon, who has already made herself an authority on this question by research work carried out at the Lister Institute. A number of treasured beliefs in the virtues of raw milk have been weighed in the balance and found wanting. One of the outcomes of this report is to show that when a young animal is fed exclusively on the milk of a different species of animal, it is immaterial, as far as the nutrition of the former is concerned, whether the milk is boiled or not. On the other hand it does make a difference whether the milk on which the young animal is fed is, so to speak, a foreign milk or whether it is derived from an animal of the same species. This is the most striking positive evidence obtained by the inquiry. As regards boiling, however, infants who are fed on milk which has been drawn from the breast of a wet-nurse, and boiled previous to use, appear to thrive just as well as when the same milk is given fresh. But the moral that clearly emerges from this report is that, since the dangers of boiled milk are so problematical they may be neglected, and since the danger of infection from unboiled milk is so real, it is wisdom to boil all milk before it is given to an infant to consume. It also demonstrates very clearly the importance of remembering that Cow's milk is intended for calves and not for human beings and that, no matter what care be taken, it is never as good for a child as mother's milk. *No one, therefore, is justified in bringing up a child by hand, especially in India, unless it is absolutely impossible for them to obtain a wet-nurse.*

Germs develop very rapidly in milk, especially if it is warm ; it should therefore be stored most carefully in a cool place—if possible, an ice chest in India—either immediately after being milked or after pasteurisation.

Cheese :—Cheese does not receive the amount of consideration it deserves in Indian dietaries. " It is much better as a food than beef, and equal nourishment can be obtained from cheese as from beef at one-sixth the cost."

It is satisfying, and it can easily be handled, as it requires no cooking, but its very virtues have been its undoing. Its cheapness has led to its being voted vulgar by polite society, and also to its being cold-shouldered by the working man, who has been induced to exchange it for the meretricious attractions of a too often ill-cooked joint. Even the pervasive odour which roasting develops in it, and which, it must be assumed, has especially endeared it to the Welsh, is quoted as an offence against it because roasting makes it indigestible.

That cheese is not readily digested by delicate persons is well known, but this indigestibility is very often a fault of the consumer rather than of the cheese. Properly eaten by a person of fair digestion it is one of the most digestible of foods. The fat, which forms one-third part of its composition, forms a waterproof coating which prevents the access of the digestive juices to the casein. The larger the lumps of cheese which reach the stomach, the slower will the access be. Hence the importance of reducing it to a state of fine division before it is swallowed. This may be done by careful chewing with some farinaceous substance, such as bread or biscuit.

To bolt cheese in unmasticated lumps, as some people do, and then to complain of its being indigestible, is folly of the worst description. •

Now it is more easy to pulverize a hard morsel than a soft one, for the latter tends always to elude the teeth. For this reason a piece of dry hard cheese is more digestible than a soft piece. The process of mastication may be assisted by grating the cheese, but the best plan for those who find any difficulty in digesting raw cheese is to dissolve it and mix it with some other food, preferably a carbohydrate, which is the natural complement of a proteid and fatty food.

The best solvent of cheese is bicarbonate of potash, because casein forms soluble compounds with the alkalis. As much bicarbonate of potassium as will lie on a two-anna piece, *i.e.*, about five grains, is sufficient to dissolve a quarter of a pound of cheese either grated or chopped in small fragments. By the addition of milk and eggs a very savoury and exceedingly nutritious pudding can be prepared in this way at a comparatively small cost.

It must be understood that the proper place for cheese in a well arranged dietary is a substitute for, and not as an appendage to, meat. There is, however, one exception to this rule, and that is the correctness of taking a small piece of cheese at the end of even a meat meal, for, paradoxical as it may seem, digestive reasons.

According to the old adage, cheese is a " crusty elf, digesting all things but itself," and in this there is the element of truth : all cheese contains elements of the character of ferments, which tend to set up a fermentative process in the food when it passes into the stomach, and thus to promote digestion. But if cheese be taken in excess at such a time the digestive action is paralysed and indigestion is the natural consequence, thus justifying the wisdom of our forefathers.

The cheaper cheeses are often more nourishing and more digestible than the expensive ones.

FATS.

Butter :—Butter is the fatty portion of milk, obtained by churning, either from the milk directly or from the previously separated cream.

Good butter should be of a yellow colour, which deepens with the richness of the pasture. Cows kept in the house on hay or dry food give an inferior product, whilst buffalo cream always yields a dead white butter. Various substances, as annatto and an Indian nut called *lutka*, are added to increase or produce the popular colour. Butter from moderately ripe cream has a fine flavour, and when well made ought to remain good and sweet for a week. Butter prepared from pasteurized cream is lacking in flavour.

As an article of food, butter furnishes most people in easy circumstances with the principal part of their fatty food : it is extremely palatable and digestible when fresh and of good quality.

The average amount taken by Europeans is from 1 to 2 ounces daily.

Ghee or clarified butter takes the place of butter in the dietary of most Indians. It is a wholesome and nutritious fat, but the peculiar flavour does not appeal to Europeans.

The Vegetable Foods.

These may be divided into six groups.

Group I.—Cereals.

These comprise the edible grains, such as wheat, oats, Indian-corn, rice, etc. Of these, wheat is preferred as a food for the following reasons :—

(1) The grain is easily separated from the chaff, whch does not adhere to it, as in the case of barley, oats, rice, etc.

(2) The yield of flour is very large.

(3) Owing to the peculiar constitution of wheat, light and spongy bread is readily made from it.

(4) The proportion of the chemical constituents present render it well fitted for the general sustenance of man.

In order to render flour suitable for human consumption it must be cooked. The simplest plan is to mix the flour with water and bake it. It is in this way ship's biscuits are made. The word " biscuit " means " twice-cooked " or twice-baked, and is not applicable in strictness to these articles as now generally made. The product is close, hard and dry, and not easy to masticate. Hence the problem arose in the early days of civilization, how to cook the flour in such a way that it would be light and easy of digestion. The problem was solved by causing gas to develop in the mixture of flour and water, so converting the latter into a kind of sponge, which was subsequently baked, and into which the digestive juices can easily penetrate. In other words, man learnt to make *bread*.

Bread can be manufactured in a variety of ways, but all methods aim at the aeration of the mixture of flour and water and subsequent cooking at a temperature of about 450°F.

A good sample of bread should be well baked (not burnt), light and spongy, the crumb being well permeated with little cavities. It should be thoroughly kneaded, of good colour (white or brown), not acid to the taste, not bitter, and not too moist. When set aside, the lower part should not become sodden. A 4-lb. loaf loses about $1\frac{1}{4}$ oz. in 24 hours, about 5 oz. in 48 hours, and about 7 oz. in 60 hours. This loss will vary with the temperature, draughts of air, etc.

Bread may have many defects :—

(1) It may be *sodden and heavy* owing to imperfect baking or in consequence of the use of bad flour or yeast, the sponge never having risen properly.

(2) It may be *sour* owing to bad flour, or to fermentation having been allowed to proceed too far. A slight degree of sourness in leavened bread is not objected to.

(3) It may be *bitter* owing to bitter yeast.

(4) Finally, it may be *mouldy*, which is due to the bread having been too moist originally, having been stored in a damp place, or kept too long, or to bad flour having been used.

Biscuit should be well baked, but not burnt. It should float and partially dissolve in water. When struck, it should give a ringing sound : and a piece put in the mouth should thoroughly soften down. Being almost free from water, biscuit contains a large amount of nutritive material in an easily digestible form, and keeps for a considerable time. Three pounds of biscuits are equal in nourishment to five pounds of bread.

Oatmeal :—Oatmeal is the most nutritious of all cereals. It is very rich in fat. Oats prepared by rolling instead of grinding and heated during the rolling process, are much more digestible and easily cooked than ordinary oatmeal. The much advertised preparations of oats, sold under various fancy names, which are now so deservedly popular, are prepared in this way.

Gruel is prepared by boiling oatmeal in water or milk, and *porridge* by stirring the meal into boiling water and cooking until the compound becomes of the consistency of pudding. Owing to the fact that it is gulped down without chewing, and therefore without allowing the starchy matter of the grain to become mixed with the saliva, porridge is not easily digestible. For this reason it frequently sets up flatulence and heartburn. *Beef brose* and *kale brose* are made by stirring meal in the hot liquor in which meat or cabbage has been boiled. The product is not adapted to delicate stomachs. Oatmeal is also made into thin cakes by mixing into a paste with water, and baking on an iron plate.

In the form of porridge, brose, and oatcake, there is a large consumption of this grain in Scotland and the North of England ; but in India oats are chiefly used as food for horses.

Maize :—Maize or Indian-corn is extremely nutritious ; but it has some disadvantages. Owing to the large quantities of fat it contains, it develops a disagreeable rancid flavour on keeping, and from its deficiency in gluten it is not adapted for making bread unless mixed with wheat-flour.

It is, however, all things considered, one of the best of our Indian foods.

Cornflour is prepared from maize by washing away the proteid and fat by means of dilute alkaline solution, so that little but starch is left.

Rice :—Rice, which is paddy deprived of its husk, is the staple food of the Indian peoples. There are two principal varieties—Burma and Country rice. Burma rice has the husk, pericarp and outer layer removed by machinery. Country rice is soaked in water for at least a day and night and then steamed and dried in the sun. The husk is then roughly removed. It therefore retains most of its pericarp and outer layers which contain protein and phosphates. The use of milled rice is said to produce beri-beri owing to the absence of the organic phosphates in these outer layers. Rice is the poorest of all cereals in proteid, fat and mineral matter. On the other hand, it has fully 76 per cent. of starch. The starch has the further advantage of being present in small and easily digested grains. When boiled, rice swells up and absorbs nearly five times its weight of water, while some of its mineral constituents are lost by solution. It is preferable, therefore, to cook it by steaming.

Rice is only moderately easy of *digestion* in the stomach, 2½ ounces cooked by boiling (*i.e.,* about two-thirds of a soup-plate) requiring three and a half hours for its disposal. This is due to the fact that it is not the function of the stomach to digest carbohydrates ; it merely passes the rice on to the intestine where it is *absorbed* with very great completeness ; indeed, its solid constituents enter the blood almost as completely as those of meat. This is due to the comparative absence of cellulose. Practically none of the starch is lost, whereas the waste of protein foods amounts to about 19 per cent. It follows from this that rice is one of the foods which leave the smallest residue in the intestine, and this gives it a considerable value in some cases of disease.

The nutritive value of rice is much impaired by its poverty in protein and fat. Hence it is not adapted to be an exclusive diet, but should be eaten along with other substances, rich in these two elements, such as dál, ghee and eggs. Even as regards carbohydrate it would require about one pound three ounces of rice to furnish the daily needs of an active man. This would entail the consumption of about 5 pounds of cooked rice daily.

Rice is insipid and is therefore usually flavoured with curry powder. A good sample of rice should have been stored for some months as Indians consider new rice likely to cause diarrhœa and indigestion. It should be unbroken, clear without grit spots or evidence of insects. Many samples sold in bazaars consist of old and new rice mixed with chalk or lime to give them an uniform appearance.

GROUP 2.—THE PULSES.

This group consists of peas, beans, and lentils. In the fresh young green state these seeds are fairly easily digested, the cellular tissue is comparatively soft, and the contained nutritious principles fairly easily reached by the digestive juices.

Peas and *beans* are about equal in nutritive value. Both contain a good deal of sulphur, which is apt to give rise to uncomfortable flatulence.

Lentils, such as the various kinds of " dál," are richer in phosphates than peas and beans, and contain less sulphur.

The group is rich in protein—chiefly in the form of a substance called legumen, allied to the casein of cheese. They are also rich in carbohydrates. Salts are fairly abundant, but phosphates are less so than in the cereals. Like wheat, the seeds are weak in fat and therefore require mixture with fats and carbo-hydrates to form a complete diet. Gram and ghee with potatoes is an example of a complete diet.

A mistake is very often made, chiefly by Euro-peans, in taking leguminous seeds as a vegetable with meat. They are flesh formers and are chiefly composed of vegetable protein. Dâl should be used therefore as a substitute for meat and it is best combined with rice, which we have already seen to be deficient in proteins.

Group 3.—The Roots and Tubers.

These consist chiefly of carbohydrates, mostly in the form of starch, and very little other food material.

Potatoes.—This tuber consists of starch, sugar, and a trace of protein. When well-cooked, it is easily digestible, and, according to Von Noorden, potato starch is peculiarly well adopted to replace other starches in the dietary of sufferers from diabetes. The salts found in the juice of potatoes are a complete preventive against scurvy.

The peeling and slicing of potatoes, before boil-ing, is a wasteful process. All the valuable salts, and much of the protein matter, pass into the water and are lost. Steaming potatoes in their jackets is a better method. Roasting them is also good, as there is sufficient water in the potato to cook the starch. Perhaps the best and most economical way to cook potatoes is to stew them with meat in the form of Irish stew.

Beetroot, when young, is of some value as a food on account of the sugar it contains.

Carrots and *parsnips* are of rather less value than beetroot.

Turnips are of little value as a food, and are liable to cause flatulence and dyspepsia. It is difficult to realise that an apparently solid object like a turnip really contains more water than a fluid like milk : yet such is the fact.

GROUP 4.—GREEN VEGETABLES AND FRUITS.

Green Vegetables.—These consist of large quantities of water, much cellulose or fibre, and small quantities of sugar, gums and allied bodies. The members of this group are chiefly valuable as flavouring agents, antiscorbutics, and natural stimulants to the action of the bowels. They have little or no nutritive value.

Cabbage contains much sulphur and is apt to cause uncomfortable flatulence.

Cauliflower is one of the most digestible of the cabbage tribe, and the flower contains nearly double the amount of protein food found in common cabbage.

Onions.—These vegetables are valuable as condiments. They contain a larger amount of phosphates than any other succulent vegetable, excepting asparagus and have a slight laxative action on the bowels. They are also said to be very valuable for persons with a rheumatic tendency.

The succulent fruits have low nutritive value, but are rich in vegetable salts : they are antiscorbutics of incalculable value.

Vegetables used in salads are valuable antiscorbutics. The salts are not lost by wasteful cookery. The uncooked cellulose greatly stimulates intestinal action, but is apt to upset the digestion. Cholera, enteric, and other diseases may readily be conveyed by uncooked vegetables. For this reason only vegetables grown under personal supervision and carefully washed before use should be eaten. Both on account of their indigestibility, therefore, and the danger of contracting cholera or enteric fever, the writers are strongly of opinion that, in this country, salads should be avoided.

Watercress is often grown in sewage water, and may spread enteric fever and worms. Even when obtained from the best sources, it should be well soaked in strong salt and water and then well washed in boiled water before use.

GROUP 5.—ALBUMINOUS NUTS.

The edible nuts, such as the walnut are generally very rich in protein matter and fats and also contain some carbohydrates. They are often very indigestible; this can be lessened by grinding the nuts into a fine powder.

GROUP 6.—EDIBLE FUNGI.

This group comprises the mushroom, truffle, etc. These contain a fairly large amount of protein matter, but a very great percentage of water makes them an extravagant food. They are difficult to digest.

MASTICATION OR CHEWING.

It is especially important that every one should be instructed in the importance of perfect mastication and insalivation of food. Sir Michael Foster, who made elaborate experiments on the subject, said :—The adoption of the habit of thorough insalivation of the food was found to have a remarkable and striking effect on appetite, making this more discriminating and leading to the choice of a simple dietary, and in particular in reducing the craving for flesh-food. The appetite, too, is beyond all question fully satisfied with a diet considerably less than is ordinarily demanded. Sir Michael Foster's experiments showed clearly that perfect mastication produces great economy in nutrition and a remarkable improvement in the condition of the whole gastro-intestinal tract. The waste products of the bowel were not only markedly reduced in amount but actually became odourless and inoffensive. We think these striking results of perfect mastication should be more widely known than they are.

In order that the saliva may be enabled to do its work, the food must not only be chewed, but must be kept for a while in the mouth. When the saliva is swallowed and reaches the stomach, its powers of digestion are soon destroyed. The habit of hurrying over meals and bolting the food is thus responsible for a great deal of indigestion. Farinaceous foods especially must be acted on by the saliva, and so porridge, bread and milk, and rice, tapioca, puddings, etc., although easily swallowed without chewing must remain for a sufficient time in the mouth. Flatulence of a distressing character is a common result of " bolting " such food.

The above may be summarised in the four rules which go to make up the now well-recognised cult of Fletcherism :—

(1) Wait for a true appetite.

(2) Select the food the appetite particularly craves at the moment.

(3) Chew every mouthful so thoroughly that all the taste in it may be enjoyed.

(4) Do not swallow a single mouthful until it practically swallows itself.

If the system is carefully followed, it will be quickly evident that what was till recently considered the proper amount of food for the average man is really twice as much as he requires ; also that far less flesh-food will be required, and dyspepsia will become a dream of the past.

Decay of the teeth is often caused by neglect of brushing, and allowing particles of food to adhere around and between them. The teeth should be thoroughly brushed at night with a little soap and water, or powdered charcoal, or chalk, or a little spirits of sal-volatile and water. Brushing with powdered pumice stone or cuttle-fish bone is injurious. The use of strong acids, such as are sometimes used by quacks who undertake tooth scaling, is highly injurious. Children ought not to be fed too exclusively on slops. They should always be allowed something requiring mastication, in order that their teeth may be regularly used. Decayed teeth must be stopped as soon as possible. Overcrowding of the jaw in consequence of the first teeth remaining when the second are being cut, favours decay in the new teeth. All children must be taught to be most careful about their teeth. Eating biscuits, sweets, etc., between meals is very bad for the teeth, as well as for the digestion generally.

BEVERAGES.

We now come to the discussion of a question which is of the greatest importance, namely, the advisability or otherwise of using alcohol. It must be understood that we hold no brief for total abstinence in a general sense, but our experience at home and abroad convinces us that alcohol in all its forms should be used most sparingly in the tropics.

Alcohol is a product resulting from the decomposition of sugar. The decomposition is due to the growth of several fungi classed together as yeasts.

A certain amount of alcohol may be safely consumed as a heat-producing food. This amount is certainly very limited—not more than one or, at the outside, two ounces in twenty-four hours. Its unsuitability as a food is shown by its other effects on the body which are so well known as to need no description. It is allowable in cases when, for some reason, insufficient food is taken. *When sufficient food is taken, alcohol is unnecessary ; when excess of food is taken, the addition of alcohol does serious harm.*

In childhood, alcohol as a beverage is most injurious ; *in adult life,* a strictly moderate amount with ordinary diet may be taken or not. It is not necessary but a more or less pleasant luxury ; *in old age, with failing strength and weight,* alcohol is most useful ; *in old age, with increasing weight and obesity,* alcohol is most injurious : it increases the tendency to fatty heart, kidney troubles, and to apoplexy, with paralysis or sudden death.

Moderation for adults may be defined as one and a half ounces of pure alcohol daily, which may be consumed in either of the following forms :—

1 pint of fairly strong dinner ale.
1½ pints light table or lager beer.
½ to ¾ pint light claret, white wine, or champagne.
2 wine glasses of port or sherry.
3 ounces of brandy, gin or well matured whisky.

Total abstinence in adult life is often necessary. Each man should test his self-control in the following way :—Having fixed a daily allowance (say one ounce of alcohol), he must make up his mind not to exceed it. If he cannot keep to the limit, total abstinence is imperative ; each time the limit is exceeded, his self-control is weakened, and he is on the high road to a dreadful disease—dipsomania. Those who have once been victims to alcoholism, and have broken the habit, must absolutely abstain for the rest of their lives.

Members of gouty families should generally be total abstainers. If alcohol is taken the beverages in which alcohol is mixed with some unfermented sugar, such as beer or port wine, must be avoided. Well diluted old whisky does the least harm.

The attitude of the military authorities towards alcoholic beverages has varied from time to time, but their last word on the subject is given in the following extract from *Royal Army Medical Corps Training* :— " We can fully sympathize with a man, accustomed to an occasional glass of beer, finding himself deprived of this drink. We are bound to recognize that beer or spirits are often useful in disease and sometimes desirable in health, but in health neither beer nor spirits are a necessity, and the majority of persons are better without them. To men, tired and fagged out after a long march, a moderate issue of beer or spirits is not only an advantage, but almost a necessity. These considerations should influence our attitude in regard to these issues in the service. Where men are known habitually to abuse the consumption of these liquors they should be encouraged and helped to become total abstainers, but where such is not the case it is unwise to forbid the consumption of alcoholic drinks altogether, or to coerce men towards total abstinence. The only rules which should be laid down in regard to this matter are (1) beer or spirits should not be drunk during working hours ; (2) beer or spirits should only be drunk after the day's work is over, that is on the completion of the march and after arrival in camp or bivouac ; (3) the issue of beer or spirits at this time should be strictly limited to either two pints of beer or one and a half fluid ounces of one of the ordinary spirits ; (4) the alcoholic drink issued must not be taken fasting, but with the evening meal. If issued on these lines, there is much to suggest that, for those accustomed to drink one or other of these beverages, an allowance daily of either beer or spirits may be productive of more good than harm." In Canada the men who are lumberers and who live in camps far away from called civilization are strongly opposed to our Military doctrine. During the whole winter they fell the trees, and these are dragged along the snow to the river, where they are made up into rafts. These men will not have any alcohol near them in the winter. On one occasion a man conveyed a cask of whisky into one of their camps, and the first thing they did was to take an axe and knock a hole in the cask, so that the whole of the whisky ran out. The reason of this was, they did not dare to have the whisky there, for if it was there, they felt quite sure that they would drink it, and if they drank it, they were likely to die.

Lauder Brunton tells a story with reference to the use of alcohol in high altitudes :—A party of engineers were surveying in the Sierra Nevada. They camped at a great height above sea-level, where the air was very cold, and they were miserable. Some of them drank a little whisky, and felt less uncomfortable : some of them drank a lot of whisky, and went to bed feeling very jolly and comfortable indeed. But in the morning the men who had not taken any whisky got up alright : those who had taken a little whisky got up feeling very unhappy : the men who had taken a lot of whisky did not get up at all : they were simply frozen to death. They had warmed the surface of their bodies at the expense of their internal organs.

Some time ago the late Sir Joseph Fayrer was out deer-stalking in the North of Scotland. He offered his flask to the keeper. The keeper said : " No, Sir Joseph, I will not take any to-day, it is too cold." And yet, if he had drunk the whisky, he would have felt, for the time being, very much warmer than before.

Cantlie wrote :—" The natives of warm climates, both by their religion and their habits, shun alcohol." But he was apparently unaware that in India this statement requires considerable modification.

In hot, moist climates, English beer can rarely be taken with impunity ; but light wines, white or red, champagne and good whisky well diluted and taken either with meals or after excessive fatigue in the quantity indicated on page 118 do no harm.

On the contrary it is evident that a weak " peg " or glass of wine with the evening meal is beneficial to the harassed Indian official at the end of a strenuous day's work. It promotes digestion and has a soothing effect on the nerves.

What does most harm in India is the practice of " pegging " or taking " short drinks " at the club bar before dinner.

If we choose to continue this most undesirable custom, we should honestly admit that we have our " pegs" and our " short drinks " because we like them and not on account of any pretended good they do us.

TEA AND COFFEE.

Tea and Coffee.—These substances contain active principles known as thein and caffein respectively, which act similarly on the body. They are stimulants to the nervous system ; they act on the heart, in small doses, as a tonic ; in excessive, or too frequent doses they make its action irregular and weak. Tea also contains a volatile oil that is an irritant, and increases stimulation of the nervous system, sometimes to the extent of making the patient nervous and irritable.

Contrary to popular idea, five minutes " drawing " of tea does not make it more injurious, apart from the fact that a stronger infusion is made. The plan of pouring boiling water on tea, and immediately pouring it off and throwing the leaves away is only wasteful. Less tea leaves and longer infusion makes tea that is no more injurious.

As a stomachic tonic and as a safe way of introducing fluid into the system, the use of tea as a beverage is beneficent and hygienic. It was evidently introduced by the Chinese, owing to the calamities arising from drinking unboiled water. Deep well water is almost unknown in China, and the shallow wells and streams are so apt to become polluted, owing to the habits of the Chinese, that experience dictated the necessity of boiling the water. But boiled water being insipid, and the object of its being boiled not being evident to ignorant and thoughtless people, the water was " flavoured " by the leaves of the tea plant, a custom which has become widespread. It was, no doubt, for hygienic purposes tea was introduced, but the abuse of tea drinking has brought many evils in its train. The Chinese drink tea after finishing their principal meal, and in fact as a drink at any time. They do not drink tea during their meal, but after the meal is finished. The pernicious system of drinking tea during a meal is one peculiar to British folk, and the habit is the cause of many dyspeptic troubles. The best China tea, properly prepared, is a wholesome fluid, calculated to aid digestion, especially when taken after the meal is finished. Tea taken with animal food, be it eggs, fish, flesh or fowl, is a certain means of producing dyspepsia, for when the tea is " drawn " for a long time, and when the tea used is of an inferior quality—the method and material usual in Britain and Australia—the tannic acid of the decoction, uniting with the albumen of the animal tissues, produces a leathery compound which no gastric juice, however potent, can penetrate and digest. Tea, used in the Chinese fashion, is a hygienic drink : as ordinarily consumed in Britain and by Britishers throughout the Empire, it is detrimental to the public health. "Afternoon tea" is an unnecessary and useless meal, especially when tea-drinking is merely an excuse for the eating of large amounts of hot buttered buns, scones, rich cakes, and such like indigestible articles.

Coffee.—Coffee is the seed of a tree familiar in some parts of India. In the berry it cannot be adulterated, but ground coffee as usually sold is a mixture of coffee and chicory, the chicory varying in quantity from 25 to 75 per cent. Chicory is the root of the wild endive dried, roasted and ground. Chicory is held to improve the taste of coffee, but it detracts from its stimulating effect as it contains no caffein.

Coffee should not be boiled ; it should be made by pouring boiling water over it. Two or three mouthfuls of good coffee after a meal are an aid to digestion : taken in breakfast-cupfuls, it is an impediment to digestion, and, diluted with half milk and taken with a meal of eggs, fish, fowl, or flesh is still more so. Taken at night, it frequently causes insomnia.

Cocoa contains a similar alkaloid to tea and coffee. It is, however, present in smaller quantity. In the way cocoa is generally taken the whole seed is consumed, so that in addition to a stimulant, some food matter, principally of a carbohydrate kind, is taken. It is, however, inconsiderable in amount, as the total weight of cocoa is so small.

Condemnation of the habitual consumption of the drugs, *coca and kola* cannot be too strong. They contain stimulating alkaloids, whose action on the system is insidious, and a craving is often set up that leads to a form of insanity known as cocainomania. Unhappily, at the present day, the cocaine habit is increasing in India. Great danger lies in habitually drinking wines impregnated with kola or coca, or in using snuffs and foods that have been similarly treated. Such drugs should be taken only under constant medical supervision. It is sometimes more easy to break the cocaine habit than to check the craving for opium or alcohol ; but, even though the habit be checked, the damage to the mental faculties is apt to be permanent.

Aerated drinks consist of water, or solutions of salts, with or without sugar and flavouring agents, aerated with carbonic acid gas. Carbonic acid gives a brightness and a pleasant flavour to the water. Provided no metallic poisons are added from lead, etc., in the machinery used in preparing the waters, simple aerated waters are not injurious, but it is wrong to suppose that aerated waters are safer than plain water. The mere addition of a little carbonic acid to water does not kill off the germs it contains, and it is safer, therefore, in cases of doubt, to drink plain water which you know to have been boiled rather than pin your faith upon aerated waters from an unknown source. The only microbe which we know to be destroyed by carbonic acid is the cholera bacillus. The gas acts slowly even on it and therefore the aerated water should be kept for a week or ten days to obtain the germicidal effect.

COOKING.

· The objects of cooking are two-fold :—

1. *Æsthetic,* to improve the appearance of meat of all kinds and to develop in it new flavours.

2. *Hygienic,* to sterilize various articles of food to some extent and to improve their keeping powers.

It is an error to suppose that cooking increases the digestibility of food. This is only true with regard to vegetable foods. The digestibility of meat is diminished by cooking, although the increased attractiveness of cooked meat may render it indirectly more capable of digestion by calling forth a more profuse flow of digestive juices.

Ordinary cooking or pickling affords little protection if meat is infected with the germs of specific diseases.

DISEASES CAUSED BY FOOD.

Overfeeding.—An excess of food, due to too large or too frequent meals, may accumulate in the intestine, causing fermentation and also dyspepsia, with constipation or ineffective diarrhœa. Gout, obesity, diabetes, and other conditions may also arise from excess of food. Absorption of the products of putrefaction may give rise to a septic condition marked by fever, furred tongue, fœtid breath, heaviness, and possibly jaundice. Diseases of the blood may also arise from retention of waste products in the intestine.

Underfeeding.—Protracted insufficiency of diet is followed by wasting of the tissues. Fat is naturally the first to suffer, and may be almost completely absorbed, the other tissues following mainly in the inverse order of their importance to life. Physical and mental weakness ensue, followed by a debilitated condition that powerfully predisposes to certain diseases, notably relapsing fever, phthisis, and pneumonia, and perhaps to all infectious diseases. Diarrhœa is apt to occur, adding still further to the general emaciation and prostration. Ophthalmia, ulcers, and skin diseases of various kinds are common : and any disease that may have obtained a hold upon the system is aggravated by the impairment of nutrition. Death ensues when the loss reaches about 40 per cent. of the normal weight of the body.

In conclusion, health may become affected by articles of food in the following ways :—

1. The essential constituents of diet may be deficient or in excess.

2. Poisonous substances may be derived from the vessels in which the food has been stored as in the case of tinned provisions.

3. Injurious substances may be added by way of adulteration or by improper manufacture.

4. Certain kinds of shellfish are occasionally liable to be poisonous, even in the fresh state, and disease may be conveyed by oysters, uncooked green vegetables, etc., grown on polluted soil.

5. Putrefactive changes may have commenced in the food and produce grave intestinal disturbance.

6. Poisonous substances, such as tyrotoxicon, may be developed, either as a result of fermentation or from unknown causes.

7. The flesh or milk of an animal suffering from certain specific or parasitic diseases, such as tuberculosis, trichinosis, hydatids, may impart the disease.

8. Vegetables may convey actinomycosis.

9. Food, especially milk, may become infected in various ways by the virus of diphtheria, enteric fever, cholera, or scarlet fever.

10. Disease in the individual, or, more rarely, idiosyncrasy apart from disease, may render injurious certain kinds of food such as shellfish which are wholesome to ordinary persons.

11. Finally, there are certain accessories of diet such as alcohol, coffee and tea which may be injurious if used injudiciously.

CHAPTER VI.

CLOTHING IN THE TROPICS.

Our comfort, our health, and even the preservation of our lives may largely depend upon the clothing we select:—(The Philosophy of Clothing).

THE principal use of clothing is to assist in the maintenance of animal heat by affording protection against the changes and inclemencies of the weather, and generally by adding to bodily comfort. The warmth of the body is, of course, solely derived from food, but clothing, inasmuch as it prevents the too rapid escape of animal heat, really acts as an adjunct to food, so that in cold climates the warmer a person is clad, the less food will he require. Some substances absorb heat rapidly and part with it very slowly, and are therefore called non-conductors, while others are better adapted for reflecting than for absorbing heat. Hence, by a judicious selection of materials, clothing can be made suitable either for cold or warm climates, or for seasonal changes. Thus, in very warm weather or in hot climates, the surface of the body is best protected by a material which will readily reflect the sun's rays, and during the cold weather or in a cold climate, by garments which are bad conductors. But clothing has also to be regulated according to its power of absorbing moisture, and to its non-interference with the healthy action of the skin and the free movements of all parts of the body. Moreover, its subsidiary uses, such as the protection of certain parts from pressure, as in the wearing of boots and shoes, and its adaptability to keep out wet, are points which merit consideration.

We obtain all our clothing from a few animals and birds, a single insect, a couple of small plants and several varieties of grass.

Animals yield us wool, furs and leather, birds yield us feathers ; the silk-worm provides us with silk ; whilst the cotton and flax plants and several grasses provide us with the remainder of our clothing materials.

Wool.—Wool forms the natural covering of animals in cold and temperature climates. It owes its value to the fact that it contains an oil or fat, and that, when woven into cloth, it has numerous interstices, which imprison air and prevent heat passing through it, hence flannel is not only warm in winter, but cool in summer. It should always be worn during the Indian cold weather and in the hills. During the hot season its desirability is doubtful.

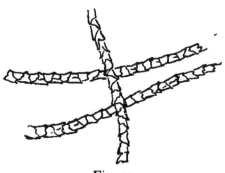

Fig. 11.
Wool Fibres, Semi-Diagrammatic
x about 200

The natural oil of the wool which is well known now as a toilet preparation, under the name of "lanoline," is one of the most important constituents of flannel, but unfortunately bad washing frequently removes this natural grease and leaves the material practically worthless. Woollen goods should therefore be washed in water which is only just warm, and soap, which should be of very good quality, should be used sparingly. A little kerosene oil added to the water will remove gross dirt.

It is not necessary that underclothing should be of pure wool. For hot climates it is difficult to obtain it either thin enough or soft enough for comfort, but various mixtures of wool and cotton, and loosely woven cotton materials, possessing all the advantages of pure wool, are on the market.

In the choice of woollen underclothing the touch is a great guide. There should be smoothness and great softness of texture; to the eye the texture should be close; the hairs standing out from the surface of equal length, not long and straggling. The heavier the substance is, in a given bulk, the better. In the case of blankets, the closeness of the pile, and the weight of the blanket, are the best guides.

In woollen cloths the rules are the same. When held against the light, the cloth should be of uniform texture, without holes; when folded and suddenly stretched, it should give a clear ringing note. It should be very resistant when forcibly stretched as the " tearing power " is the best way of judging if " shoddy " has been mixed with fresh wool.

Silk.—Silk, next to wool, is the best material for underwear, but its price places it beyond the means of all but the well-to-do.

The soft and soothing feeling of a silken vest is due to the fact that silk fibres are beautifully smooth, whereas wool, which is merely a variety of hair, presents a rough surface. (Fig. 11.)

Cotton.—Cotton has the great practical advantage of being hard, durable, and cheap. It is introduced into most woollen materials to increase their durability, and to prevent shrinking; it constitutes nearly a quarter of the excellent flannel from

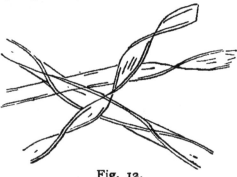

Fig. 12.

Cotton Fibres. Semi-Diagrammatic
× about 200.

which the familiar grey shirt of the soldier is made.

In the form of various types of cellular clothing it is a capital material for hot weather wear, and even for use in cold climates these cellular materials have many medical advocates.

Specially woven and dressed it is very largely used as " flannelette." This material is cotton in its worst form, and on account of its inflammability it is positively dangerous.

Linen.—Linen as an article of clothing possesses no advantages over cotton. It can be woven into finer materials and takes a higher finish, so that it must be judged from an æsthetic rather than a hygienic point of view.

India-rubber, oilskin and waterproof.—Special waterproof fabrics have a very wide use during the rainy season. The following is a useful recipe for waterproofing ordinary materials :—

Take five ounces of lanoline or wool fat and dissolve it in a gallon of petrol. The clothing is then immersed in the solution ; the garment wrung out and the excess of solvent allowed to evaporate rapidly in the air.

Clothing impregnated with wool fat in this way may be worn both in rain or sun without ill-effects. It permits the rapid evaporation of perspiration, and affords a better protection against rain than do fabrics waterproofed with alum preparations or other chemicals. Such garments are even more permeable to air than ordinary clothing, and also absorb less watery vapour. Moderate washing has no effect on the waterproofing, so that the effects of the procedure are fairly permanent. The expense is inconsiderable, the cost of waterproofing a suit of clothes being less than two rupees.

Boots.—Boots should be carefully fitted at all times, but require special consideration in India.

They should be· invariably "tried on" over a thick pair of socks and may well be a size or two bigger than is actually necessary to allow for the swelling of the extremities which is associated with hot weather and for expansion of the foot in active exercise. They must not be tight over the instep and great pains should be taken to see that there is plenty of room for the toes, especially the little one. The soles should be pliable ; nothing being so tiring as a long walk in shoes with stiff soles. New boots should be frequently used for short distances before being worn for any length of time.

Castor oil is one of the best materials to rub into boots used for sporting purposes to render them soft and pliant. In Europe it is not very largely used for this purpose on the score of expense, but in India it can be obtained extremely cheaply from the jails and elsewhere.

In India boots should always be worn in preference to shoes in order to protect the ankles from the bites of mosquitoes.

Leggings and putties.—Experience has shown that a well-fitting legging is the best covering for riding, whilst the puttee forms an excellent protection for the lower extremities for walking. Like boots and socks, these articles require careful attention, as a tight-fitting legging or a carelessly applied puttee spells misery to the individual wearing them. No man can either ride well nor walk far when the leg muscles are cramped by undue pressure from the legging or puttee.

Drawers.—Everyone should wear drawers in the Tropics. They promote cleanliness and protect the internal organs from chills.

Cholera belt.—The official publication "Hints on the Preservation of Health in India," says very wisely that the flannel cummerbund generally fails to answer the purpose for which it is intended. It

is very difficult to keep in position and either rucks
up under the ribs or lies in a roll above the hips.
In either case it is of little value as a protection,
and after exercise it becomes converted into a wet
poultice over the abdomen.

We would restrict the use of the belt to night
wear when we consider it most useful. If a blanket
is relied on in hot weather, it is frequently tossed
off by the restless sleeper with the result that the
abdomen is chilled by the draught of the punkah.

In the Tropics this is undoubtedly a source of
danger, and it should be carefully explained to those
recently arrived in this country that, whereas chill
in temperate climates usually leads to nothing
more serious than a cold in the head, in hot countries it is very liable to be followed by a severe
attack of either diarrhœa or dysentery.

The colour of articles should be carefully considered when deciding the question of general suitability. It is well known that different colours
possess, in varying degrees, the power of absorbing
heat. Black has the highest capacity for absorption—white has the least—the order in which
different colours absorb heat being as follows :—
Black, dark blue, light blue, dark green, turkey
red, light green, dark yellow, pale straw and white.
Under the name of " solaro," a cloth is now sold,
which has a red lining. This is supposed to keep
off the chemical rays of the sun, to which the
symptoms of " sunstroke and heat apoplexy " are
said to be due, but recent experiments in Manila
do not confirm this view.

The clothing of children.—An infant requires to
be especially protected by clothing because it loses
heat quickly by evaporation, its surface being in
large proportion to its bulk, as is the case with
everything small.

Young children should wear wool next to the
skin all the year round, only varying the thick-

ness to suit the season. It shows a poverty of resource to expose the upper and lower parts of the bodies of children in order to give them greater freedom of movement. This can be accomplished without depriving them of clothing. Deprivation of clothing has a distinctly injurious effect upon children who require a large amount of heat to enable them to carry on the processes of growth and development. The habit, therefore, of tying up a baby's sleeves with ribbons, and allowing older children to run about with the legs bare, cannot be too strongly condemned, as a large part of the body is thereby exposed to sudden chilling. A child has only a certain amount of nerve force available for the vital functions of breathing, digestion, etc., and, if an undue amount of this is expended in the maintenance of bodily heat, the other functions suffer with the result that digestion is enfeebled and constipation or diarrhœa ensue.

Even in the Tropics, therefore, a child's clothing should be soft, light, warm and loose, and so arranged that it can easily be taken off. Every garment should be made to fasten with tapes and buttons, and an infant's binder should invariably be sewn on and not fastened with a safety pin.

Long clothes are a relic of barbarism and universally condemned by all medical men. Much money would be saved if children were put into short clothes at birth and young mothers should be brave enough to defy convention and refuse to make their infants unhappy by swathing them in long sweeping garments during the first three months of life.

All children should wear a vest of natural wool in cold weather and silk in hot weather, and it is important that the remarks with reference to flannelette should be properly appreciated by mothers. Older children should wear combinations

as these garments avoid undue pressure round
the waist.

Children's bedclothes should be light and warm
and, wherever possible, the insanitary coloured
blankets, which are so popular in India, should
be replaced by white blankets which *do* " show
the dirt."

Mackintoshes should be placed over children's
mattresses, but they must *never* be put on over a
baby's napkin, as the rubber causes irritation of
the skin. Eider-down quilts are undesirable for
children's beds as they are not porous and cannot
be washed.

Soiled napkins, even although they are merely
wet with urine, must never be used a second time
without washing ; and good soap, free from excess
of alkali, must always be used for this purpose.

Stockings long enough to extend from the feet
to the napkin must be worn in cold weather, and
for older children they should join the leg of the
combinations, covering and protecting the knees,
except in the hot weather. Garters which interfere
with the circulation and thus hinder the development of the limbs must never be used.

The stockings can be easily supported by a piece
of tape sewn on the outer side and buttoned by a
loop on to the bodice of stout jean which takes the
place of stays. They should fit the foot easily and
not be mended too much. Economy in the way of
too much darning is the cause of many a tear.

With regard to foot covering, boots or shoes
must not be worn until the child begins to crawl
about, *i.e.*, at about the ninth or tenth month. To
cramp its feet with boots or shoes before this time
is both unnecessary and harmful.

Shoes should be properly made. The use of
improperly made footgear spoils many a shapely
foot. Boots should be " square-toed," but not
necessarily shapeless, and they should *fit*. Many

parents spend large sums on their own boots, but think anything good enough for their children. This is absolutely wrong.

Children's boots should be made by a good bootmaker, and the only point parents need insist on is that the inner edge of the sole should be in a perfectly straight line and not inclined towards the outside from the ball of the toe towards as is the case in all " fashionable " footgear.

Children's boots should invariably be made to lace up and not to button. This method of fastening allows of making one part tight and another loose as circumstances require. They should only be laced as far as the last hole but one and tied *loosely*. If laced right up to the top the bootlace often slips on the leg and chafes and constricts it. One of the commonest causes of cold feet in children is wearing boots too tightly buttoned or laced.

Sandals have been strongly advocated for children and they have much to recommend them. It is obviously undesirable to keep a growing organ shut up all day long in a leather bag—which is after all what a boot really is—but sandals are only suitable for fine weather, as children's feet must be kept warm, and it is impossible to do this with sandals in really severe weather. Moreover, they do not protect the feet from the bites of mosquitoes. Sandals are now made with a piece of leather to protect the toes. This variety must invariably be obtained ; otherwise the child's toes are apt to be wounded or even severely injured by gravel and sharp stones.

Plimsolls must not be used. The undesirability of enclosing a portion of the body in a waterproof bag must be obvious to any one after a moment's consideration.

With regard to head covering, babies' heads should not be wrapped up except in the most severe weather. The adage " keep the head cool " applies even to infants. As they grow up, light loose-fitting hats and caps should be used, and headgear of the type of Dutch bonnets avoided : sunshine and fresh air are essential to a vigorous growth of hair, and these cheap and invaluable hair tonics are not to be obtained if the head is tightly wrapped up. A light broad-brimmed mushroom-shaped topee is all that is necessary for wearing in the sun, whilst a similar covering in light straw is easily devised for use after sundown. The topee must be worn out-of-doors, even in the early morning : the sun is just as likely to produce sunstroke in the morning or evening as in the middle of the day.

Corsets should not be worn by children, and indeed the whole endeavour of mothers should be to make girls' clothing as much like boys as possible. A school uniform for girls on these lines has been advocated and largely adopted in better class girls' schools.

Girls should wear an easy fitting blouse, knickers and skirt suspended like a boy's trousers by straps over the shoulders ; but " braces," strictly so called " for improving the figure," should not be used.

The best way to develop a graceful figure is to indulge freely in field sports. This is now recognised by nearly all schoolmistresses, some of whom, however, are apt to go rather to extremes in this direction.

General remarks.—Cleanliness of the person cannot be maintained without due attention to cleanliness of clothing, and this applies not only to the garments which are worn during the day but also those that are worn at night.

In order to ensure thorough cleanliness, persons should avoid sleeping in any garment worn during the day, and bedding and bed-clothes should be thoroughly aired every morning. All clothes, after being washed, should be dried in the open air, and otherwise well aired before they are put on : indeed, clothing of every description should be frequently exposed to the sun and air, and should never be kept shut up in closed boxes and drawers for long periods. It is needless to add that under garments, no matter of what colour or texture, should always be kept clean and well brushed.

Supervision of laundry work is a point with reference to clothing which receives too little attention from Indians and Anglo-Indians.

The Indian *dhobi* is generally an abominable washerman. It is no uncommon thing to see clothes being violently beaten on stones, a process destructive of all fabrics, and notably so in the case of flannel.

In addition to the absence of all ordinary skill and care, the washing is carried out in any dirty stream or pool that may happen to suit the Indian's idea of convenience. In many stations the washing is carried out in streams which, owing to their receiving the drainage of the city, are horribly foul, and in this way garments become contaminated with disease-germs in the so-called process of washing. It is no far-fetched idea to suggest the spread of cholera, dysentery, enteric fever, and other diseases by *dhobies* and the subject is in consequence fully worthy of the earnest attention of the authorities, and, in fact, of all residents in India. When India really awakes to her sanitary necessities, properly equipped laundries will be considered essential in every part of the Empire.

The ironing and storage of the *clean (?) clothes* is usually as badly carried out as the washing process itself. Too often the clothing is ironed in the bazar and stored a night or two in the *dhobies'* living room before it reaches the owner's bungalow. This may account for many mysterious outbreaks of smallpox and measles amongst the European community.

CHAPTER VII.

HOUSES AND THEIR SURROUNDINGS IN THE TROPICS.

In olden times the fashion in many parts of the East was for each king to build a new city, which no doubt originated from the fact that after a certain number of years each city became so unhealthy that it was advisable to leave it.—(Simpson's " Principles of Hygiene.")

INDIA is essentially an agricultural country. To appreciate, therefore, the sanitary necessities for the immediate environment of the Indian, it is necessary to consider primarily the social and economic position of the peasant population. The large towns and even villages of importance are few or far between, and the vast bulk of India's two hundred million of inhabitants live and work in the fields. Now the common labourer in India is about as poor as man can be. He is very nearly as poor as a sparrow. His hut, built by himself, is scarcely more substantial or permanent than the sparrow's nest, and his clothing compares very unfavourably with the sparrow's feathers.

The Indian is essentially a home-loving individual, and the consideration of his house and its surroundings must be of special interest to him as there can be no sort of doubt that a large proportion of the disease from which he suffers is due to the hopelessly insanitary environment in which so many of the teeming millions of the inhabitants of this Empire eat, sleep, and work.

Although these insanitary conditions are still unrecognised by the peasant class, they are beginning to be very fully appreciated by Indians residing in our great cities, as may be gathered from the following extract from a paper read before the Bombay Medical Congress :—

" Bombay, with its area of about 14,300 acres and a population of fully a million, may be considered as one of the most densely crowded cities in the world. Not only have all available building areas in the city been long since taken up for building purposes, but a very large number of residential quarters in the shape of tall houses, ricketty tenements, and very big chawls, have been allowed to crowd on them without much heed to the needs of the people. The scarcity of house accommodation and of available land in the city for building purposes has become so great within the last few years, owing, on the one hand, to the constantly increasing demand for a rapidly increasing population, and, on the other, to the somewhat hasty demolition of several insanitary areas by the City Improvement Trust in the first year of its existence, without much regard to the sudden displacement of the people occupying them, or without any adequate provision for their temporary accommodation, that the evil of overcrowding and insanitary dwellings has been greatly accentuated. Notwithstanding this wholesale demolition of a large number of houses unfit for human habitation, and the partial improvement of others, under the Epidemic Diseases Act, a considerable number of insanitary and overcrowded tenements still remain in almost every ward of the city, and it will take perhaps another twenty or twenty-five years before the slow progress of the operations of the Improvement Trust will have beneficially touched a fairly large proportion of them.

" There are but very few open air spaces in the shape of parks, gardens, or other places of public resort, to act as ' lungs ' to the city, compared to the urgent needs of its teeming population, dense-

ly packed in every nook and corner of it. The
extent of this overcrowding can only be realized by
a nocturnal visit to one or two of the many Goanese
residential clubs, or to one of the larger tenement
chawls in some of the most crowded parts of the
city. In these, sometimes as many as 15 to 30
persons sleep in each room at night, while in some
of the big four and five storeyed buildings in the
city, from 300 to 500 people, and even more, can
be counted as their daily occupants.

"No wonder, overcrowding should thus stand
far and away as one of the largest, if not quite the
largest, factor in the very high rate of disease and
death in our midst. But, as if this baneful overcrowding was not enough of a curse for the City,
the poor of Bombay, who probably form more
than 90 per cent. of the entire population, have
perforced to put up with all the attendant filth
and refuse lying unremoved, for several hours at
times, near their doors. In this, of course, it is
the people themselves who are chiefly to be blamed
even more than the insufficiency of appliances
or of the minor staff, or the ineffective supervision
of the executive, because of the peoples' perverse
and filthy habits contributing to this accumulation
of refuse at their very doors, and because of
their apathy to, and ignorance of, even the first
principles of sanitation.

"Most of these tenements consist of very small
rooms, ill-ventilated, damp, and unwholesome,
and are literally crowded with people, many of
whom go out for work during the greater part
of the day, and who on return home can scarcely
get more breathing space than that which is
obtainable in the shape of the barest sleeping
accommodation at night. Their drains and house
connections are faulty, and their adjoining 'open?
space,' if there happens to be one at all, in the
shape of a dark and narrow 'gully,' is oftener

than not of a very filthy character, and reeking with all kinds of noxious odours and poisonous emanations from decomposing night-soil percolating through leaky privies. And yet, to a very large number of such residential quarters in the city, these sweepers' passages constitute the chief, if not the only, ventilating space for those living in rooms adjoining. Generally speaking, these gullies are badly paved and badly drained, and some of them are in the most filthy condition imaginable. A European can scarely conceive such a state of things in the heart of a town like Bombay. Thus, these 'open passages,' instead of bringing the fresh draughts of pure air into the houses abutting on them, serve as so many storages for decomposing materials, and help to slowly but most steadily poison and undermine the health and constitutions of the unfortunate inmates in their close vicinity. To add to their sufferings there are also the sickening emanations from the accumulation, for several hours in the day, of household sweepings, street refuse, and decomposing stable litter, heaped up to overflowing in one or more unsavoury dust-bin carts, often located right under their bed-room windows. Add to these, the poisonous exhalations night and day from all the paraphernalia of leaky ventilating pipes, syphons, and taps of various kinds attached to these houses ; the sum total of the miseries can scarcely be more complete.''

A recent Health Report for Calcutta speaks out with no uncertain voice, with reference to the relation between bad housing and consumption or phthisis.

There were 2,110 deaths returned as due to tubercle, of which 2,049 were ascribed to phthisis and 52 to other forms of tuberculosis. The death-rate from phthisis in Calcutta is 2.5 per 1,000 of the population. In England the rate is 1.9 per

1,000. This is about the same as for the past four years. The rate in the Indian Army is ·52 per 1,000, but in the jail population of India it reaches 3·2 per 1,000. The rate for males in Calcutta is only 2·0 while that for females is 3·3 per 1,000.

The severe incidence of the disease amongst Mahomedan women is very striking—the rates amongst them being 5·8 per 1,000, whilst amongst Hindu females it is only 3 per 1,000.

The relation of the incidence of phthisis to the density of the population has been worked out, and in making the calculation the error of mistaking the density of an area such as a ward with the density of population per house or per room has been carefully avoided. From the average density of population in huts and pucca houses, respectively, as given in the Census, it would appear that phthisis is twice as common amongst the population living in huts. This is partly a question of overcrowding, as the average number of occupants per hut is 6·47, and, for each room in a hut, 2·41 ; whilst for pucca houses the corresponding figures are 10·44 (per house) but only 1·72 per room. Most pucca houses are more or less paved and comparatively dry, whilst the floors of huts are kutcha and more or less perpetually damp. This latter condition has long been recognised as favouring the development of this disease.

" The varying incidence of phthisis in the several wards of the city seems to depend upon the different constitutions of the populations in the several wards. Where there are large Mahomedan populations the phthisis rate is high, because the female death-rates in these wards are so excessive. In other wards the phthisis rate is low, either because there is an enormous excess of males or because there are comparatively few Mahomedans. The conditions of female life must be particularly favourable in the Mussulman wards because in these wards the female death-rate from phthisis varies from 3·9 to over 5 per 1,000. Phthisis is a disease largely dependent upon the insanitary conditions of the home, and so long as the vast majority of the houses in Calcutta remain in their present state, there is little hope of affecting the prevalence of the disease."

The requirements for a healthy dwelling, whether it is situated at the Pole or at the Equator, are six in number, namely :—

1. A site which is dry and an aspect which gives light and cheerfulness.

2. A system of sewage-removal sufficiently adapted to modern life that the Institutes of Vishnu and the Laws of Manu be observed.

3. Proper means of ventilation.

4. Proper system of construction which will ensure perfect dryness of the foundation, walls, and roof.

5. Proper means of warming the house in winter and cooling it in summer.

6. Efficient means of lighting.

I.—Site.

The health of a locality is intimately connected with the nature of the soil on which the houses are built and the best site is a gentle slope on a gravel soil. Clay soils should be avoided as they foster dampness, and if a house become damp, malaria, rheumatism, dysentery and diseases of the chest are apt to occur. Sandy soils are undesirable unless covered with short grass. As turf is hardly ever seen in India without irrigation and super-abundant vegetation, the bare sandy soils which are common are very hot. If any choice is available, always build on the highest ground available, and invariably provide surface drainage so as to prevent pools forming which may become mosquito nurseries.

Marshy and swampy ground should on no account be used for building purposes, and what are called "made soils" must be especially avoided. Such sites consist of hollows filled up with rubbish of all kinds and are obviously full of impurities which must, and do, produce emanations prejudicial to health.

2.—Sewage and Refuse Disposal.

Sewage and refuse disposal is fully dealt with in the next chapter.

3.—Ventilation.

Ventilation has already been referred to in Chapter III, but we must emphasize the fact that an opening opposite the door or window is an absolutely essential requirement in order to secure cross ventilation. Too often houses in every part of the Empire have all their doors and windows at one side, and cooking, sleeping, and eating are all carried on in one tiny room. Cooking is done in the living room with green wood, and the result is dense volumes of smoke which find their way out as best as they can. This smoke is very irritating to the eyes and induces many of the eye diseases so common in this country. In the houses of the comparatively well-to-do, punkahs are relied on to act as ventilators. They are practically useless for this purpose as they merely agitate the air of the room and do not draw pure air from outside.

4.—Construction.

When we realize that the houses of so many Indians are no more substantial than the sparrow's nest, it is obvious that the fourth requirement must be a dead letter to a large section of the community.

The following are what should be aimed at in the houses of the well-to-do :—

ASPECT.—Having chosen a suitable site, the next question is in what direction the house should face : in other words, the relation of the building to the four points of the compass. In India the house should front the north so as to avoid having the sun pouring in and to have the principal rooms as cool as possible.

PLAN.—The bed-rooms should also face north, or if that is not possible, then south, whilst all rooms intended for storage of food must have their windows to the north.

FOUNDATIONS.—These should be sufficiently solid and deep-rooted to afford stability. If firm foundations cannot be obtained on the site, it is necessary to make artificial ones out of large blocks of concrete, on which the walls may rest. Each of these should be at least four times the breadth of the wall it supports, and at least 18 inches in depth.

MATERIALS.—The shell of a house may be constructed of a variety of materials, such as concrete, mortar, stone, bricks, wood, plaster, iron or canvas, but in India we are only concerned with the ordinary stone, brick or mud houses.

Concrete—Consists of cement, interspersed with broken brick, stone, or gravel. Portland cement is made from lime and a peculiar dark blue mud-clay.

Mortar.—Properly made mortar consists of lime with clean sharp sand, but unfortunately mud mixed with *bhoosa,* or chopped straw, takes its place to an alarming extent in India, indeed, it is difficult to know what the native architect would do without this useful but sordid material in this country.

Stone.—The rocks most commonly used in building are the sandstones and limestones, both of which are very plentiful and easily worked. In certain parts of this country where it is plentiful, granite is largely used, and is specially suitable for foundations.

Bricks.—In India bricks are of two kinds, *kutcha* and *pucca*. The former is made from mud dried in the sun, while the latter are made from " brick earth," which may consist of pure clay, clay loam, and clay marl baked in a fire. A brick should be well shaped, and all its angles should be right angles. The edges or solid angles should be sharp and clean. It ought to weigh five pounds, be twice as long as it is broad, and be homogeneous in character and colour, both externally and on section. The common dimensions are 9 inches by 4½ inches by 3 inches. A brick can absorb as much as 1 pound of water, but it should not be what builders describe as " over-thirsty."

Wood.—For structural purposes deal, deodar, teak, and shisham are chiefly used. The quality of timber depends on its rate of growth and its original position in the stem of the tree. The slower the growth and the nearer the centre of the tree, the better the specimen. A rough comparative test is the musical note given out by the wood when it is struck by a hammer. A good dense wood gives a clear, ringing note.

No timber can withstand alternate wetting and drying, or heat and moisture without adequate ventilation. Under such conditions decay sets in, especially if lime be adjacent, hence the ends of beams are liable to early degeneration. Two peculiar diseases affect timber, namely, dry and wet rot, the exciting causes being fungi. Wood suffering from either form of rot must be condemned and removed. Protection from decay is best secured by forcing creasote into the wood under pressure where the wood is to be hidden out of sight and by painting and varnishing in the case of external woodwork.

Plaster.—The best quality consists of lime or cement bound up with sand and hair, but the lime plaster generally used in India consists of bricks ground up with lime.

WALLS.—The walls, to ensure stability, must rest on a broad base. These broad bases are called the " footings," and rest upon the foundations. In heavy or main walls they must extend on both sides of the wall, and must project on each side to a distance equal to one-half the thickness of the wall. It is most important that foundations should be of the best material as work is very apt to be scamped when hidden away underground. The same remark applies to the concealed parts of the walls and therefore wainscotting or lining with wood is most undesirable in the Tropics.

Damp-proof Courses.—As water can rise in the house walls by capillary attraction to a height of 32 feet, it is essential that moisture interceptors be placed in them. These are called damp-proof courses, and may consist of Portland cement, glazed stoneware and slates embedded in cement, or tarred bricks.

Tarred bricks are made by first heating them and then plunging them into a bath of boiling tar. On removal from the tar they are rolled in dry sand. Failing even tarred bricks, a mixture of fresh slaked lime and vegetable oil is useful. It is spread evenly over the foundation course with a trowel, in a layer about $\frac{3}{4}$ inch thick and left for one day to set firm. In laying the first courses of bricks over this preparation care must be taken not to break or disturb the cement.

In a properly constructed house one damp interceptor is required where the footing ends and the wall begins : a second, 6 inches above the level of the external earth : and as damp may enter the wall from above, a third on the very top beneath the roof timbers. If only one damp-proof course is feasible, it should be placed in the second position.

The inner or room walls of a house may be composed of brick, tiles, or of wood and plaster.

The modern fashion of papering rooms in India in the same way as in England is to be deprecated. Paper is expensive and cannot be often renewed. Moreover, one of the greatest enemies of the mosquito is the half-yearly colour washing which ensures the brushing down of our bungalow walls at least every six months. Papers therefore should be dispensed with, and some form of silicate paint substituted for them.

All sharp angles should be rounded off to facilitate cleansing and prevent deposits of dust.

Walls should invariably be coloured or papered in the lightest shades as we have seen that mosquitoes dislike all the lighter colours.

CHIMNEYS.—The flues should be straight, circular, separate from each other, and smoothly lined, so as to prevent the risk of fire, to facilitate cleaning, and to aid the upward draught. All chimneys should rise at least 3 feet above the roof.

ROOF.—There should always be an open space between the ceiling of the highest rooms and the roof. Tile roofs are very common in Bengal and the Punjab : when unprovided with a ceiling they are insanitary abominations. They also harbour rats, and thus tend to spread plague. The tiles are good conductors of heat, and in the hot weather are a source of very serious danger. A room may also be rendered absolutely uninhabitable by the heat radiating from a metal roof in the absence of a properly constructed ceiling and air-space.

Double roofs of non-conducting materials, and high rooms, are essential to comfort in the tropics. The heat radiated from a roof is in inverse ratio to the square of its distance. The direct heat reaching a person from a roof 5 feet above him is four times as much as would reach him if the roof were 10 feet above him. Ceilings should always be insisted on, as they act as powerful heat interceptors. The air-space between them and the roof should always be ventilated.

Thatched roofs, consisting of long wiry grass laid in bundles on a bamboo frame, or of palm leaves, are very cool and dry, but harbour squirrels, rats, insects, and other animals, and are liable to take fire. Plantain fibre (not leaves), forms an excellent roof, and is not inflammable, but it is liable to run into channels, leaks, and often requires repairing.

Corrugated or galvanized iron is largely used as a roof covering. The sheets should never be laid on rafters only. Such roofs render the huts excessively hot during the day and cold at night. The sheeting should be laid on close boarding, or should be lined with felt underneath, or should have an earth ceiling put under the roof. It is indeed remarkable how few houses in the Indian plains have ceilings.

FLOORS.—Indian floors consist of wood, bricks, tiles, slate slabs, concrete, or rammed earth.

Concrete is the best and most sanitary of these materials, as it necessitates fewer gaps or cracks than any of the others.

Rammed earth and kutcha brick floors are insanitary abominations as it is impossible to keep a room clean with such a floor. The plan of covering one of these floors with *chillai*, or matting, and leaving it down for months without moving it is comparable with the disgusting insanitary habits of the Middle Ages.

All floors should have a good plinth, that is, they should be raised at least two feet above the ground level to prevent dampness.

A well-constructed house should have pucca drains to carry off water which drops from the eaves.

A belt of sharp gravel round the house keeps off snakes.

Mosquito-proofing of windows and doors.—This consists· in carefully protecting all windows and doors with fine wire gauze. The gauze may be tinned iron, copper, or brass, and must be secured with nails of the same metal to prevent galvanic rust.

This is an expensive measure, but it adds greatly to the comfort of life in the tropics. It excludes not only mosquitoes, but flies, moths, and other insects, bats and birds.

Where, from the score of expense, mosquito-proofing with wire gauze is impracticable, ordinary cotton netting may be used. If painted four or five times with a solution of commercial silicate of potassium in its own volume of water, its durability is greatly increased, and it is rendered comparatively rain and fire-proof.

The Italians have long advocated double swing doors with a protected entry, but this is necessary only where the insects abound very much. Automatic swing doors generally suffice. Of course, in order to protect a room or a house completely, every possible orifice, including key-holes, chimneys and chinks round doors and windows should be properly closed or guarded : but the details are so numerous that it is useless to give them in this book.

The various hints given above show the ideal at which we should aim. What actually exists in this country is shown in Figs. 13 to 17.

Fig. 13 shows the appearance of a common type of Indian dwelling. The walls are built of unhewn stone plastered together with mud and

Fig. 13

in an almost constant state of disrepair. The roof affords ample shelter for rats beneath the country tiles. If we enter a room in the upper storey of such a house, a picture, much like the one depicted in Fig. 14, will confront us. We will have entered a small room 10 feet by 10 feet with a sloping roof. The roof at its highest part is perhaps a little over 6 feet above the floor, and, gradually sloping downwards, it meets the floor at one side of the room. It is difficult to move about in such a place, yet this room may be inhabited by three or four adult persons. There is usually

no window in the room.   What light enter comes in
through the door and through gaps in the tiled
roof.

Fig. 14.

Fig. 15 shows another house with a stable
below it.   In the towns of India no bye-laws exist
which prohibit the keeping of horses and cattle
within a limited distance of a dwelling-house.   At
least if such laws have been enacted, they are seldom
enforced.   In almost every part of an Indian town,
stables will be found immediately below dwelling-
houses, and their presence in such situations appear
to occasion no repugnance on the part of the inhabitants.   Wealthy Indians sometimes even convert the porch over their front door into a stable.

In some streets even in large towns the   ground
floors of all the houses are used as stables or store
houses.   The ground floor of practically every building in one of the districts of Bombay is used as
a godown, while people live in the upper storeys.

The walls of the building are solidly constructed
of brick raised on a high masonry plinth.   The

floors are made of concrete or patent stone, and the building is roofed with Mangalore tiles. The verandahs and corridors are paved and are wide and airy. The lighting and ventilation of the whole building leaves nothing to be desired. The sanitary arrangements are excellent : there are no gullies. In short, the insanitary condition of the buildings is entirely due to the habits of the

Fig. 15.

people in the matter of disposal of their household belongings and food-supply. Grain and grocers' shops are to be found on the ground floors, and here rats find food and shelter. In the upper storeys the inhabitants construct shelves and on these materials accumulate which are seldom disturbed, and which provide homes for rats. In the plague season of 1906 these tenements were so badly smitten by plague that they had to be vacated, and the curious spectacle was presented of empty houses and the inhabitants living in matting huts.

Fig. 16 shows the interior of an ordinary Indian dwelling. The accumulation of rubbish and general disorder is evident. The walls of the room are soft and readily penetrated by rats, for mud or inferior lime is often used to hold the stones together. The floor is made of rammed earth covered with a layer of cowdung. The furnishings are of the simplest kind : a lamp, a few earthenware and brass pots, some boxes and baskets make up the complete domestic outfit. Scattered

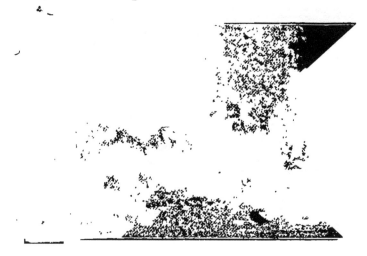

Fig. 16.

about in various parts of the room are collections of firewood and bundles of sticks. A grinding stone usually occupies one corner.

Fig. 17 is a picture of a small room measuring 5 feet by 5 feet by 7 feet, tenanted by four adults. The roof sloped towards one end of the room and at its highest part only measured 5 feet from the ground, so that it was impossible to stand in any part of the room.

There is another habit of the people which favours the presence of vermin amongst them, namely, that of keeping animals, particularly cows, goats, and hens in their dwelling rooms. These animals during the day feed upon grain and all sorts of food material which becomes scattered about the street, affording food for rats.

Amongst the poorer classes in India, about 85 per cent. of the population live in a single roomed house, and it is the constant practice of the people to keep either hens or goats in their dwelling room.

Wherever you go in India the same story holds good.

Fig. 17.

The village cattle enjoy themselves in the village tank. The cattle will at night share their owner's dwelling. On entering one of the dwellings we find the stall or room for the cattle, and passing from it through the sleeping room of the family, we enter by another door, a room in which the grain supply for the year is kept stored in large earthen vessels. In addition we may find a number of earthen pots within the room, in which spices, chillies and onions are stored. The rooms are generally very dark, as there are no windows. Outside the door at one side of the house a ladder or staircase leads to the roof. The flat roof of the house is used as a store for all sorts of materials and in the courtyard below are nearly always some animals tethered.

This is what is going on in and around the homes of the vast bulk of the Indian population, but although high ideals are as yet impracticable, the following seven simple rules can be carried out in the poorest dwelling, and their observance might well be enforced by municipalities and cantonment authorities.

1. *Floors.*—The use of cowdung as a covering for floors is a dirty and unwholesome habit. Cowdung attracts flies and moisture, and is a breeding ground for microbes.

Mud floors should have the surface dug up and removed at least twice yearly.

Fresh mud should be laid down and beaten until quite smooth.

This should be done in the dry weather.

2. *Walls.*—These should be whitewashed twice yearly, inside and outside.

3. *Windows.*—Every room should have two windows at least 2 feet square opposite each other, or else one window 3 feet square opposite the door.

Windows must open to the outer air. They must be left open most of the day and all night.

4. *Cookroom.*—A chimney or outlet for the smoke must be provided.

5. *Refuse and Waste Water.*—Refuse must be placed in a receptacle and waste water emptied into a drain as far away from the house as possible.

6. *Latrines.*—The necessaries should be outside the general house buildings, and must have a window. They should have a solid floor and must be easily accessible to the sweeper from behind.

7. Whilst a few plants and small trees in the neighbourhood of a house are pleasant, there should be no interference with the free passage of

air and light to all parts of the dwelling, and all animals, fowls, and pets should be separately housed outside the house and its enclosure.

Purdahs and hangings are to be avoided as there is no proverb truer than the one which says " Where the sun does not enter the doctor does."

5. WARMING OF HOUSES.

This is accomplished in India by open fires and stoves.

Heat may be transmitted by conduction, convection, or radiation.

Conduction is the means whereby heat passes directly by contact, either from the hotter to the colder parts of the same body, or from a hotter to a colder body.

Radiation.—Heat is said to be radiated when it passes from one point to another, without raising the temperature of the medium through which it travels.

Convection is the conveyance of heat by means of the movements of masses of heated air. Hot air is lighter than cold air and tends to rise. Currents are formed and the heated particles part with some of their heat to the colder particles with which they come in contact.

Heat travels by rays and if we stand in front of a fire we are warmed by these rays given off by the fire. If a screen is placed between us and the fire, the rays do not reach us and we feel no effect from the fire. Heat passes from the fire in a stove to its walls by conduction and is given off from the walls to the air of the room by radiation.

Open Fires—Construction of a fireplace and grate.—As coal is now so very largely used in India, it may be of interest to point out that the present types of grate consisting of iron baskets which have been dumped down in the old type of fireplace are neither economical of fuel nor effective as regards heating.

An ideal form of fireplace which favours complete combustion, while there is less loss of heat than in any other form, is made as follows :—

1. The back, base, and sides of the fireplace should be constructed of fire brick, and should be solid.

2. The solid base of the fireplace should be about 6 inches in depth, *i.e.*, the part on which the fuel has to rest should be that distance above floor level. Its length from before backwards should be from 9 to 11 inches.

3. The sides should converge towards the back, which is thus rendered narrower than the open front.

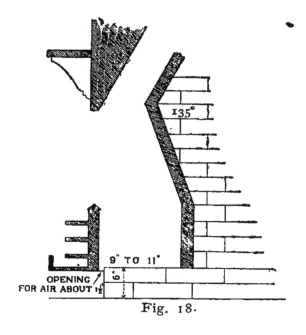

Fig. 18.

4. The back should overhang the fuel cavity, so that the throat of the chimney is narrowed and the base of the fuel cavity wider than the top. The

chimney flue and the fireplace should, in this way, be inclined towards each other at an angle of 135°.

5.   The fuel should rest directly on the bottom of the grate, no iron bars intervening.

6.   The bars should be movable, narrow, vertical, and far enough apart to just admit a poker.

7.   Air is to be admitted through a horizontal space, 1 to 1½ inches in depth beneath the bars, and this place can be closed at will by a shield.

Stoves made of brick and tiles, cast or sheet iron, are now largely used for heating in India.

There are two types, (1) *close* and (2) ventilating. In the close variety no arrangements for assisting the ventilation of the room exist, but in the latter kind fresh air from outside the dwelling is drawn into the room and heated without coming in contact with the fire.

Their advantages are :—1. More uniform warming of the room, the hot stove walls drawing cold air to them and warming it, after which it ascends towards the ceiling, and circulates through the apartment.

2.   There is less loss of heat, there being a greater radiating surface, and less extraction of warm air as compared with the open fire.

3.   Economy in fuel consumption.

The disadvantages of all kinds of stoves require careful consideration ; they are :—

1.   Stoves do not act as such efficient ventilator as open fires.

2.   They diminish the relative humidity of the air rendering the air of the room too dry and unpleasant to the nose, eyes and skin. This, however, may be combated by placing vessels containing water on the stove.

3.   If the walls of the stove get very hot, and especially if they are composed of metal, there is a nuisance produced by the smell of scorched organic matter in the air.

4. Further, carbon monoxide may be formed in the stove owing to imperfect combustion, and pass into the room owing to bad jointing and the permeability of hot iron. Carbonic acid, moreover, the product of combustion, in passing through the heated iron, may be converted into carbon monoxide, or the atmospheric carbonic acid coming into contact with the hot external surface may undergo a similar transformation.

Oil stoves are extensively used in the Indian Hills, and as they are only used for short periods, there are no serious sanitary objections to them, provided efficient ventilation and complete combustion of the oil is secured. It is very important that the best oil should be used in them in order to be certain that poisonous waste products are not passed into the air. Oil stoves should have diffusers or radiators placed above them to increase their action.

Cooling of Rooms.

Punkahs, thermantidotes, khus-khus tatties and electric fans form the means of reducing the temperature in our Indian houses. Electric fans are by far the best of the four. The custom, formerly popular in India, of avoiding the extreme heat of the summer by living underground is happily disappearing. Cellar rooms, so popular in former days in India, are dark, ill-ventilated and unhealthy.

We would remind the reader that a dark room is no cooler but far unhealthier than one into which every ray of indirect sunlight is admitted.

Lighting.

The agents employed in India are sunlight, candles, oil, coal-gas, and electricity.

Sunlight is essential to health, and no room should be without its cheering rays. It promotes human growth, and prevents germ growth. No house is healthy unless sunlight has access to each room. It is one of the most potent and one of the cheapest agents for the destruction of the disease-causing bacteria.

Candles.—These may be made of tallow, wax, spermaceti, or stearin. The products of combustion are watery vapour and carbonic acid, and two sperm candles produce as much carbonic acid as one man. They are comparatively feeble illuminants, but in themselves produce little or no ill-effects on the health.

Oil.—The chief illuminating oil is kerosene. It consumes the oxygen of the air to a greater extent than candles, and gives off watery vapour and carbonic acid. A good oil lamp of moderate size is, as we have seen, equivalent to seven men in its power of producing carbonic acid. Weight for weight, kerosene oil is twice as powerful an illuminant as candles. Inferior oils are liable to explode and cause fire, and therefore their use for bath-room lamps and similar purposes is one of the most dangerous of our little economies in the tropics.

Coal Gas is the most widely used illuminant in Europe, but is comparatively little used in India. It possesses many disadvantages, being poisonous and explosive, whilst its use renders the air impure. It is, however, a cheap and fairly powerful lighting agent. Coal gas is a purified product of the distillation of coal, and consists of a mixture of no fewer than eight or nine gases. One gas jet produces as much carbonic acid as five or six men. The introduction of the incandescent burner undoubtedly postponed the universal adoption of electric light as it renders the light more brilliant for a smaller consumption of gas, and consequently diminishes the production of impurities, uses up less oxygen and produces less heat.

', *Acetylene Gas.*—Acetylene is one of the constituents of coal gas. It is evolved when water comes in contact with carbide of calcium, a compound prepared from a mixture of lime and carbon which have been formed into a chemical compound by the intense heat of an electric furnace. It is colourless, has a strong odour, and can be storéd in gasometers or burned in special lamps. It easily explodes when mixed with air in a proportion of 7 per cent., but it is only very slightly poisonous. For household use improved apparatus for its combustion is required, as at present lamps have to be re-charged with carbide frequently and the process is both difficult and offensive.

Petrol.—A large number of lamps are now in use in India which burn petrol. They give a white light of great intensity.

Electricity.—From a hygienic point of view, electric light is preferable, especially for the tropics. It has none of the disadvantages of the other forms of lighting. It does not vitiate the air, deprive it of oxygen, nor yield to it carbonic acid, watery vapour, or much heat, while it is clean and does not discolour walls or ceilings. It may be necessary to moderate the intensity of the light, which is often trying to the eyesight.

SUMMARY.

By no means the least important of the causes of the bad hygienic condition of the Indian city is the peculiar social customs, habits, and prejudices of the people, and their dense ignorance with regard to even the first principles of sanitation. In the Tropics, notwithstanding some progress of recent years, the habits of the poorer classes of the population still remain very uncleanly, and there is a considerable amount of filth and squalor in their midst, both within and without their dwellings.

Owing to these factors, a large amount of disease and illness prevails amongst them, and, what is perhaps of equal importance, their energy for work is greatly diminished, and their powers of resistance against attacks of disease considerably lowered. All this economic waste could be considerably lessened, if only the poorer classes could be made to understand, appreciate and observe the first principles of household sanitation and personal hygiene.

CHAPTER VIII.

THE DISPOSAL OF REFUSE IN THE TROPICS.

Filth is the mother of sickness. (Gulistan.)

IN any community of persons, arrangements must be made for the collection and removal of their excreta; of the waste water from houses; and of the dry refuse (ashes, dust, and refuse food). The solid and liquid refuse matter from stables, cowsheds, and slaughter-houses, street sweepings, and the waste waters from works and manufactories, must also be removed.

On the efficiency with which refuse matters and especially human excreta are removed, the health of that community will largely depend. The question of the disposal of refuse in the Tropics may be considered under two heads:—

(A) *Disposal of Excreta, or Conservancy.*

(B) *Disposal of Refuse, or Scavenging.*

(A) DISPOSAL OF EXCRETA, OR CONSERVANCY.

The Law of Manu directs that the adherent of the Hindu faith should leave his house in the early morning, taking a bow and arrow with him. When the outskirts of the village are reached an arrow is to be shot from the bow as far as possible. Where the arrow falls, the bowel should be emptied and the excreta covered with dry loose earth. In country districts this plan is quite satisfactory, but for congested places it is, of course, impossible of application. The principle, however, remains that the excretions of the body must not be allowed to remain in the vicinity of man. The system advocated by this law was the forerunner of the dry method of conservancy which is still the one most generally adopted in all tropical lands.

Including this method we have four ways of disposing of excreta in the tropics, viz. :—

1. The Dry System of Conservancy.
2. The Wet System.
3. Incineration.
4. The Biological Method (i.e.,—by means of " septic " tanks or " contract beds ").

Let us consider them in this order :—

1. The Dry System of Conservancy.

Latrines usually consist of corrugated iron sheds with partitions of the same material. They are fitted with glazed gumlahs or tarred or enamelled iron pans into which urine and fæces are passed, the contents being emptied into receptacles and removed daily, by means of iron carts, to a piece of ground outside the town or cantonment, where it is deposited in shallow trenches and covered with earth.

Latrines should always be placed on an impermeable base, made of concrete, and whatever variety of latrine may be adopted, the following points must be borne in mind :—

1. The sun's rays must be brought to play upon the whole of the inside of the latrine for as many hours in the day as possible.
2. Free ventilation must be provided.
3. Rain must be kept out.
4. Privacy must be maintained.

The ground used for trenching is cultivated and rich crops of jute, cabbages, sugar-cane, makki, etc., are grown. Under such circumstances trenching grounds give little trouble and are quite sanitary, but those under the control of some Indian Municipalities are too often entirely neglected, with the result that the improperly cared for trenches and conservancy carts become regular fly nurseries, and the system is the cause of grave nuisance and danger to health.

For the efficient working of this system the cardinal principle to be observed is that filth, refuse, and all other putrescible matter, etc., must not be exposed to flies, or be allowed to contaminate the ground, but should be safely transported and disposed of. A close observance of this principle will not only improve the health of the community, but will also afford a source of income to the municipality.

Water-tight receptacles for night-soil must be provided and maintained on a system by which all danger and discomfort can be avoided.

In like manner, water-tight filth carts must be used on a similar system.

A system of removal by day, instead of night, which latter cannot be watched effectively, and leads to many abuses especially on cold winter nights, must be carried out. An effective watch must be kept upon the removal carts during the whole of their transit.

A sufficient area for trenching ground must be provided to meet requirements, i.e. : (a) suitability of soil ; (b) presence of irrigation ; (c) suitability of distance from inhabited areas ; and (d) a succession of quick-growing crops.

Sufficient ground must be set aside to ensure that each plot is only trenched once in four years, in order that the soil may not by any possibility be overcharged with manure.

All the arrangements at the trenching grounds must be reduced to a system that leaves nothing to chance, and provides that all trenches are ready at least twenty-four hours before they are required.

The thorough cleaning of all filth carts and receptacles that are taken there, and the preparation of washing trenches for this purpose must be arranged for.

A due proportion of spare sanitary plant, on a regular scale, to be used in lieu of articles under repair, and for emergent calls on the conservancy system, must be provided.

The strict enforcement, as most highly important, of the rules to be observed at trenching grounds, and the absolute elimination of any conditions favourable to the production of flies must be secured.

The objection to seeing filth carts plying by day is more or less a sentimental one. Everyone admits that they are eyesores, but when it comes to a question of which is the lesser evil of the two, disease or unsightly appearance, there can be no doubt as to the answer. Working hours can, however, be so fixed as to cause the least amount of inconvenience to the public, but there must be no yielding on this point. As already noted, filth carts should not be offensive if they are properly looked after. They will be odourless if proper lids are provided, and if the rules are strictly enforced.

The defects in this system are two in number :—

1. The first is the fact that fæcal matter, many dirty buckets and receptacles, etc., are left exposed for many hours at a time, open to the air, and accessible to flies. This constitutes a most serious defect. There is no doubt, as will be shown in the next chapter, that the ordinary house fly plays a very important part in the dissemination of some diseases in tropical climates, and the more opportunities this insect has of gaining access to human discharges, the greater the danger to the health of

the community at large. Furthermore, the presence of a large quantity of night-soil or highly
contaminated ground increases the number of flies,
so that the best method of reducing the pest is a
rapid and satisfactory disposal of all excreta and
rubbish.

Very little, indeed, need be said on the intolerable nuisance created by the hand-removal system,

'Fig. 19.
COUNTRY REFUSE-DISPOSAL CARTS.
Photograph by Lieut.-Colonel Blackham.

as the horrible smell caused by the passing of a
night-soil cart is within the experience of all who
have set foot in the East. Further, it does not
require any great power of imagination to understand what would be the result of emptying half a

dozen buckets of night-soil into a cart. On this account alone, we consider that it is better, when possible, to make use of handcarts, rather than larger vehicles, in order to obviate this handling of night-soil, for it is generally admitted, by all who have had any experience of sanitary work, that the amount of nuisance caused by night-soil increases in direct proportion to its bulk and to the amount of handling that is necessary.

2. The second flaw in this method is that it involves the use of dust-laden latrines. Bearing in mind what has been said in the first chapter on the subject of enteric fever " carriers," it is obvious that the dry earth latrine renders every facility for these individuals to carry out their baleful function for spreading the disease.

There are few medical officers who do not regard latrine infection as a most potent factor in the causation and spread of enteric fever and cholera in Indian communities. That these diseases are water-borne no one will deny : but every observer in the tropics has had to deal with epidemics where the water-supply was above suspicion, and where, after eliminating every possible known cause, he has been driven to believe that the attacks do not arise from a common origin, but are communicated from one individual to another.

2. THE WET SYSTEM.

As carried out until quite recently in India there can be no doubt that hand removal of dejecta was fraught with great difficulty, and accompanied by nuisance, soil pollution, and danger to health at every step. But during the past few years the difficulty of carrying out the so-called dry-earth system and the necessity for preventing infection by flies and other insects has been fully realized and the system has been replaced in all Indian cantonments by the reception of fæces in a fluid disinfectant.

This procedure is known as the wet system of conservancy and it is directed towards the destruction or inhibition of the growth of bacilli at the moment they leave the human subject. It is especially directed against those bacilli of disease, which are found in dejecta and the inhibition of their action or destruction by disinfectants.

This system may be carried out with either a coal tar disinfectant, such as saponified cresol or a solution of perchloride of mercury. The cresol solution which is now in use in all military cantonments is made up by adding half an ounce of cresol to a gallon of water. One pint of this solution is placed in each receptacle.

A pan having been used, the *mehter* removes it, places the contents in the receptacle, cleans the pan, places a pint of cresol solution in it and returns it. Urinals are treated as follows :—A tin receptacle or *gumlah* is suspended at the highest point of the trough and filled with the disinfectant solution and a small hole is made in the bottom sufficient to allow the solution to fall drop by drop and trickle slowly along the trough.

The test of a safe latrine or urinal under this system is absolute freedom from smell. If an unpleasant odour is present an insufficient amount of disinfectant has been used.

Anyone who doubts the benefits of the wet system has only to visit latrines in which it is working and others where the dry-earth, or litter modification of the Goux system, is in vogue. In the former, flies will be few or absent ; in the latter, they will be found in large numbers at all seasons of the year.

Whether carried out by the dry or wet methods the hand-removal system is not economical from a financial point of view. It necessitates a very large staff of sweepers, many carts, bullocks to pull the carts and a very heavy incidental expenditure. The wear and tear of carts, buckets, etc., is enormous, and the difficulty of getting repairs done to conservancy appliances is well known.

The appreciation of some of these difficulties led to the introduction of the next system.

3. INCINERATION.

As far back as the Crimean War, the British troops burned their camp offal · in improvised incinerators, built much in the fashion of lime-kilns, but of recent years the disposal of refuse by burning has been advocated as a novelty, and taken up with the greatest enthusiasm by many medical officers.

A vast number of incinerators or apparatus for burning excreta have been devised and given special names, but all of them may be divided into two classes, viz. :—1, slow combustion ; 2, rapid combustion.

The type of the former class is the Raitt incinerator, which consists of a circular iron framework without sides, and with or without an iron cover.

The incinerator is set going by placing a quantity of litter and dry refuse on the framework, and setting fire to it.

When combustion has proceeded for some time, the total contents of latrine pans are directed to be emptied over the smouldering material. We frankly confess that we do not believe in this form of incinerator. In our experience heavy rain invariably puts these incinerators out, and the exposure of smouldering material to the strong gales of the winter must and does result in the addition of much objectionable matter to the dust which is blown in all directions.

2. In the second pattern forced draught is obtained by enclosing the matter to be burned in a brick

or metal furnace. There can be no doubt · this pattern is the better. The objections noted against the first variety are not present ; waste matter is more completely and more quickly consumed and the actual cost of construction—an important matter in municipal institutions—is not very much greater. In this pattern a further improvement is made in that fluids are mixed with some absorbent dry material such as litter, wood, coal or saw-dust to promote combustion.

A method which has been used of recent years, *viz.*, the placing of stable litter in the receptacles, cannot be recommended as the litter undoubtedly attracts flies.

The following conditions for the proper incineration of night-soil are absolutely essential if the method is to be a success :—

A.   A properly designed incinerator.

B.   Constant intelligent supervision and efficient stoking.

C.   A liberal supply of fuel.

D.   A mixing platform provided with a roof and a storage godown for the combustible material in wet weather.

If any of the four conditions are absent, sooner or later the process breaks down.

A.—PROPERLY DESIGNED INCINERATORS.

The great mistake of most types of incinerators is that the draught is not sufficient : the consequence is that there is a great deal of smoke which is often highly offensive. The presence of smoke is nearly always due to one of two things : (1) defective design of the incinerator ; (2) insufficient supply of dry and inflammable material.

A drawing of a very good pattern is given at Fig. 20.

SPECIFICATION.

Incinerator dome shaped, 1st class brick in mud lime pointed.

Two openings 1′ 9″ × 2′ 3″ on opposite sides, 4′ from ground level for feeding incinerator with fuel and night-soil, etc. Each opening is provided with an iron lid.

Four ventilating openings at bottom 1′ 3″ × 1′ 6″. Iron grating 1′ 3″ from ground consisting of 1½″ flat iron ring 5′ 6″ in diameter to which is rivetted either 1″ angle or round iron bars 1½″ between bars. The grating is built 3″ into the masonry all round. If round iron bars are used, additional support is given by means of two cross pieces of angle iron.

There is a 4′ masonry chimney and a 4′ sheet iron chimney 12″ in diameter.

The total height is 15′. External diameter 6′ 6″.

Section.

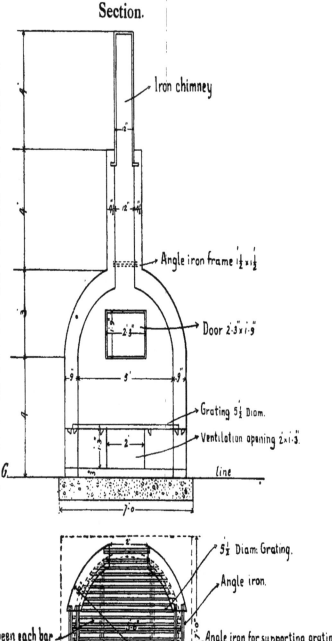

Iron chimney

Angle iron frame 1½ × 1½

Door 2·3″ × 1·9

Grating 5½ Diam.

Ventilation opening 2 × 1·3

line

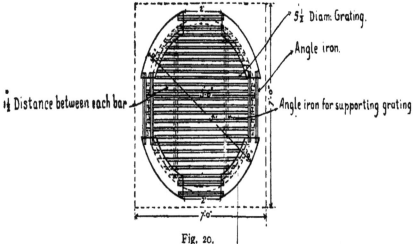

5½ Diam: Grating.

Angle iron.

Distance between each bar

Angle iron for supporting grating

Fig. 20.

It gives better results than any we have yet met with, but it is somewhat expensive to erect. The small types of incinerators, built of mud or iron, cannot be regarded as satisfactory and are only suitable for camps of brief duration.

. In the particular kind of incinerator illustrated. comparatively little smoke comes from the chimney, even when large quantities of night-soil are being burnt.

The type approved by Army Head-quarters is known as the Umballa B pattern.

B.—SUPERVISION.

Constant supervision is necessary because the native sweepers will never make a proper mixture of the night-soil and the inflammable material : they are always inclined to be sparing with the fuel. Sweepers do not know how to stoke properly. If left to themselves, they almost invariably put the mixture into the incinerator either too wet to burn, or too much of it at a time, so that the fire smoulders, instead of blazes, with the result that much smoke is generated.

C.—FUEL.

In order to burn night-soil a large quantity of combustible material is required, particularly if urine is to be disposed of as well. The best materials are wood shavings, saw-dust, coal dust, damaged bhoosa, or pine needles.

The greater the amount of combustible material that is mixed with night-soil, the less the smoke and the possibility of nuisance. If any of these materials have to be purchased in the open market, the incineration of the night-soil cannot, as a general rule, be carried out economically. Consequently an insufficient quantity is used : the night-soil is imperfectly incinerated ; and the nuisance arising from the incinerator is often great.

There is an impression amongst persons who have only partly studied the subject of incineration that street rubbish in any part of India is an inflammable substance. This is a serious error, The street rubbish from most Indian towns will *not* burn. It requires some combustible material to burn it, even when put in the latest pattern incinerator. Therefore, Sanitary Officers should be chary of making the recommendation that nightsoil and town rubbish be consumed together in an incinerator unless it has been distinctly established that the rubbish is itself inflammable. In places where the rainfall is small, street sweepings may be combustible, but the rubbish that is collected during the rains in any part of the tropics will not burn : therefore, if street rubbish is to be relied on for incineration of night-soil, a quantity of the dry material must be stored for use in wet weather : and this is not a procedure which can be advocated.

The method in use with most incinerators in India is a form of the Goux system. A modification of this method of sewage disposal, which is still in use in various French towns and at Halifax in Yorkshire, was introduced at Dagshai in 1901, and fully described in a paper by one of the writers, " The Goux system and its application to India " in the *Journal of Royal Army Medical Corps* in June 1906.

The Dagshai plan was to mix pine needles with both liquid and solid excreta and was, therefore, only applicable to certain hill stations, but the method has been made applicable to plains stations by adopting stable litter as the absorbent material. This involves the carting of litter into bungalow compounds.

The introduction of stable litter into compounds is obviously objectionable, for horse droppings, as will be shown in the next chapter, are a favourite breeding ground for flies, and these insects are now regarded as hardly less important than mosquitoes as disseminators of disease. It must be remembered, moreover, that the intestines of the horse are the home of the bacillus of tetanus, and that pollution of the soil with horse droppings is the cause of this disease in human beings. The greatest care, therefore, should be exercised to prevent the smallest quantity remaining any length of time without being passed through the incinerator. Moreover it is necessary to see that the manure is destroyed and not merely toasted as is sometimes the case. The history of the present war brings home to us the enormous danger of tetanus, whenever wounds become contaminated with earth from richly manured soil or from a road where there is much traffic. Many a life too has been lost in tropical countries from neglect of the proper precautions when dealing with contused wounds (often of the slightest description— as from a fall from a bicycle) occurring in crowded cities. The writers wish, therefore, to impress upon the reader the vital importance of inoculation with antitetanic serum as soon as possible after the infliction of the wound. If this precaution is taken there is practically no risk of the supervention of tetanus.

D.—Fuel Sheds and Mixing Platforms.

In a heavy downpour of tropical rain it is impossible to keep any material, be it saw-dust, wood shavings, or litter, in a readily inflammable condition. Therefore it is necessary that shelters should be provided for any mixing procedure adopted and for the storage of fuel.

Where litter is used in incinerators, fuel sheds often constitute a grave nuisance as they develop into veritable fly nurseries. The original advocates of this type of fuel do not appear to have studied the life-history of the house-fly as given in Chapter IX.

Fuel sheds should be only large enough to contain two days' supply of fuel ; surrounded with wire gauze which will admit of drying and will exclude flies ; and, most important of all, provided with concrete floors.

The difficulties with reference to incineration may be considered under four headings :—

1. Disposal of fluids.
2. Supervision of stoking.
3. Æsthetic.
4. The supremacy of the sweeper.

1. *Disposal of fluids* :—The point with reference to incineration which appears to be debatable is the disposal of fluids.

It is calculated that 3 maunds of coal, or 12 maunds of wood, would be required to evaporate the total amount of urine from a battalion of infantry per diem. It would, therefore, appear that if complete destruction of fluids is really achieved in incineration, stable litter and refuse constitute a fuel of higher economic value than is generally supposed.

In practice the evaporation of fluids is not always carried out. It was ascertained by one of the writers that, in a cantonment where incineration has been adopted, fluid excreta were being tipped into a drain and flushed out from a specially constructed channel connected with the irrigation system.

2. *Stoking* :—The success or otherwise of the incineration depends on effective stoking or the individual technique of the sweepers. Now these useful members of the Indian community are not naturally energetic, and themselves say the dis-

posal of urine is their greatest trouble, so being ingenious as well as slothful, they endeavour to get over their difficulty with the least possible inconvenience to themselves. Obviously, it is easier to throw away fluids than to burn them and, if not constantly looked after, they are likely to adopt this simple solution of, to them, a difficult problem. It must, however, be remembered that this evil is not a new one, as the drivers of conservancy carts have been known to empty the fluid contents of their carts into convenient nullahs to avoid the tedious journey to the trenching grounds.

3. *Æsthetic :*—A serious æsthetic objection to incineration is the smell and smoke associated with it. These are undoubtedly nuisances, and it seems that this objection is more than purely æsthetic as the prevalence of sore-throat in an Indian cantonment has been attributed to incinerator smoke.

The appearance of the incinerators with their unsightly sheds containing heaps of litter is hardly less objectionable than that of the conservancy carts of former days.

4. *The supremacy of the sweeper :*—The gravest of all the defects in this method is that whilst in the other systems the sweeper is important, in the practice of incineration he stands supreme, and the whole of the conservancy arrangements of a community depends on the good-will and behaviour of the sweepers. This is a very great weakness. The entire sewage disposal of a town may be upset by a single dishonest overseer. Within recent times strikes amongst the sweepers are not unknown, and have caused great inconvenience to everyone concerned, and endangered the health of many large and thriving communities.

The question of cost :—There can be little doubt that it was largely the claim of its advocates that it could be carried out for next to nothing, that commended it to many authorities and led to the introduction of incineration.

W.e are inclined to think that the original savings were due to cheap and inefficient incinerators; cheap sheds and imperfect fuel, which have succeeded in bringing the system into considerable discredit. When carried out with proper apparatus and fuel, it is more than doubtful whether incineration will be much cheaper than trenching.

The question we have to answer is, can we design any arrangement that is cheap; that requires a minimum of staff to work it; that rapidly puts all undesirable matter beyond reach of the omnipresent fly; and that does not cause a nuisance?

We believe that this question can now be answered in the affirmative, and that the method now to be described is, *wherever a liberal water-supply* and the necessary funds are available, by far the best method of disposing of dejecta in the Tropics.

4. BIOLOGICAL TREATMENT.

This method is one of the means of disposing of water-carried sewage and for its introduction a liberal water-supply is essential. It consists in the purification of sewage by means of the action of bacteria.

The process depends on the action of two main groups of organisms.

The first group is able to break down and liquefy solid organic-matter, and the second has the power of converting liquid sewage into simple inodorous substances.

Some systems depend on the free exposure of the sewage to the oxygen of the air and others rely on the action of the bacteria on sewage in closed tanks from which light and air are carefully excluded.

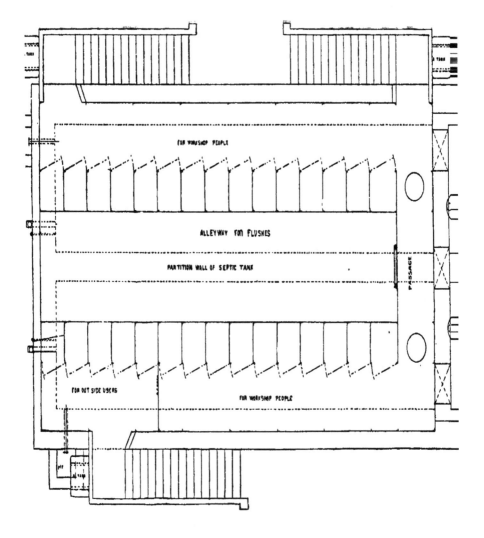

Fig. 21,
SEPTIC TANK LATRINE.

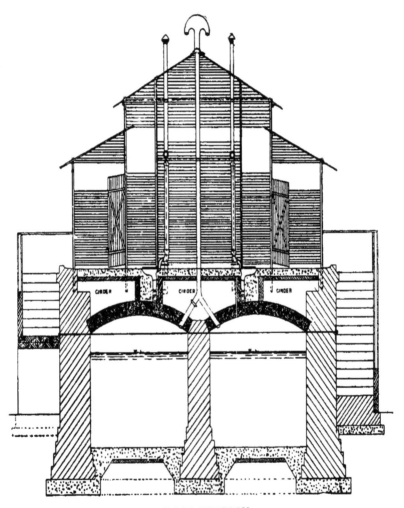

CROSS SECTION.

Fig. 22.

SEPTIC TANK LATRINE.

Missing Page

The first system consists in the free exposure to the air of sedimented sewage on beds of coke, clinker, or gravel.

The necessary organisms exist in the sewage and the beds act well at first, but are apt to become clogged and inactive after a time. We do not advocate this method for the Tropics, but advocate the second system which consists in the reception of the sewage in what are known as septic tanks. In this process the sewage is flushed by water from a suitable latrine into a long thin closed tank, varying in size with the number of individuals who are to use the latrines connected with it.

The most economic and satisfactory working depth for a septic tank is 6 feet ; but 5 feet does fairly well and may be used in places where, on account of the latrine being used in rushes, as at railway stations, very ample seating accommodation is required with a comparatively small tank capacity.

Figures 21, 22 and 23 show the general arrangement of the Septic Tank Latrine.

In most active septic tanks there is about 8 to 12 inches of light sludge and the scum is frequently some 6 inches in thickness, so that it is obviously not desirable to decrease the depth below 5 feet.

A tank capacity of 12 to 15 gallons per user, per diem, gives the best results. A grit chamber is provided for the collection of solid material and its removal if desired.

When the sewage enters the tank, a leathery scum forms on the surface, from 2 to 6 in. thick : below this is the zone of fermentation, in which the sewage is clear, but permeated by bubbles of gas that constantly keep rising, and maintain a quiet movement throughout the whole body of the fluid : at the bottom is a layer of peaty material, very small in amount : small masses of organic matter are seen to fall from the top layer by their own weight, but on reaching the bottom gas is evolved from their constituents by bacterial agency, and the particles are floated up again ; on reaching the top the gas bubbles burst, and the solid matter again sinks. This cycle is repeated, until practically the whole of the suspended solid material is liquefied through ·bacterial action.

With a tank working properly sludge accumulates very slowly.

This sludge is drained off at rare intervals into a pit filled with gravel or stones.

The fluid part of the sludge soaks away into the subsoil : the sludge itself, which is quite odourless,. is removed and trenched.

The fluid sewage after treatment escapes by means of pipes at a point half way between the scum and sludge.

Large quantities of gas are developed and shafts to carry it away are necessary. The gas generated in tanks has been utilised for lighting and power purposes in Europe.

Septic tank effluents must always be looked upon as potentially dangerous. The effluents from bacteria beds ought to be regarded as hardly, if at all, more safe in their possible relation to disease than the raw sewage before treatment. Therefore septic tank effluent, however good in quality, must not be discharged into a river or stream, from which a large proportion of the population of a town draw their drinking-water.

The most satisfactory of all methods is the passing of the effluent over land. This method has been tried in Southern India, notably at Ootacamund, with great success.

Probably the most satisfactory and elaborate scheme of this type is the one at Malabar Hill in Bombay. In this case 281 houses of the better class with a population of 3,211 persons are connected by means of underground drains with septic tanks. The kitchen waste water is also passed down the same drains. The effluent runs into the sea. Without the use of septic tanks, it would be impossible to dispose of the crude sewage of this community by passing it into the sea at this point. The scheme is more elaborate than is possible or advisable for ordinary bazaar work, but it is a good example of minor schemes, in which a septic tank plays an important part.

Prior to the introduction of biological treatment *the* difficulty in the way of installing the water-carriage system has always been that no suitable plan for the ultimate disposal of the sewage could be suggested. By proper use of septic tanks it is now possible to convert the sewage into a clear, non-putrescible and non-odorous fluid which can safely be treated over land or, if it is sterilised,' passed into a stream.

(B) Disposal of Refuse, or Scavenging.

The effective disposal of town waste, consisting of street sweepings, stable-litter, household refuse, paper, rags, and other more or less combustible material, constitutes one of the greatest difficulties which Sanitarians in or out of the Tropics have to face. The difficulty is increased by the fact that the material to be dealt with varies in quality and quantity according to the season, the kind of fuel used, and the habits of the people.

In this country it is accentuated by the national habit of using the street as a depository for filth and refuse.

One has only to visit any Indian city or village to see quantities of rice and other food material thrown out of the windows, whilst the odour of the drainage channels indicate that both liquid and solid filth has been thrown into them from the house-tops.

Figure 24 is a photograph of a gully taken an hour or two after it had been swept out. Observe the

refuse accumulated in the central channel. The
marks on the wall show that the gully has been

Fig. 24.

badly infected by plague. Each " P. R. " with
date indicates that on that particular date a rat has
been picked up here which was proved to be infected with the plague. There is here a record of
at least ten plague-infected rats picked up on different dates between the 5th December 1905 and 5th
January.

The magnitude of this problem of refuse disposal
is apparent when we realise that, for urban areas,
the quantity of ash in refuse averages from four to
five thousand maunds annually for each 1,000 inhabitants.

A proper system of scavenging is the *A. B. C.* of
sanitary administration. Water-works, drainage
schemes, etc., are the learned books which the
people of India are often called upon to master
before they have acquired the alphabet of sanitation.

Amongst populated centres in tropical latitudes, cleanliness and freedom from refuse matters of all kinds is the first essential to the public well-being.

" Town-refuse " may be described as domestic household refuse with, in most cases, some limited admixture of trade and shop rubbish, and, in many districts, a small proportion of vegetable or garden waste. The chief methods employed for the disposal of such materials from towns are as follows :—

1. Depositing upon waste or low-lying land and filling up pits or excavations or raising the level of marsh land.

This method often gives rise to intolerable nuisance and cannot be recommended in the Tropics generally. Too often made soils are, as we have seen in the last chapter, used as building sites with disastrous results.

2. *Selling by tender yearly :*—As in India, town refuse is found to be a good top-dressing for the production of grass ; it will sometimes command a sale. This method appeals to municipal authorities as it enables them to get over a great difficulty without expense and even with profit, but it is not to be recommended as the contractor is very often dilatory and unsatisfactory in carrying out the process of removal.

3. *Destruction by fire :*—This is far and away the best method, but the method of disposal in different districts has hitherto depended largely on local circumstances and conditions, the cheapest plan available having always the preference in India. Often this has been but a mere makeshift, and the means of disposal for many years has been nothing better than a hunting about from one makeshift to another, until, at last, all other means having been exhausted, a refuse destructor of some sort has become an absolute necessity.

Given a good destructor and proper management, town waste and house refuse can be reduced to about one-third their original bulk, the residue being innocuous clinker, metallic refuse and dust.

The adoption of incineration of excreta has the advantage of rendering the disposal of other refuse comparatively easy, as destructors of a kind are always available, but unfortunately in actual practice in one community at least, to the writers' personal knowledge, an attempt was made to burn urine whilst garbage was being carted for a long distance and dumped on fields.

Proper receptacles for refuse should be provided by all municipalities. They should be small, covered and made of some kind of metal so as to be unabsorbent and they must be thoroughly emptied at least once daily.

HOOKWORM DISEASE OR ANCHYLOSTOMIASIS.

This disease about which much has been written in America also exists in India, especially in parts of Assam and the Dooars. It is found, in fact, in all countries which lie in the tropical or sub-tropical zone. It is caused by certain small white worms about half an inch long and as thick as a number 30 thread, which live in the bowel and feed on its delicate lining. These worms are called hookworms or anchylostomes, and in some parts of India they are found not only in people suffering from the symptoms of the disease but also in 8 out of every 10 healthy persons. Hookworms in the bowels only cause symptoms of disease when they exist in considerable numbers. The symptoms of the disease to which they give rise are anæmia, indigestion, and gradually supervening dropsy, and in many cases this dropsy leads to a fatal termination. Children suffer. more severely than adults. The way in which the disease is transferred from man to man is as follows: These hookworms cannot live anywhere except in the bowels of human beings, but whilst they live there, they lay eggs, and these eggs pass out of the body with the excrement. As the excrement lies on the ground, a tiny larva develops inside each egg, and after a few hours it hatches out. It then remains in the excrement for a period of from one to two weeks after which it is necessary for its continued development that it should enter a human being and again become a parasite in the intestines. In order to accomplish this, it now leaves the excrement and is found both in water and in moist earth. It can climb up the stalks of grass if they are wet with dew, and it is very hard to kill, and it easily enters the body by piercing its way through the soft skin of the feet or ankles, but especially between the toes, where the skin is fine and tender. It then passes through the body until it finally reaches the bowels, where it attaches itself to the mucous membrane and grows into an adult worm. Whilst the hookworm larvæ are boring through the skin, they often cause much irritation and give rise to a disease which is known as " ground-itch."

The full-grown hookworms attach themselves to the mucous membrane of the small intestines by means of their hook-shaped jaws. They then not only suck large quantities of blood, but they secrete a poisonous fluid which causes anæmia as well as inflammation of the bowels. Much blood, moreover, is lost by oozing from the small wounds caused by the bites of the worms.

From this life-history of the hookworm, it is obvious how very important it is to prevent fouling of the site round houses and round native latrines, and it is an additional reason for insisting on the most perfect scavenging and disposal of all excrement. Prophylaxis, in this disease, must be based upon an attempt either to kill the parasites in the human beings who are acting as " carriers,' or to prevent

human beings from being infected by the parasite;
but in order to ensure success, it is absolutely
necessary to educate both the rich and the poor
in a district as regards the causation of the disease.
This may be done by illustrated lectures and
pamphlets in the vernacular. The people should
also be urged to submit to regular medical inspection and systematic treatment. The first method
is the most successful, but it requires skilled
medical assistance. In order to protect your-
self from these worms you may adopt three
methods :—

(1) You can attack them whilst they are still in
the excrement, and in order to do this, it is necessary that all excrement should be deposited in one
place, preferably into a pail latrine, and that your
servants should not be allowed to use the fields
and jungles for the purposes of nature. For this
reason it is important, on all tea-plantations, to
allow a clear area between the tea-bushes and
the coolies' lines. This area should be treated from
time to time with quicklime. Further, every alternate row of bushes might be left out in the
half-acre adjoining the lines, and in the vacant
spaces latrine-holes, lined with lime, might be
dug. When the excrement is collected, it is not
very difficult to kill the eggs and the young
worms, and there are several ways in which this
can be done. One is by burning the excrement
and another is by taking it away to some distance
from the house and burying it two feet deep
in dry earth. The third method is to keep it
in a concrete pit for 3 months, but if this be
done there must be water in the pit, and it must
be screened so that flies cannot get to it.
Possibly the best plan is to dispose of the fæces in
a small incinerator. There is, however, no need
for incurring great expense. A simply constructed
incinerator will often work well if a little smell is

not objected to. (See Chapter XIII, for details of a cheap incinerator.)

(2) As regards attacking the young hookworms in the soil, the only method of dealing with them is to keep the soil clean by collecting all the excrement and destroying it in one of the ways mentioned. If this be done and no more hookworms are allowed to get into the soil, those buried in the soil will die in time. We know, however, that they can live for at least a year, so that it probably takes two years of clean habits in your compound before the soil round about your latrine can be considered perfectly innocuous.

(3) The third way is to prevent these small hookworms from getting into the skin. This you should do by protecting your feet and ankles with boots and socks ; by never allowing your children to go out into the compound bare-footed ; and by insisting on the wearing of boots or shoes by all your native servants.

It is obvious therefore that the question of the destruction of hookworms is in your own hands, and if you can persuade or compel all those in your vicinity to be clean in their habits, you can stamp the disease out from your immediate vicinity. This is one of the strongest arguments in favour of careful sanitation of the surroundings of the house in the tropics.

CHAPTER IX.

INSECTS AND DISEASE IN THE TROPICS.

Tropical Medicine has directed our attention more and more to the rôle which insects play in the transmission of disease.—(Sir Rubert Boyce in "Mosquito or Man.")

WITH the exception of domestic animals, there is no single group in the animal kingdom which enters more into the daily life of man than that of insects. They live on us and around us : in our food, our clothes, our furniture, our houses : we eat them or their products, we collect them and even sew them on our clothing. Most people eat honey, use bees-wax, and, occasionally at any rate, clothe themselves in silk, and there is certainly no one who has not, at one time or another, been dependent upon some member of the insect world.

It has been the custom of authors in all ages to refer insects in some way to man's well-being and economy. Every insect was, to them, created with some definite object from man's point of view : but this is an impossible attitude and it might be easier to classify our activities as they affect insects than to refer each insect to its " use " to us.

Indeed, impartial judgment and a dispassionate consideration of facts will show that insects have fully exploited man, and, that, although man may think that he is dominant, he really is not, and that not least amongst his functions is that of providing food and occupation for insects.

In number, in species, in all but one form of mentality, insects are the dominant form of life on the earth at the present time, but the limitations. put on them are of such a nature that their dominance must remain within bounds, and unless man is removed cannot be actual and entire.

Insects are of all sizes, from one-fiftieth of an inch or less in length to over six inches, and even more, their numbers are incalculable, the number of their species alone being put at three millions. Their lives may be as short as a week or as long as ten years and more, but they seldom live for more than three years and are seldom active for more than three months. On the surface of the earth and in fresh water they are found wherever nutriment is available and also thrive in the bodies of warm-blooded animals and in man.

It was the work of Manson on the mosquito in 1877 that first drew attention to the important rôle which insects play in the spread of disease, and of recent years a large amount of evidence has accumulated against them as foes of man.

They may be the agents in the transmission of both the bacterial and the parasitic diseases.

In the dissemination of bacterial diseases insects were formerly thought to act entirely as passive agents.

It was taught that they conveyed infection by taking up the specific material on their wings, legs, proboscis and body and depositing it on the food or water-supplies of man, but it has recently been shown that flies which have had access to tuberculous sputum retain the tubercle bacilli in their digestive tubes for several days, and that the tubercle bacilli multiply there more rapidly than in cultures. Furthermore, it has been observed that the tubercle bacilli are present in abundance in the droppings of the flies, and therefore it is obvious that the fly can act as a vehicle for tubercle by depositing its infected droppings on articles of food. Although the fly is only a simple vehicle and does not itself become tuberculous, its digestive fluids appear to be a favourable medium for the cultivation of the tubercle bacilli.

Still more recently it has been shown that the fly also takes the organisms of enteric fever and cholera into its intestines and that they grow and multiply there.

The house-fly, before sucking material, moistens it with a fluid which it ejects from its craw and it is this fluid, when infected by bacteria, which is more dangerous and more lasting as a means of conveying disease than the mere mechanical methods of carrying microbes on the exterior of the fly's body.

In the transmission of *animal* parasites, insects may be merely passive agents, as in the case of flies of various kinds ; intermediate hosts in which the parasite develops, as in the case of mosquitoes and sandflies, and possibly also active agents as in the spread of Yellow Fever by a day-flying mosquito.

The following is a list of injurious insects and the human diseases they are known, or supposed, to transfer :—

1. *Ants :*—These insects may readily convey all the diseases due to contamination of food, such as cholera, dysentery and enteric. There is no definite proof that ants act as carriers, but considering their habits in tropical countries, it is far from unlikely.

2. *Bed-Bugs :*—These loathsome insects are charged with the conveyance of kala-ázár, leprosy, some skin diseases, tuberculosis and yaws.

3. *Fleas :*—It has been definitely proved that plague is conveyed by rat-fleas, and there are good reasons for believing that the infantile type of kala-ázár, which occurs along the Mediterranean littoral, is conveyed by the fleas which infest the dog.

4. *Non-biting Flies :*—The list of diseases laid to the door of the common house-fly, or as the

Americans have re-named it " The Filthy Fly," is a long one ; it includes :—(1) cholera, (2) diarrhœa, (3) dysentery, (4) enteric fever, (5) maggots in wounds, (6) leprosy, (7) oriental sore and other skin diseases, (8) consumption, and (9) eye diseases.

5. *Biting flies, apart from mosquitoes and sand-flies :*—The tsetse fly conveys sleeping sickness. It has recently been stated that Pellagra is conveyed by midges.

6. *Lice :*—Body lice have been charged with conveying tubercle, leprosy, and they undoubtedly convey both typhus and relapsing fever.

7. *Mosquitoes :*—These insects are the sole agents for the spread of Malaria, Filariasis, Dengue and Yellow Fever. " No mosquitoes, no malaria " is an universally accepted sanitary dogma of to-day.

8. *Sandflies :*—A variety of these insects is believed to convey the three and five-day fevers which are common all over India, whilst recent observations go to prove that one form of oriental sore is conveyed to man by a small sand-fly (Phlebotomus minutus), the intermediary host being the gecko, a kind of lizard.

9. *The Itch Insect :*—This is a member of the spider class which, in addition to causing the disease known as "itch," is charged with conveying leprosy and skin diseases.

10. *Ticks :*—These pests are the agents for the conveyance of a large number of the diseases of animals, and it has recently been shown that in Africa they convey the germ of a fever which closely resembles the Relapsing Fever of India.

The Insects constitute a distinct zoological class and are divided into numerous Orders and Families, but of these we are only concerned with the following :—

  1. The Diptera, including flies of all kinds.
  2. The Hemiptera, including bugs.

3. The Anoptera, including lice.
4. The Siphonaptera, including fleas.
5. The Hymenoptera, including ants.

The itch insect and the ticks, which we have included in the list, are not, strictly speaking, insects, as they have different characters, notably the fact that they possess eight legs instead of the six which are characteristic of the insects. They belong to the same class as spiders, mites and scorpions, a tribe rejoicing in the name of Arachnida.

The bodies of insects are covered with a tough skin and are divided into three distinct parts :—(1) the head, provided with two antennæ or horns, and eyes and mouth of variable form : (2) the trunk or thorax composed of three segments, which has always attached underneath it six jointed legs ; and usually attached above it two or four wings ; but in some insects there are no wings : and (3) an abdomen, composed of nine segments, some of which may be difficult to recognise.

In addition to these characteristics they are not provided with an interior skeletons, and their nervous system is formed of a double cord, swelling at intervals, and placed under the head and along the underside of the body. Insects are not provided with lungs, but breathe by special organs, termed *tracheæ*, extending parallel to each other along each side of the body, and communicating with the exterior air by lateral openings termed *spiracles*. In all insects the sexes are distinct and all are reproduced from eggs. But the perfect insect is not complete until the tiny creature has passed through a wonderful and perilous process of development.

There are four stages in the life-history of most of the members of this great family, *viz.* :—

1. The egg stage in which the insect usually attracts no attention.

2. The larva in which it is most destructive as a maggot, grub or caterpillar.

3. The pupal or chrysalis stage in which the insect again becomes inoffensive, and

4. The stage of full development.

THE DIPTERA.

The members of this family with which we are concerned are divided into two groups, *viz.* :—

1. *Group A* :—Containing the mosquitoes, sand-flies and midges.

2. *Group B* :—Containing the great family of house flies.

Group A.

General Characteristics :—Flies with slender bodies and long antennæ which are often plumed.

The group includes perhaps the most important disease-transmitting insects from an Indian stand-point, *viz.*, mosquitoes, sandflies and midges.

1. MOSQUITOES.

The first three stages of these insects are spent in the water, the last only on the wing. It follows, therefore, that water is essential to the existence of all mosquitoes.

There are two chief tribes or sub-divisions—

1. The Culicinæ which carry filaria and probably dengue fever, but not malaria.

2. The Anophelinæ or malaria carriers.

1. THE CULICINÆ OR NON-MALARIA CARRIERS.

The Eggs :—The female mosquito haunts the vicinity of stagnant water with weeds growing in it and dead leaves floating about on it.

To deposit her eggs she alights on one of the float-ing fragments, forms her hind legs into a form of receptacle and drops the eggs one by one on to it.

The eggs are surrounded by a gelatinous material which binds them together into a little mass which falls on the surface of the water and floats about like a little raft when the mother insect flies away.

The little raft-like colonies contain two or three hundred eggs and in the common varieties are not unlike carraway seeds, in form and colour.

The Larva :—In about three days the eggs open by a sort of little trap door near their blunt end and out comes the tiny grub or larva which is just big enough to be seen by the naked eye. From the first it swims about actively in the water.

Fig. 25 shows the little creature much enlarged. It will be seen to consist of a head with two very large eyes, a globular thorax and an abdomen of nine segments.

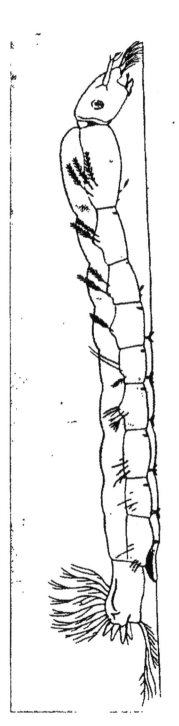

Fig. 25.

LARVA OF ANOPHELINE MOSQUITO.

It has a nervous system, a heart and organs of digestion, and two curious structures at its tail end. One a sort of fin and the other a hollow breathing tube protected by valves which open and close as required.

It is very voracious and is continuously on the move in search of food which consists of small aquatic plants and animals, and often, as we shall see, the carcases of its friends. It is, however, obliged to come to the surface to breathe.

The end of the breathing tube is surrounded by a fringe of fine hairs which prevents it from sinking. The culicinæ larva (Fig. 26) spends a considerable part of its life thus suspended by its siphon fringe to the surface film of the water, but if frightened or desirous of feeding at the bottom it can shut up its fringe and its own weight then causes it to sink.

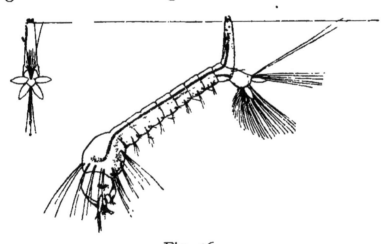

Fig. 26.
CULEX FATIGANS LARVA.
In breathing position at surface of water.
(*After Howard, Bull. United States Dept. Agr.*)

The larva is very much preyed upon by small fish and to avoid its natural enemies has a great predilection for aquatic weeds, which provide it with grateful protection. It grows rapidly and moults its skin four times.

The Pupa :—When fully grown the larva swims about in a fitful purposeless way and finally comes to rest. After a short stationary period it swells and a slit suddenly appears in the back. After a few wriggles a new creature emerges from the skin.

The pupa (Fig. 27), as it is now called, is shaped somewhat like a comma with a comparatively large anterior portion and a whip-like posterior. It has no mouth, and so cannot eat. It is, however, very active, swimming rapidly by lashing the hinder part about. When disturbed, it darts to the bottom of the pool, but soon rises again on account of its buoyancy. The pupa unlike the larva does not breathe through its tail, but has two trumpet-like bodies on each side of its chest. It is kept right side up

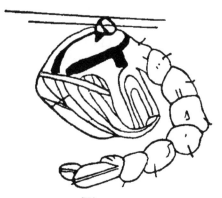

Fig. 27.
PUPA OF MOSQUITO.

and at the surface of the water by little air-tight compartments, and as it floats back upwards, its head appears to be tucked underneath it.

The full grown insect :—After two or three days the pupa case splits and the perfect insect emerges from it. It raises itself on its legs, withdraws its wings, and standing on the buoyant pupa case, lifts itself well into the air, and flies away on its mission of annoyance and death. Sometimes the insect is unable to deliver itself ; at other times a slight puff of wind upsets the raft on which it balances itself and the young mosquito is drowned. The carcase of the insect is not wasted, but forms food for the larvæ of others, who thrive on their cannibal propensities.

A puddle is not essential for the development of the pupa, as a moist piece of ground does equally well, but complete dryness is fatal to mosquitoes in all these stages.

2. THE ANOPHELINÆ OR MALARIA-CARRIERS.

The members of this tribe constitute the malaria-carriers. Only a few of the tropical varieties have been shown to carry the disease.

Eggs :—Readily distinguished from Culex, as they are found separately on the surface of water, arranged in triangles or other geometrical figures. Boat shaped, ribbed laterally. Found in natural or terrestrial collections of water.

Larvæ :—Attitude on surface of water is characteristic.

Fig. 28.

PERFECT MOSQUITO EMERGING FROM PUPA.

An anopheline larva, instead of lying with its head and body sloping downwards beneath the surface in an oblique direction, lies flat at the surface, nearly the whole of its body parallel to and touching the surface film. See Fig. 25. There are two reasons for this attitude, namely,—(1) Anopheline larvæ do not possess the characteristic air-tube of the Culicinæ ; and (2) on the upper surface of the abdominal segments are little cup-

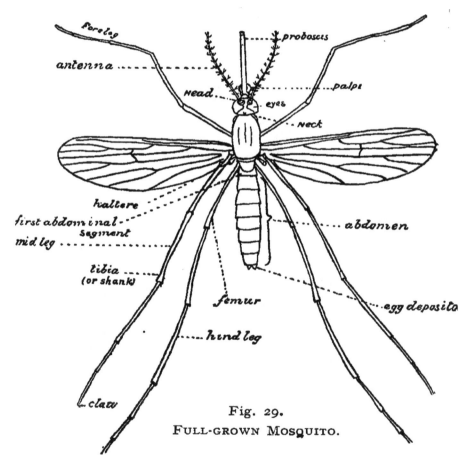

Fig. 29.

FULL-GROWN MOSQUITO.

shaped structures called " palmate hairs," which open at the surface of the water, and, acting like floats, keep the body of the larva in contact with the surface. These palmate hairs can be easily seen by examining in a drop of water under a low power of the microscope. They are not present in the larvæ of any other kind of mosquito, and, together with the straight and short air-tube render anopheline larvæ easy to recognise.

Pupæ :—It is not easy to distinguish anopheline from Culex pupæ, and the matter is not of sufficient importance to concern the ordinary person.

We have now arrived at the stage of the insect when it is familiar to all of us.

On reference to Fig. 29 it will be seen that it has a globular head, with large eyes, and a prominent proboscis, or trunk, a relatively large thorax or chest, a long segmented abdomen, six jointed legs, and a pair of beautiful wings.

1. *The Head :*—The head is connected with the thorax by a slender neck and bears the mouth and

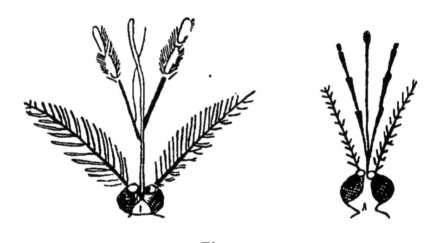

Fig. 30.

Male.　　　　　　　　　　　　　　Female.

HEADS OF MALE AND FEMALE MOSQUITO.

organs of special sense. Two large compound eyes occupy the anterior part of the head and in front of them are the *antennæ* which are organs of hearing.

Fig. 30 illustrates the heads of a male and of a female mosquito.

It will be noticed that the male has whiskers or plumes on either side of his head which readily distinguish him from his mate.

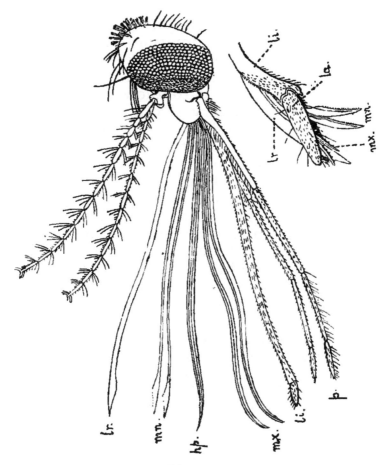

Fig. 31.

MOUTH-PARTS OF MOSQUITO.

2.. *Proboscis :*—Below the antennæ at the very front of the head, are the mouth-parts or " proboscis." This consists of gutter-shaped lower lip (the labium), roofed in by the upper lip, composed of labrum and epipharynx, so as to form a complete sheath and support for the inner parts. These consist of a flattened, blade-like "hypopharynx," or tongue, and four sharp serrated needles—the two mandibles and maxillæ. It is these last six parts of the organ which do the actual work of piercing and sucking. The epipharynx and hypopharynx form by their approximation a central tube through which the blood is sucked.

The labium does not pierce the skin at all, but can be seen to bend so as to allow the labrum to be inserted to a satisfactory depth.

Attached to the end of the labium by a hinge joint on either side are two leaf-like processes— the labella. It is through the angle made by the two labella that the stylets pass, as a billiard cue between the thumb and index-finger.

The labium proper stops short at the point of junction of the labellum, but is continued on its upper surface as a blunt point covered with fine hairs. It may be likened to a pen, continued on beyond the penholder, the junction of the pen ·and penholder being the point at which the labella are hinged on.

The outer surface of the proboscis is covered with scales. Only the labium and upper surface of the labrum are ordinarily visible.

In the male the mandibles are lacking, and the tip of the labrum is blunt and unfit for piercing, so it is unable to suck blood.

3. *The Palps :*—On either side of the proboscis there are two long pointed appendages, the *palps*, which serve as organs of touch. In the female anopheline they are slender, whilst in the male they are larger and bear long hairs. In both sexes of the Malaria Mosquito the palps are long, equal in length to the proboscis, and covered with fine scales. In the common Culex Mosquito, the palps of the female are not more than half the length

of the proboscis : those of the male are long,
but their terminal segment is not enlarged though
set with long hairs. This furnishes a ready
means of distinguishing the Malaria Mosquito from
Culex.

4. *The Chest :*—This portion of the insect is
comparatively large to accommodate the strong
wing-muscles and the legs. It consists of three
segments.

5. *The Wings :*—The Malaria Mosquito is distinguished by the presence of dark spots on its
wings, and hence its name " maculipennis " or
" spotted-wing." The margin of the wings bears
several rows of scales, long and slender scales
alternating regularly with rows of shorter ones,
producing a beautiful fringe.

6. *The Legs :*—Each of the segments of the chest
or thorax bears a pair of legs. The legs are connected to the body by joints, which are constructed
so as to permit great freedom of movement. Each
leg consists of seven pieces, the last of which bears
a pair of *claws.*   •

7. *The Abdomen :*—The abdomen consists of
eight segments and tapes gradually towards the tip.
The last segment in the female mosquito bears
the egg depositor by means of which the eggs are
laid, and with the aid of the hind legs, arranged
on the surface of the water.

The colour of mosquitoes ranges from a light-
yellow or transparent pale-green shade to the
darkest brown.

The Malaria Mosquito is usually brown.

The Internal Anatomy of the Mosquito.

The Stomach :—When a mosquito bites, blood
is pumped up into the " sucking-tube " by two
pumps and passes into three food-reservoirs, two

small ones above, and a third below, which reaches far into the abdomen.

The stomach is a continuation of the gullet and is tubular in shape. It ends in a valve-like construction beyond which it discharges into the intestines.

The Respiratory Apparatus :—All mosquitoes breathe by a system of air-tubes which open to the exterior by two main openings, one either side of the chest and by several smaller ones in the abdomen.

The Circulation of the Blood :—The circulation of the blood is maintained by the heart which is situated in the abdomen.

The Salivary Glands :—These important glands, of which there are two, supply the irritating poison of the mosquito bite and are situated on either side in the anterior part of the thorax. The secretion from each gland is conducted into the head by a fine tube. In the head the two ducts join and discharge into the salivary pump. This pump connects with the salivary channel in the hypopharynx and forms a syringe by which the saliva is automatically forced out at the tip of the proboscis during the act of feeding.

Fig. 31 shows the five lancets and stylet, like the point of a hypodermic needle, which are driven into her victim. when the mosquito bites.

All of us in India are familiar with the pain of mosquito bites and most are doubtless aware that it is not the bite itself that is painful but the poison which is injected when the insect bites.

It is generally said that this poison is instilled to produce irritation and thus attract more blood to the part.

This can hardly be the case, as the insect bites, sucks and flies away in a very short space of time.

The painful bite is a distinct disadvantage to the biter—it is like a thief making a noise—and it is now generally taught that the poison has the power of keeping the blood liquid, and thus preventing it from coagulating in the proboscis.

It is a pity that this treatment of the blood is necessary, as it is the injection of parasites mixed with the saliva which makes the insect the serious enemy of man she is.

The constant use of the feminine pronoun in the foregoing paragraphs has doubtless been observed by the reader. The reason for this is that the male mosquito is a harmless vegetarian, whereas his mate is a greedy bloodsucker.

The habits of mosquitoes :—We have now learnt something of the structure and life-history of mosquitoes and may now briefly consider their habits.

The staple fare of both sexes is the juice of vegetables, but the female loses no opportunity of sucking blood whenever she can.

Birds and all sorts of animals suffer from varieties of malaria and are bitten by mosquitoes. Much experimental work on malaria has been done on the malarial fevers of various birds. But it must be clearly understood that the malaria of birds is quite different to human malaria and due to entirely different parasites.

Mosquitoes can be kept alive in captivity for several weeks on bananas, but the desire for blood is so strong that they will even bite a corpse, so that in malarious districts even the dead are dangerous.

In cool climates the mosquito becomes lethargic, and either goes back to vegetarian habits or hibernates.

Mosquitoes in various stages of their development can live for many months, and we know that in the North of India they can withstand long periods of cold and wet. Even the intense rigors of a Norwegian winter to which the cold of even Peshawar is as nothing, cannot kill them, and the insects appear in clouds every summer, even in the land of the midnight sun.

Water is an absolute essential to the development of mosquitoes, and stagnant water or the edges of picturesque marshy pools are especially attractive to many varieties.

Generally speaking, they are night prowlers and only turn out at sunset, but in darkened rooms they are active enough in the day, hence our frequent recommendations in previous chapters that all rooms in India should be brightly lighted.

We are all too familiar with the humming and buzzing noise made by mosquitoes. This noise varies with the sex and with the species of the insect. It is said to be produced by the vibration of the wings and the proboscis, the wings producing the deeper notes and the proboscis the higher ones.

The malarial parasite :—The organisms which cause malaria are minute animals consisting of a single living cell, but have none the less well-marked characteristics distinguishing the sexes.

There are three varieties of the parasite which produce the three kinds of malaria, *viz.,* Benign Tertian Ague, Quartan Ague, and Malignant Tertian Ague.

The process of development starts from the bite of the mosquito which injects into the blood small seed-like bodies which we will call " spores " whose origin will be explained later. These small seeds of malaria fix themselves on to the red corpuscles and bore their way to their interior.

In the second stage of development we have, therefore, the parasite inside the red blood corpuscle forming a curious ring shape, which is shown on the extreme left of Fig. 32.

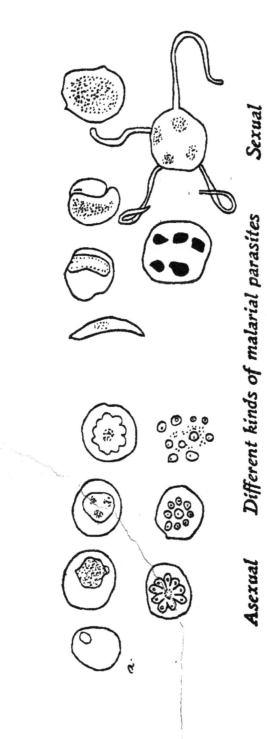

Fig. 32.

Different kinds of malarial parasites

Asexual   **Sexual**

a—Shows the " ring shape " from which both varieties of parasite start.

From the ring shape the parasite may take on a sexual or asexual form ; let us follow the asexual cycle first. We find that the parasite grows at the expense of the corpuscle, absorbs its fluids and rapidly increases in size.

In the interior of the corpuscle the parasite is actively motile and throws out processes which alter in shape. It grows at the expense of the blood corpuscle and when it comes to occupy the greater part of its host cell, the material of which it is constituted, begins to split up into eight, twelve or more segments.

On the completion of this process of segmentation, fragments of the parasite are arranged in the form of a daisy or rosette with colouring granules in the centre, forming the stamen of the " daisy " or centre of the rosette.

The petals of the daisy, or loops of the rosette, constitute the small bodies originally referred to as "spores," and when this curious malarial blossom is full-blown, the remains of the red cell rupture and its baleful contents are set free to attack fresh red blood corpuscles and start the malarial cycle anew.

The melanin, as the colouring granules are called, passes into the blood stream, and is carried by the white blood cells to the tissues producing the darkening of the skin which is so familiar in subjects of malaria.

The process detailed above constitutes the asexual cycle of development in the three varieties of the parasite. The period occupied in the process occupies in ordinary Benign Tertian Ague only 48 hours from spore to spore.

If quinine is not given, this goes on until, owing to the exhaustion of the reproductive power of the parasite under the strain of repeated division, the process ceases, and specially differentiated male and female forms appear in the following way :—

Starting from the ring shape the sexual cycle proceeds at first in much the same way as the asexual.

When the parasite is fully grown, it nearly fills the red cell and develops male or female characteristics. If the patient is not bitten by a mosquito at this particular period, the parasite dies, but if the organism passes into the stomach of a mosquito, its true sexual life begins.

Ten minutes to half an hour after the blood has been swallowed by the mosquito the male parasite throws out four to eight filaments.

These little filaments are actively motile and are soon set free. They unite with the opposite sex forming a worm-like body which reaches the wall of the mos-quito's stomach, b u r r o w s its way through the tissues, and comes to rest between the layers of the muscular wall of the stomach,

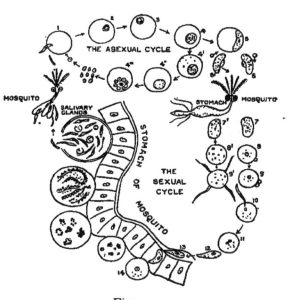

Fig. 33.

in which situation it can be seen with an ordinary lens.

A tough resistant membrane develops round it which soon begins to split up into a mulberry-shaped mass which consists of the small seed-like bodies called " spores." This mass eventually bursts and the spores are accordingly set free in the general blood stream of the mosquito. Most of them find their way to the neighbourhood of the salivary glands from whence they enter the salivary cells and ducts, so that when a mosquito bites an animal, she injects, with the venom which, as we have seen, she always instils, a large number of these fully-developed spores which proceed to attack the red blood corpuscles and start the malarial cycle.

The time occupied in the development of the malarial parasite in the blood varies from 36 hours to 15 days according to the variety of the parasite.

The frontispiece indicates in a graphic way the two methods of development of the parasite, but the diagram Fig. 33 will be helpful to the reader.

1. Spore entering blood corpuscle.
2. Ring-shape or early form of parasite in blood cell.
3. Ditto   ditto   ditto.
4. Parasite in cell.
    4″   Ditto.
    4″   Ditto.
    4″ Rosette or " Daisy."
5. Parasite taking on crescent shape.
6′, 7′, 8′ and 9′. Male parasite.
6, 7, 8, 9, 10 and 11. Female parasite.
12, 13 and 14. Impregnated female parasite in various stages.

2. *Sandflies.*

The sandfly is a keen rival to the mosquito in making things unpleasant for man in India.

There are two distinct families of insect popularly known as sandflies. One of them, scientifically known as the Simulium, and popularly as the Buffalo gnat, is a humped back little fly with broad wings (Fig. 34) which in some parts of America does great damage to live-stock of all kinds and even to dogs and cats.

Fig. 34.
BUFFALO GNAT.

As in the case of mosquitoes, the males are harmless, but the females suck blood, and their attacks not infrequently result in the death of their victim, whose eyes, nose and ears are the points to which the pest directs its attention. The bite leaves a small purple spot-like a blood blister and causes intense irritation.

The larvæ live in quickly running water and are peculiarly adapted for this mode of life as they have a sucker at the end of the body which enables them to cling to stones. Moreover, they are able to spin threads which anchor them to suitable projections in the stream.

The fly does not come to the surface to be born from the pupa, but emerges under water and floats to the surface, protected from getting wet by a bubble of air or gas entangled amongst the hairs of the legs and body.

The other insect known by the name of sandfly is the Owl-Midge or Phlebotomus.

This variety is like the other in appearance, but is more hairy (Fig. 35).

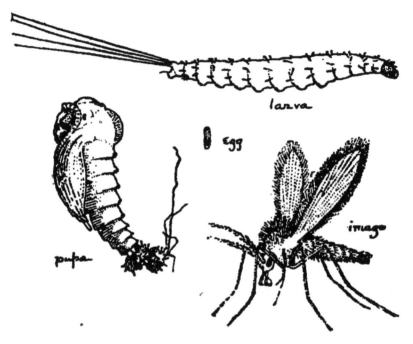

Fig. 35.
THE OWL-MIDGE.

The larvæ are found in damp earth and are very curious; they have a large head with big jaws, and the body is covered with toothed spines and furnished with two long bristles at the tail end for the first fourteen days and afterwards four, as shown in the picture.

The insect has been found to propagate itself in the dejecta of lizards and wood-lice and is only prevalent where walls and roofs are badly constructed and in bad repair, thus favouring the development of the indirect hosts of the insect.

Here, again, it is the females who give all the trouble to man. Their small size gives them a great advantage over mosquitoes since they are able to get through ordinary mosquito netting without difficulty. The ankles are favourite points of attack and the flies will even crawl under the bed-clothes in their lust for blood. They are found in bath rooms, especially near the floor and under bricks or stones, in the interstices of *chittai*, or in similar damp shady places during the day. At night they emerge from their seclusion to bite.

This little fly is believed to be the carrier of a disease which has long been known in various parts of India. It is a form of fever which lasts about three to five days, and is sometimes followed by much weakness and prostration. It is common in Austria and Malta, and three Austrian military surgeons have investigated the matter and carried out a series of interesting experiments which fully established the relations of the sandfly to the disease.

A number of flies were caught and allowed to feed on a patient suffering from the fever and were then transported to London and Vienna where the disease does not occur. At the Royal Army Medical College, London, and in Vienna, they were permitted to feed on healthy volunteers, 50 per cent. of whom contracted the disease and went through typical attacks.

The chief methods of prevention are :—

1. Good walls to houses.
2. Painting or distempering instead of white-washing walls.
3. Good floors and the disuse of matting.
4. Removal of old walls and ruins.
5. Formalin spray to walls of rooms.
6. Removal of all old woodwork, and painting and varnishing of all doors, etc., yearly.
7. The use of a fine-mesh mosquito net.

It is well known that newcomers to a sandfly district in this country always acquire Sandfly Fever, whereas old residents who know how to protect themselves, and take the trouble to do so, enjoy complete immunity.

3. MIDGES.

Fig. 36 is a sketch of the midge which shows its structure.

Midges are easily confused with mosquitoes, but may be distinguished by the short proboscis, or trunk, and the absence of scales on the wings. In the resting attitude they raise the forelegs and hold them above the head, whereas mosquitoes raise the hindlegs above the rest of their body.

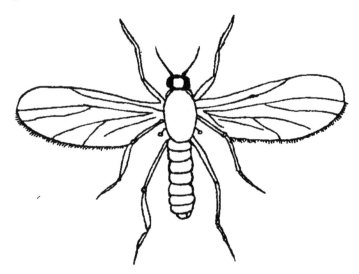

Fig. 36.
MIDGE.

As everyone knows from experience, they are often bloodthirsty little beasts and cause annoyance out of all proportion to their size. Nearly all varieties deposit their eggs in water and these eggs go through much the same stages as those of the mosquito, but one variety is terrestrial, and its larvæ live in rotten vegetable stuff, under damp bark and similar places.

The " blood-worms " which are familiar objects in water receptacles are the larvæ of the aquatic variety of these little flies.

Recently a variety of Buffalo-gnat or Simulium (see page 206), which has been described in some text-books as a midge, has been suspected to be the agent for the transmission of Pellagra, a disease common in some parts of India, and characterised by a special rash, debility, pains in the back, sleeplessness, and digestive disturbances.

Group B.

General Characteristics :—This group consists of a large family of insects of the familiar shape of house-flies and having short three jointed antennæ and a proboscis which may be short or long, but is always polished in appearance.

HOUSE-FLIES.

There are several species which are commonly found in houses, but only two of these should be called the house-flies, *viz.*, the Common House-Fly and the Lesser House-Fly (Appendix II). The Common House Fly or *Musca domestica* is a medium-sized, greyish fly, with its mouth-parts spread out at the tip for sucking up liquids. It breeds in a great variety of substances of a filthy nature, and is found in practically all parts of the world. On account of the conformation of its mouth-parts, the house-fly cannot bite, yet no impression is stronger in the minds of most people than that this insect does occasionally bite. This impression is due to the frequent occurrence in houses of another fly which is called the stable fly (see Appendix II), and which, while closely resembling the house-fly (so closely in fact, as to deceive anyone but an expert), differs from it in the important particular that its mouth-parts are formed for piercing the skin.

Several kinds of flies of metallic greenish or bluish colour are occasionally found in houses, the commonest of which is the so-called blue-bottle fly. This insect is also called the "blow-fly" or

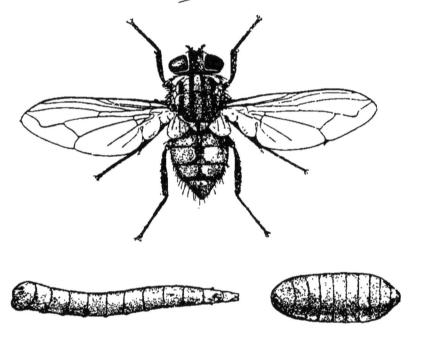

Fig.-37.
THE HOUSE FLY.
Larva.   Perfect insect.   Pupa.

"meat-fly" and breeds in decaying *animal* material. It feeds on the fæces of man to a great extent and is very partial to fruits of various kinds, hence it is very likely to be a carrier of disease.

In most parts of the world the common house-fly prefers to lay its eggs upon horse manure, this substance being its favourite larval food, but in India where in many parts of the country every scrap of manure is made into cakes and used as fuel, it is frequently not available. In this country it has perhaps from necessity developed a taste for human excrement, and from this habit it becomes very dangerous to the health of human beings, carrying, as it does, the germs of intestinal diseases such as enteric fever and cholera from excreta to food-supplies. It will also lay its eggs upon any decaying vegetable and animal material, but of the flies that infest Indian houses a vast proportion comes from either human excrement or horse manure, and the maggots of these flies can

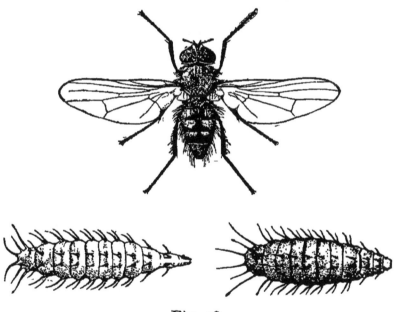

Fig. 38.
THE LESSER HOUSE-FLY.
Larva.   Perfect insect.   Pupa.

readily be found in the soil under scattered deposits of human dejecta. As the fæces dry and crumble the maggots bury themselves in the earth, finding a passage by way of cracks and the holes made by worms or dung-beetles.

The excrement of dogs has also been found to serve as a breeding-place for various flies, which haunt houses and hospital wards. Cow-dung, and the earth under it, harbour fly maggots, but experiments have shown that house-flies do not breed in ordinary ground as distinguished from organic deposits.

To attract the house-fly, ordinary household refuse must be in a state of fermentation as flies breed in relatively small numbers in ashpits where no fermentation has taken place. They do not breed at all in refuse receptacles which are emptied at short intervals, but the use of disinfectants, as ordinarily carried out, does not prevent them breeding in such receptacles unless they are regularly emptied. Very dry or excessively wet ashes or moist cow-dung does not harbour them.

Fowls, but not ducks or geese, devour larvæ and pupæ in stable litter greedily, and there are certain species of ants which destroy them with great rapidity.

The duration of the egg state of the house-fly is eight to twenty-four hours, the larval state from three to five days, and the pupal state from five to seven days. (Appendix II.)

The periods of development are influenced largely by the temperature of the breeding place and this varies not only with the climate and season but also with the amount of fermentation going on in the organic refuse. The pupal form of the insect hibernates in manure or at the surface of the ground under a manure heap. In the adult form it hibernates in houses, hiding itself like the mosquito in dark nooks and crannies. The unceilinged roofs of Indian bungalows and native houses offer limitless facilities for flies to enjoy undisturbed winter repose.

The number of eggs laid by an individual fly averages about 120, and the enormous numbers in which the insect occurs is thus plainly accounted for, especially when we consider the universal presence of appropriate food.

Indeed, their fecundity, the rapidity with which one generation succeeds another, and their great voracity, added to the extraordinary quickness of their production, are such that *Linnæus tells us that three flies, with the generations which spring from them, could eat up a dead horse as quickly as a lion could.*

The presence of flies in a house means that filth is close at hand. It may be just outside the kitchen window, in the refuse receptacle, in the adjacent stables, or in the garden soil around the house, but the kitchen itself is the feeding place, *not* the breeding ground of the fly.

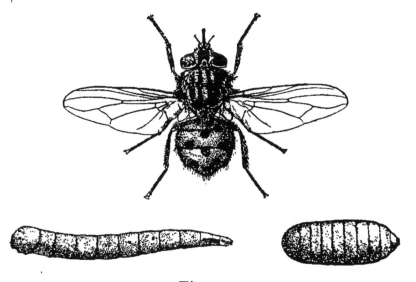

Fig. 39.
THE STABLE FLY.

Larva.   Perfect insect.   Pupa.

The table in Appendix II shows the characters of the two chief varieties of House-fly and the Stable Fly.

Remedies and Preventives.

The house-fly has a number of natural enemies. The common house centipede destroys it in considerable numbers, and there is a small reddish mite which frequently covers its body and gradually destroys it. Various predatory beetles and a variety of ant also render good service to man by waging an endless vendetta against the fly.

Its most effective enemy, however, is a fungus disease which carries off flies in large numbers, particularly towards the close of the season. The epidemic ceases with the onset of cold weather, but although many thousands are killed by it, the remarkable rapidity of development in the early summer months soon more than replaces the thousands thus destroyed.

The general means of preventing flies are :—

1. Careful screening of all windows and doors during the summer months.

2. The use of sticky fly papers.

3. The prompt gathering of horse manure and its removal within 24 hours or storage in special receptacles.

4. The use of disinfectants in latrines.

5. Absolute domestic cleanliness.

6. The use of trap breeding places, consisting of shallow trays containing horse manure. These are emptied every third day, their contents being burnt.

The prompt gathering of horse manure, and its removal or destruction by fire or storage in specially prepared receptacles, and the proper use of latrines, would greatly abate the fly nuisance in this country, but even under existing circumstances absolute household cleanliness will always result in a diminution of the numbers of the house-fly.

The following rules for dealing with the Fly Nuisance might be published in the vernaculars, distributed to all residents in Indian towns and enforced by Indian Municipalities.

1. Keep flies away from the sick, especially persons ill with communicable diseases. Kill every fly that strays into the sick-room as this body is covered with disease germs.

2. Do not allow decaying material of any sort to accumulate on or near your premises.

3. All refuse which tends in any way to fermentation, such as bedding, straw, paper waste, and vegetable matter, should be promptly burnt.

4. Keep all food in *doolies*.

5. Keep all receptacles for garbage carefully covered, or sprinkle them daily with kerosene oil.

6. Remove all stable manure daily or dry and burn it.

7. Cover food after a meal, and burn or bury *deeply* all table refuse.

8. Cover with muslin all food exposed for sale.

9. Protect all windows and doors, especially in the kitchen and dining-room with wire gauze.

10. Don't forget that flies are bred in filth near where you find them. It may be behind the door or under the table, but is probably a large or small heap of refuse near at hand.

If there is no dirt and filth, there will be no flies.

THE HEMIPTERA.

The only members of this great order of unwinged insects with which we are concerned are the family called Cimicidæ or Bed Bugs.

These insects, like fleas, have lost their wings owing to their habits no longer affording any use for them. Their origin is obscure. They were well known to the Greeks and Romans. It is possible that the insect was originally a parasite of birds and mammals, and gradually included man among its hosts. Its distribution is almost world-wide, as it is readily carried in steamers and can survive long periods, even a year, without food. It is this accomplishment which enables the species to continue its existence even under the most unfavourable circumstances, as they live from season to season in permanent camps, summer residences, empty apartments and the like.

It has been found experimentally that mice, both living and dead, are attacked by bed-bugs and that young mice particularly seem to provide an excellent supply of food for them. It seems not unlikely that other small animals, including even rats, may also be hosts ; therefore this parasite must be taken into account in the spread of many diseases.

The bug is a most disagreeable insect, and abounds in dirty houses, principally in towns, and above all in those of warm countries. It lives in beds, woodwork, behind pictures, under *chittai* and carpets : indeed, there is no crack, however narrow it may be, into which it is unable to slip.

It is nocturnal in its habits as a rule, but may be active at any time, and the bite is irritating to most persons, though repeated inflections appear to confer a certain degree of immunity. Travellers are aware of the ingenuity of the insect in reaching its prey, and it has been observed that when all other means of access failed, it went to the ceiling and fell on its victim from that position.

Its body is oval, about a fifth of an inch in length, soft, of a brown colour, and covered with a little hair.

The eggs are laid in cracks in the floor, in the furniture, or in any convenient position to which the female can obtain access. They are beautifully shaped and sculptured, and about five to ten days after they are laid the young escape by a round door at one end. The young are similar to the adult, but smaller, more transparent, and less darkly coloured. There are probably five moults, and if the insect is under favourable conditions where it can get blood easily, the whole life-history will probably occupy not more than two months. A meal of blood seems to be required before each moult and before egg-laying, and if it cannot be obtained, the interval between the moults may

be very greatly prolonged. When the insect
wishes to suck blood, it injects a liquid which is an
irritant and causes a flow of blood to the spot on
which it gorges itself. The adult insect feeds
about once in from thirty-six to forty-eight hours,
taking nearly fifteen minutes to get its fill of blood.
At earlier ages, the feeding period is much shorter.

When attention was directed to the part played
in the dissemination of disease by biting insects,
it was soon shown that the bug, besides being a
common household nuisance, may be important as a
disease carrier.

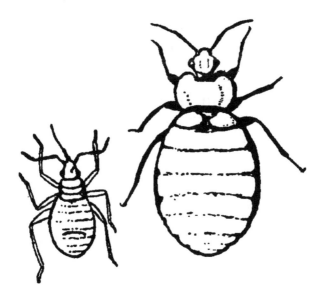

Fig. 40.
BED-BUG.

There is a definite tradition in Russia, frequently
referred to in lectures at the Pasteur Institute, that
the bed-bug forms an intermediate host, or is at
least an agent in conveying intermittent fever,
so common in certain districts of that country.
The possibility of its acting as intermediary in
cerebro-spinal meningitis is still the subject of

investigation, and it is suspected to be one of the means by which kala-azar is conveyed from man to man.

Fumigation with formaldehyde is a good agent for freeing railway carriages and other vehicles from this pest. Cleanliness, washing the floor and wooden bedsteads with kerosene oil or turpentine emulsion, the use of pure pyrethrum powder, and fumigation with sulphur, are other means available, but cocoanut oil is the most effective insecticide against bugs. All that is necessary is to smear a little of the oil over places where the bugs are found. Where there are cracks or crevices requiring treatment the oil should be dropped into them. By an intelligent use of cocoanut oil any room or articles of furniture or bedding, can in a short time be freed of bugs. Cocoanut oil will destroy ova as well as the adult insect, so the systematic use of the oil in places where bugs are likely to breed will keep the place free from them.

THE APTERA.

This order includes the Pediculidæ or lice family which are closely allied to the bug tribe. Three species infest man in India, viz. :—(1) The Head Louse ; (2) The Body Louse ; (3) The Crab Louse. Other varieties occur in horses, cattle, goats, pigs, camels, dogs, etc.

1. *The Head Louse* :—This is an insect of a greyish colour, with a flat slightly transparent body. It is spotted with black on the spiracles, soft in the middle and rather hard at the sides. The head, which is oval, is furnished with two thread-like antennæ, composed of five joints, which are constantly in motion while the creature is walking. Its eyes are black and round and of simple structure. In the front of the head is a short, conical, fleshy nipple. This nipple contains a sucker, or rostrum,

which the animal can put out when it likes, and which, when extended, represents a tubular body, terminating in six little pointed hooks, bent back, and serving to retaining the instrument in the skin. This organ is surmounted with four fine hairs, fixed to one another. It is by means of this complicated apparatus that the louse pricks the skin of the head. The limbs are very thick, terminating in a strong nail, which folds back on an indented projection, thus forming a pincer. It is with this pincer that the louse fastens itself to the hair.

Head Lice develop from long white eggs which remain sticking to the hair and are commonly called " nits." The young are hatched in the course of five or six days : and in eighteen days are able to produce their kind. It has been calculated that in two months two female lice could produce ten thousand. The second

Fig. 41.
THE HEAD
LOUSE.

generation of a single individual can amount to two thousand five hundred, and the third, to a hundred and twenty-five thousand, whilst the prodigious rapidity of their reproduction has led to the widespread popular impression that their appearance in such annoying numbers is often due to spontaneous generation.

Happily for the victims of these disgusting parasites, their actual reproduction is not usually up to the prodigious development which is possible.

2. *The Body Louse :*—The body louse is larger than the head louse. It infects beggars and people of unclean habits, producing the complaint called Phthiriasis.

It is not the least of the minor horrors of the present war.

3. *The Crab Louse :*—The variety is found on the parts of the body covered with short hairs

usually in the vicinity of the private parts. It is very readily communicated from man to man.

It has recently been shown that the parasites of Typhus fever as well as those of the Indian type of *relapsing fever* are conveyed by pediculi, so that the prompt destruction of these insects is very important from a health point of view. Recently an interesting discovery has been made as regards the method by which these diseases are conveyed by infected lice. It has been shown that the bites of these insects are harmless to man. The poison only exists inside their body cavity, so that a man can only be infected if the insect is crushed and the poison rubbed into the raw places caused by the constant scratching, or if the conjunctiva of the eye is infected by rubbing the eyes with soiled fingers. This emphasises the extreme importance of refraining from scratching oneself if one has been unfortunate enough to become infested with pediculi—a point which has received considerable attention in connection with the present trench-warfare.

Destruction of Lice.

For the head louse :—In women the hair need not be sacrificed. The lice can be killed by smearing the scalp with white precipitate ointment or rubbing in kerosene and olive oil, equal parts. The hair must be combed with a fine comb dipped in vinegar to get the nits out. The vinegar dissolves the glutinous material which fixes the eggs or " nits " to the hair. Scrupulous cleanliness and care are sufficient to prevent recurrence.

For the body louse :—The clothing should be placed for hours in a disinfecting oven or exposed to direct sunlight. To allay the itching a warm bath containing 4 to 5 ounces of bicarbonate of soda is useful. The skin may be rubbed with a lotion of carbolic containing 2 teaspoonfuls of pure carbolic acid and 2 ounces of glycerine to the pint.

For the crab louse :—White precipitate or ordinary mercurial ointments are reliable remedies, and the parts should be thoroughly washed two or three times a day with soft soap and water..

THE SIPHONAPTERA.

The Flea :—The fleas were originally flies and had wings, but their form and structure has in the course of ages become profoundly altered in consequence of their parasitic habits.

The common flea has an oval, somewhat flattened body, covered with a hard horny skin of brilliant chestnut brown colour. Its head, small in proportion to the body, is compressed, and carries two small antennæ, of cylindrical form, composed of four joints, which the animal shakes continually when in motion, but which it lowers and rests in front of its head when in a state of repose. The eyes when present are simple, large and round. The beak is composed of an exterior jointed sheath, having inside it a tube, and carrying underneath two long sharp lancets, with cutting and sawlike edges. It is with this instrument that the flea pierces the skin, and sucks blood. The bite, as everyone knows, is easily recognised by the presence of a small darkish red spot, surrounded by a circle of a paler colour.

The quantity of blood absorbed by this little creature is enormous, when compared with its size.

The limbs are long, strong, and spiny. The foot has five joints, and terminates in hooks turned in opposite directions. The two anterior limbs · are separated from the others and are inserted nearly underneath the head; the posterior ones are particularly large and strong. The strength of fleas is herculean and the jumps they can make gigantic when compared with their size.

The female flea lays from eight to twelve eggs, which are of oval shape, smooth, and white. She drops these on the ground, between the boards of floors, or old furniture, and amongst dirty linen and rubbish. There is always found mixed with the eggs a certain number of grains of a brilliant black colour, which are simply dried blood. This is a provision

Fig. 42.
RAT-FLEA.
Order Siphonaptera.

which the foreseeing mother has prepared at our expense to nourish her young offspring.

In two to five days in summer, and in about eleven days in winter, small, elongated larvæ come out of these eggs. They are of cylindrical form, covered with hair, and divided into three parts, the last provided with two small hooks. The head is scaly above, has two small antennæ, and is without eyes. The larvæ are without limbs, but they can twist about, roll themselves over and over, and even progress by raising their heads. Though at first white, they soon become of a reddish colour.

About a fortnight after they are hatched they cease to eat, and become motionless. They then surround themselves with a small, whitish, silky cocoon in which they are transformed into pupæ. In another fortnight these pupæ become perfect insects.

Certain circumstances particularly favour the multiplication of this insect. It is most abundant in dirty houses, in deserted buildings, in ruins, and in places frequented by people of uncleanly habits. Several species of fleas live on animals, as, for example, the cat-flea, the dog-flea, and those of the pigeon and poultry.

The rat-flea is an insect whose study has become of the first importance as its bite constitutes the chief way whereby plague is spread. The rat-flea is a parasite of the rat, but does not confine its attacks to these animals, and will bite man, especially when there are no rats on which it can feed. It is well known that before plague attacks the men of a village, it attacks the rats. When the plague-stricken rats die, the rat-fleas leave their bodies and are then particularly apt to bite men, and thus infect them with the plague bacillus which the fleas have previously sucked up with the blood of the rats on which they last fed. Martin has shown recently that normal fleas, even when they have sucked the blood of infected rats, do not convey plague to man : plague is only conveyed to man by certain diseased rat-fleas, whose gullets have become blocked by large masses of plague bacilli, and who are constantly unable to swallow the blood they suck, and are consumed therefore with a raging thirst. Such fleas suck blood constantly, and then regurgitate it mixed with the plague bacilli which block their gullets, and in this way man is injected through the small wound made by the flea when biting.

The *chigger or sand-flea* is not unlike the common flea, but is smaller in size. It is flat, brown in colour, with a white spot on the back, and is armed with a strong pointed beak provided with lancets. It is with this instrument that the female attacks man. The favourite haunt of the *chigger* is dry, sandy soil, and the dust and ashes in badly kept native huts, the stables of cattle, poultry pens, and the like. It greedily attacks all warm-blooded animals, including birds and man.

The *chigger* attacks chiefly the feet. It slips in between the flesh and the nails, or gets under the skin of the heel. Notwithstanding the length of the animal's beak, introducing itself beneath the skin does not cause at first any pain, but after a few days irritation appears, which, though at first slight, gradually, increases, and ends by becoming unbearable.

The insect, when under the skin, becomes as large as a small pea, and surrounded by a large brown bag containing matter. In this bag are collected the eggs, which issue from an orifice in the posterior extremity, but are not hatched in the wound itself.

As a cause of suffering, invaliding and indirectly of death, it is an insect of some importance. It is now extremely prevalent on the East Coast of Africa and is causing a large amount of invaliding amongst the Indian coolies there, by whom it has been introduced into India.

The Hymenoptera.

Ants :—This order embraces some of the most interesting of insects, including bees, and wasps, but the only members with which we are interested in relation to the transmission of disease are the *Formicidæ* or Ants.

These insects are very familiar to us in India. They are in general small creatures of a brown or black colour.

Like bees, ants are what are called social insects. They live in communities in which there is a considerable amount of specialisation of form to serve the purpose of a useful division of labour. Their little republics consist of males and females, and various forms of workers, but the degree to which this specialisation goes, varies very much with the species. Commonly there are two or three forms of workers, the soldier with large head and mandibles, and the workers, major or minor, with more normal structure. A nest may consist of a greater or smaller aggregation of individuals, and there are a few species which share the light-shunning habits of white-ants, but most varieties nest in soil, trees, etc., and work in the light.

In general, the ants are scavengers, the workers bringing to the nest the food for the whole community. This food consists of dead insects, any available nutritious animal matter, the sap of plants, and any edible vegetable matter that can be obtained. In this sense ants are excellent scavengers, and as they are practically everywhere in the open, they serve an extremely useful function in the tropics. In some species this habit is specialised in one direction : some are " harvesters," storing in their nests seeds of grasses, small millets, and rice.

The life-history of these wonderful little workers is very similar to that of bees.

The eggs are laid by the female and tended by the workers in the nest. The larva hatches out in about a fortnight and is a white helpless grub without legs and incapable of locomotion, which is fed by the workers. In some varieties the pupa is free, in others in a silken cocoon which the larva itself prepares. The larvæ and pupæ live in specially built galleries in the anthills and one may often see an ant republic being moved, the little white larvæ and pupæ being carried by the workers.

The workers are the only members of the ant family which are recognised as such by the popular mind.

They have the charge of the building, provisioning, and as we have seen rearing of the larvæ, in fact, all the care of the household, and the defence of the nest.   Deprived of the wings they are bound to the soil, and condemned to work.   As compensation to them belong strength, authority, and power. Nothing is done in this community but through them.   Born protectors of an immense family still in the cradle, by their vigilance, their tenderness, and their solicitude without being mothers themselves, they share in the duties and joys of maternity. Alone, they decide on peace or war : alone, they take part in combats : head, heart, and arm of the republic, they ensure its prosperity, watch over its defence, found colonies, and in their works show themselves great and persevering artists.

Hitherto no conclusive evidence has been produced against the ant as a disseminator of disease : on the contrary, a certain Indian species is said to render valuable service by destroying the eggs and pupæ of flies.

The Arachnida.

This is the last group of parasites we have to consider.   As already pointed out, they are not insects but allied to spiders and scorpions.   The members known to affect man are :—

The Itch Parasite :—This little member of the spider tribe produces troublesome and distressing skin eruptions in man.   The male is rarely seen, but the female can be seen with the naked eye and has a pearly white colour.   It lives in a small burrow which it makes for itself in the skin forming the web of the fingers and toes, the backs of the hands and the armpits.

The lesions which result from the presence of the parasite are very numerous and result largely from the scratching which it induces.

It has been accused of acting as an agent for the dissemination of leprosy so that its early destruction is desirable not only for the individual but for the community.

It is destroyed by sulphur ointment or Balsam of.Peru which should be applied after a good scrubbing with hot water and soft soap, but treatment often results in distressing irritation of the skin. The parasite lurks in the patient's clothing which must be most carefully disinfected.

Ticks :—These little animals constitute a large proportion of this section of the animal kingdom, and recent developments in tropical medicine have shown that they play an important part in the transmission of disease. They are

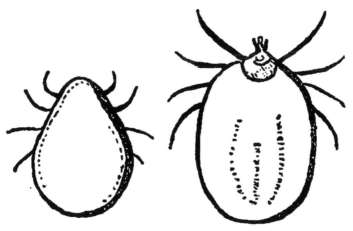

Fig. 43.

FOWL TICK.   CATTLE TICK.

widely distributed, almost every animal either having species special to itself or being liable to attack by the parasites of other animals.

They are always visible to the naked eye, and the females are almost invariably larger than the males. In some species the former, when gorged with blood, may reach a length of nearly half an inch. As a rule, they are temporary parasites, but some live in a quasi-permanent manner on the body of their host : and occasionally a few, as the sheep tick, may burrow beneath the skin.

After impregnation the female tick attaches herself to her host.   Becoming enormously distended with its blood, she drops off and secretes herself in some convenient hiding place where she deposits her eggs, which are small, yellowish, roe-like grains amounting in some cases to thousands.   In three or four weeks under favourable conditions the eggs are hatched.   The larvæ look like minute moving grains of sand, and when a suitable opportunity presents itself, they attach themselves to some animal and then undergo many curious changes both in the larval and subsequent pupal or chrysalis stage.

In some species these changes take place upon the same host, the parasite remaining attached during the process.   In other species the tick, before each moult, drops off as soon as it ceases feeding, and in consequence has to find a " host " three times during its life instead of once.   The diagram (Fig. 44) shows the life-history of a tick with three hosts.   Having reached maturity the sexes unite. After fertilizing the female the male usually dies, but the female proceeds to gorge herself with blood for the development of her ova.   On account of the difficulty of finding an appropriate host, ticks at all stages are endowed with a phenomenal capacity for fasting.   They have actually been found alive after a fast of four years' duration.

In habits the tick resembles the common bed-bug. It lives in the huts of natives, hiding during the day in cracks in the walls and floors, or in the thatched roofs, and moving about actively during the night in search of nourishment.   It feeds slowly, and is unable to get much blood from any but a sleeping person.

Ulcers and a severe form of fever which is endemic in Southern Madras are attributed to a tick very common there.

An African Tick (Ornithodorus Moubata) has been proved to be the disseminator of the " Coast "

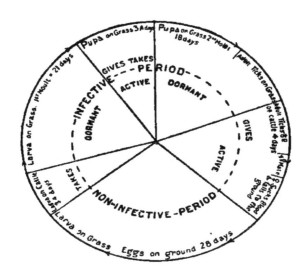

Fig. 44.

DIAGRAM SHOWING LIFE CYCLE OF TICK WITH THREE HOSTS.

or " Tick Fever " which closely resembles the " Relapsing " or " Famine Fever " of India.

The propagation of disease by body insects serves to explain the spread of epidemics of relapsing and other fevers from one neighbourhood to another at a great distance which has hitherto puzzled students of epidemiology.

CHAPTER X.

DISINFECTANTS AND DISINFECTION IN THE TROPICS.

Disinfection is no longer a vague attempt to influence the unknown as instanced by the scattering of powdered sulphur and the building of bonfires during epidemics in Mediæval times, but is now carried out in accordance with scientific methods based on amply demonstrated facts.—(Munson's " Military Hygiene.")

IT is becoming a matter of past history how plague and, to a certain extent, cholera have been driven out of Europe, and other infectious diseases promise to follow in their wake. Even in unprogressive India, relapsing fever and enteric epidemics are less frequent visitants than formerly, and not only is the mortality from other communicable diseases being reduced, but the general deathrate of the country, and especially that of the great centres, has fallen in recent years to a considerable extent. This is acknowledged to be due to the organization of the public health service of India, and to the prophylactic and sanitary measures indicated and executed.

First amongst these sanitary reforms stands disinfection, which, strictly speaking, implies dealing with infection, but in its popular and wider sense embraces purification in all its applications. The burning sacrifices of volatile substances, the libation of liquids, and the sprinklings of powdery compounds on a large scale by our ancestors, are now recognised as feeble or futile substitutes for the physical and chemical means of destroying infection. The efficacy of disinfection may broadly be said to be in inverse ratio to the scale upon which it is carried out.

In the process of cleansing and purification in its widest sense, organic and inorganic substances are dealt with either by physical or chemical means. By physical means, when applied to movable matters and without regard to their preservation, they are removed by road or water, and disposed of upon the surface, or by burial, or by burning, according to the proximity of dwellings and other conditions. When applied to objects not removable, washing, scraping, dusting, and other processes are resorted to, the resultant refuse being destroyed. These are merely parts of the multifarious methods of cleansing, which should be adopted always in addition, or in preference, to the mere temporary measures resorted to by the use of chemicals for the purpose of treating organic decomposing matters. It is this process of chemical treatment of decomposing refuse that popularly and fallaciously passes under the name of disinfection. This is fostered by the popular habit of styling many and varied substances *disinfectants,* which have not the slightest title to the name.

The object of disinfection is of course to destroy the germs of disease, but unfortunately three groups or agents are usually confused together under this single heading, *viz.* :—

1. *Antiseptics, i.e.,* substances which arrest the action of microbes but do not destroy them, such as boracic acid.

2. *Deodorants, i.e.,* substances which counteract disagreeable odours such as charcoal, toilet vinegar and many *so-called* disinfectants.

3. *Disinfectants proper, i.e.,* substances which really destroy germs, such as carbolic acid.

1. *Antiseptics :*—An antiseptic is an agent which prevents decomposition. The application of this group is limited to substances and places where removal or destruction are undesirable, temporarily

or permanently, and its members require the most careful and discriminate employment to be of value in preventing the evil results of infection by disease organisms.

Preservatives are closely allied to antiseptics in their effects upon organic substances, and the preservation of food by physical means such as cold, or exclusion or filtration of air, and by chemical means, such as smoking, salting, and the use of various chemical substances are really antiseptic processes not far removed from the methods of modern surgery.

The word " antiseptic " means prevention of sepsis or decomposition, and the whole army of antiseptics merely act by preventing the growth and development of the microbes which induce this process. They do not destroy them.

2. *Deodorants :*—Decomposition and putrefaction are now well known to be the result of micro-organic life in the beneficent work of resolving organic substances into their innocuous elements. During this transmutation malodorous gases are given off, and *deodorants* act by overpowering, absorbing, or breaking up these gases. They produce little or no effect upon the decomposing substances. Odours are the tell-tales of filth, and simply masking them is a most fallacious remedy and should never be adopted, least of all in the tropics.

3. *Disinfectants Proper :*—Disinfection in the more restricted and accurate sense, implies the destruction of the infection produced by the specific micro-organisms of diseases.

In all the recognised infectious diseases, whether the specific organisms have been found or not, disinfection properly applied constitutes the destruction of the specific infection, and the degree to which this destruction is effectually accomplished can now be accurately measured by experiments upon cultivations of known microbes.

Thus restricted to the destruction of specific infection, the process of disinfection admits of the application of various measures mechanical, natural, physical and chemical. The mechanical means includes the common process of cleansing, but although it is specially important to observe cleanliness in the presence of infection, these means cannot alone be trusted for effectual destruction of disease-producing organisms.

Happily, in addition to the practice of strict cleanliness which removes and destroys microbes we have a large group of other *true* disinfectants which may be classified under the following headings :—

1. Natural Disinfectants.
2. Physical Disinfectants.
3. Chemical Disinfectants.

1. *Natural Disinfectants :*—Fresh air and sunlight are powerful natural disinfectants and will kill most germs.

All living micro-organisms are sooner or later attenuated in their disease-producing activities and finally killed by drying.

Thus the Spirillum of Asiatic Cholera, when dried, dies in from three hours to two days, according to the degree of desiccation : the bacilli of enteric fever, tuberculosis and diphtheria resist drying for a longer time but gradually lose their vitality.

It has been shown that the bacillus of enteric fever is destroyed in from one and one-half to two hours by the direct solar rays, and in five hours by diffuse daylight. The diphtheria bacillus is destroyed by from one-half to one hour's exposure to direct sunlight : while Koch found that the tubercle bacillus is killed by the rays of the sun in from a few minutes to several hours, according to the thickness of the mass exposed.

The influence of drying on the multiplication of bacteria—for none of them develop in a dry state—

is of manifest importance, and it is shown that the maintenance of the habitation and surroundings of the Indian in as dry a state as possible is a stringent sanitary necessity. The frequent airing of bedding and clothing secures the desired dryness : and in addition the oxygen of the air exercises a destructive effect on such organisms as may be harboured in the articles, whilst the agitation to which they are subjected in a strong breeze not only mechanically dislodges and removes a considerable proportion of the adherent microbes but also markedly interferes with the development of certain species.

Nature's disinfectants are, therefore, fresh. air, winds and sunshine.

2. *Physical Disinfectants* :—The physical disinfectants consist of heat in its various forms, *viz.* :—

    A. Fire.
    B. Hot Air.
    C. Boiling.
    D. Steam.

A. Fire :—Destruction by fire is, of course, the most thorough means of disinfection, and it should always be employed for articles of little value. Where possible the material should be soaked in kerosene to ensure complete and ready combustion.

Bazaar dwellings, which are cheap and readily reconstructed, are best disinfected by fire, especially in such diseases as plague, but whenever such action is taken for portable articles, the employment of a closed incinerator is desirable as if destruction by fire is carried out in the open air small unburnt particles carrying infectious material may be scattered by the action of the wind.

It was undoubtedly the purifying influence of the great Fire which freed London from Plague in 1666.

B. Hot Air :—This method of disinfection is now largely discredited as it has been found to be unreliable.

Its advantages are :—(1) It is economical ; (2) an ordinary oven can be used for the purpose in emergencies ; and (3) within certain limits, it does not destroy articles such as furs, leather, india-rubber, and bound books.

Its disadvantages are :—(1) That it has slow and feeble penetrating power. (2) It is likely to stain certain articles. (3) It renders some articles brittle and damages others.

C. Boiling :—One of the best methods of disinfection is boiling. There are few organisms which will stand boiling for a few minutes, and still fewer which will stand a subsequent washing in soap and hot water.

The disadvantage of boiling is that it is apt to fix albuminous stains, and if it be employed, *e.g.*, for clothes, these must first be soaked in cold water, washed with soap or soda, and then boiled for half an hour. The water in which they have been soaked and washed must also be disinfected by boiling.

D. Steam :—Applied in special forms of apparatus, steam is now utilized in various parts of India for disinfecting bedding and clothing. Its superiority over hot air is due to the following reasons :—

1. The large amount of latent heat in steam. Steam in contact with the article to be disinfected, which is at a lower temperature than the steam, undergoes condensation, and in the process parts with its latent heat, thus increasing the temperature of the article. When steam condenses into water, it shrinks to $\frac{1}{1200}$ of its bulk and gives off latent heat sufficient to raise its temperature to 300°F. Hot dry air, on the other hand, has no latent heat, but, on the contrary, has its temperature reduced, owing to the fact that before the temperature of the article can be sufficiently raised, any moisture it contains

must be evaporated, and the process of evaporation uses up a certain quantity of heat.

2. Its high penetrative power. The condensation of steam is accompanied by a diminution in volume, and the creation of a partial vacuum in the interstices of the article under disinfection. To fill up this vacuum, more steam rapidly presses forward, and, in its turn, undergoes a like process, until every part of the article is thoroughly penetrated by the steam. The penetration of hot dry air, on the contrary, depends entirely on the processes of conduction and convection, and dry air is a slow conductor of heat. Further, the diminution in volume of hot dry air, by loss of heat, is trifling compared to that produced in the condensation of steam.

3. A lower temperature continued for a shorter time suffices for adequate disinfection.

4. There is less risk of fire and of injury to most fabrics and materials.

The various types of apparatus used for disinfecting by steam are classified, as follows :—

1. Stoves in which steam without pressure is employed. These are of course cheaper, but, as the temperature of the steam does not exceed 100 degrees C., less efficient than—

2. Those in which steam at low pressure (2, 3 or 5 pounds per square inch) is used. Although the temperature of 110 degrees C., which can be reached by these stoves, is generally sufficient, a higher temperature can never be employed in them. These stoves, though cheaper, are therefore less efficient than—

3. Those in which steam at high pressure (10 pounds and over) can be employed. A temperature of 115 degrees C. to 120 degrees C.—which should not be exceeded—can be obtained in these stoves : and an exposure of articles for from a quarter to half an hour will suffice for their disinfection. The

TH

higher the pressure of the steam, the more rapid the penetration, the less time required for disinfection.

Steam under pressure has not such a deleterious action on articles, with the exception of leather, as dry heat, whilst its penetrating powers are far greater. By 'saturated steam' is meant steam at the temperature at which it condenses, and the temperature of the condensation point rises as the pressure increases. By 'superheated steam' is meant steam at a temperature higher than that at which it can condense : therefore superheated steam has to be cooled down into the state of saturated steam before condensation ensues. If superheated steam is used for disinfection, it loses heat by conduction, and the rise in temperature of the articles treated approximately corresponds to the fall in temperature of the steam. With saturated steam, on the other hand, immediately it is cooled an enormous amount of latent heat is set free by the change in state from the gaseous to the liquid condition, therefore saturated steam is a far more efficient disinfectant than superheated steam. These considerations should always influence the choice of a steam disinfecting apparatus for efficient working.

There are three varieties of disinfecting apparatus in common use in this country, viz. :—

1. The Washington Lyons.
2. The Equifex.
3. The Thresh.

1. *The Washington Lyons Apparatus :*—The apparatus is oval in section, and is usually worked with a pressure of 10 lbs. per square inch in the jacket and 5 lbs. in the chamber, so that the steam in the latter is superheated, a further precaution against condensation. The articles having been introduced and the doors closed and secured, steam is first sent into the jacket so as to heat the contents of the chamber. Steam is next admitted

into the chamber itself, and soon reaches the full pressure required. It is found that penetration is more rapid if the pressure is intermitted once or twice, which is readily effected by turning a cock. Ten to twenty minutes suffice for the penetration of even bulky objects, and at the end of that time the steam is allowed to escape from the chamber, the door is opened, and the articles are removed. Further drying may be effected, if necessary, by leaving the door ajar for a few minutes, and exposing the articles to heat from the jacket.

2. *The Equifex :*—This type is worked with saturated, not superheated steam, at 10 lbs. pressure (239 degrees F.). The chamber consists of a steel cylinder made without steam jacket, so as to avoid risk of superheating. The cylinder is lagged with non-conducting composition and wood, to reduce loss of heat by radiation, and furnished with separate doors for infected and disinfected articles respectively.

3. *The Thresh Apparatus :*—In this form of apparatus current steam at a temperature a few degrees above 212° and not under pressure is used. The steam at this temperature is obtained by using a saline solution which boils at a higher temperature than water.

The process is continued for about twenty minutes and at the end of this time a current of previously heated air is drawn through the chamber to dry the disinfected articles.

The apparatus is simple, efficient, and has the additional advantage of being cheaper than the other varieties.

3. *Chemical Disinfectants :*—The number of chemical disinfectants on sale by chemists is enormous. They may be divided into :—

    A. Gaseous.
    B. Liquid.
    C. Solid.

A. The principal gaseous disinfectants are burning sulphur, formaldehyde and chlorine.

Burning Sulphur :—The gas produced by burning sulphur has been in use in nearly every part of the world for many years as the most convenient form of gaseous disinfectant. It is essential that all surfaces with which the gas is to come into contact should be thoroughly damped as the sulphur only acts in the presence of moisture.

Rolled sulphur or the specially prepared candles,. should be used, as powdered sulphur is frequently impure. Two pounds of sulphur are required for each 1,000 cubic feet of space.

Sulphur fumigation, although it was held in high repute in the 16th and 17th centuries, and has been regarded as an antidote against Plague since the time of Hippocrates, has been found to be very uncertain in its action and useless for plague-infected houses in India. Its use has therefore been abandoned in most places. Sulphur is still, however,. the official disinfectant in many European countries, and if fumigation by its means is properly carried out in an air-tight room, it is certainly efficacious in cases of small-pox, cholera, and relapsing fever.

Formaldehyde :—This gas liberated from tablets by heating in some special form of lamp, has largely replaced sulphur of recent years.

It may be readily generated by pouring formalin on permanganate of potash.

The proportion of the two substances which gives the best results and the driest residue is two parts of formalin to one part of permanganate. The method is effective, simple, rapid, and, by virtue of the inexpensive apparatus required, preferable to the older and more cumbersome methods. For a space of 2,000 cubic feet, 10 ounces of the permanganate and one pint of formalin are required, the reagents being mixed or added the one to the other in an ordinary galvanized iron pail. The crystals which are better crushed, are put in first, and then the formalin is poured on them. There is time for the operator to withdraw, and the period of disinfection should be six hours. Heat and moisture are essential for efficient disinfection. From 60 to 70 degrees F. is a proper temperature, while it is well to render the air of the room moist in a dry country.

At the Bombay Medical Congress the Lingner apparatus was highly spoken of on account of its reliability and the certainty with which all pathogenic germs are destroyed. It is economical to use, and time is economised, as a room 3,500 cubic feet in capacity can be sprayed with it in half an hour. Owing to the rapidity of discharge of the disinfecting vapour, it is unnecessary to go to the trouble of stopping up every crevice in the room to prevent loss of the vapour. This is a point of considerable importance in many Indian houses where it is impossible to render a room perfectly air-tight.

This apparatus was used in Astrachan during the last epidemic of Plague in that town, and it is stated that some 315 rooms and their contents were disinfected by means of this apparatus, and it was found unnecessary to undertake any further disinfection owing to the complete extinction of the disease.

Chlorine :—This element which is prepared by adding an acid to bleaching powder, is a useful disinfectant, but is a powerful bleaching agent, and should only be used where the other two gases mentioned are not available. Half a pound of acid will liberate the gas from two pounds of chloride of lime.

It should be borne in mind that the *air* of an infected room can be readily changed, and therefore does not require disinfection. Moreover, microbes have weight and do not remain in the air, but sink on the floors, walls and furniture, so our attention should be devoted to them.

B. Liquid Disinfectants :—There are seven substances or groups of substances in common use in India as liquid disinfectants, *viz.* :—

1. *Perchloride of Mercury or Corrosive Sublimate* in solutions of various strengths :—It has the advantage of being a most powerful disinfectant and cheap. Its disadvantages are that it is very poisonous to man but slightly so to insects, it corrodes metals and its solution has neither colour nor smell.

2. *Cyanide of Mercury* :—This substance is quite as powerful a disinfectant as corrosive sublimate. It has the advantage of not being rendered inert by coming in contact with albumen and is therefore well adapted for use with mud floors smeared with cow-dung. Unfortunately it is five times as expensive as perchloride of mercury and goes no further.

3. *Carbolic Acid* :—This is a good disinfectant, but expensive and poisonous. It has now been largely replaced by cheaper and less poisonous products of coal tar.

4. *Saponified Cresol* :—This is the preparation officially adopted by the Military Department out of a great mass of tar oils now on the market. It is cheaper and more efficient than carbolic acid and not nearly so poisonous.

5. *Formalin* :—This has an irritant odour, but is harmless to colours and metal work with the exception of iron. It is a fairly cheap, rapid and reliable disinfectant in one per cent. solution.

The bulk of the infection of phthisis is communicated in the home and the work-room. During the lifetime of a phthisical patient it is necessary to take measures to minimise the risk of infection to others from this disease, the more so when such a patient shares a single room, in a crowded tenement, with others.   In such cases, a systematic disinfection of the rooms occupied by the patients is required at least once a week.

It is claimed for Izal that it is eminently suited for a room in which a phthisis case exists, because it is non-poisonous, it gives off an odour which is not irritating to the sensitive breathing organs of the sufferers, it does not injure textile articles to which it is applied, and its germicidal properties are not lessened even after prolonged exposure. The method of employing it is to use a solution of 1 in 50 for sputum, and 1 in 100 for spraying on the walls and floors of rooms.   Some sort of systematic disinfection of rooms occupied by consumptive patients with a coal tar disinfectant should be insisted on by Indian Municipalities.

7.   *Phenyle* :—This popular disinfectant is a feeble disinfectant compared with other tar oils as it is little more powerful than carbolic acid.

C. *Solid Disinfectants* :—We shall only refer to five substances under this heading, *viz.* : (1) Lime, (2) Chloride of Lime, (3) Permanganate of Potash, (4) Ferrous Sulphate, (5) Soap.

1.   *Lime* :—Freshly burnt lime is a cheap and useful germicide. In the form of whitewash it is a disinfectant which plays a most useful part in our Indian life.   It is important to see that lime used for disinfecting purposes is fresh, as if stored for any length of time the action of the air converts a large amount of it into chalk which has no germicidal properties whatever.

Some authorities have found that ordinary whitewashing destroyed all micro-organisms except those of anthrax (or splenic fever) and tuberculosis.

Prior to the application of whitewash, the surface should be well scraped as we should aim at the removal of bacterial life from our houses rather than its burial even underneath a germicide.

2. *Chloride of Lime :*—Bleaching powder is a powerful but disagreeable deodorant, and a disinfectant of considerable power when fresh. It consists of lime saturated with chlorine, and is of very unstable composition. It corrodes metals and blocks drains.

It used to be largely *misused* to hide offensive odours. Its chief legitimate use in India is to keep off flies, but for this purpose as it keeps very badly in this country crude petroleum is much better.

3. *Permanganate of Potassium :*—This is a powerful disinfectant in five per cent. solution, but, as generally used, in less than half per cent. solution it is merely a deodorant. Even when prepared in strong solutions it has three disadvantages :—(*a*) It is expensive. (*b*) It stains fabrics. (*c*) It is too easily reduced to an inert form. Its use in the disinfection of wells has already been alluded to.

4. *Ferrous Sulphate :*—Green copperas acts mainly by what is called its reducing action, a process in which it absorbs oxygen. It is a feeble disinfectant, unless used in great strength (20 to 30 per cent.), but it is a good deodorant, absorbing ammonia and sulphuretted hydrogen. In practice it is suitable only for excreta, as it stains badly, and tends to form iron moulds.

5. *Soap :*—Common soap must be regarded as one of the most generally useful of the chemical disinfectants and a most powerful agent against the germs of disease.

The alkali in ordinary household soap not only actually destroys germs, but also tends to dissolve the outer covering of their spores or seeds. It also washes away the greasy materials which frequently protect bacteria from the action of the great natural disinfectants, sunlight and oxygen, and is therefore a very valuable purifier. There is no doubt that one of the great reasons of the healthiness of the Anglo-Saxon race is its firm belief in the gospel of soap.

So much for the property of disinfectants generally. We now turn to the practical application of disinfectants in India.

When a case of infectious disease occurs in the absence of a competent medical adviser, the following simple rules should be observed :—

1. Whenever a steam disinfector is available all articles of bedding, carpets, hanging, etc., which are not likely to be injured by steam, should be sent to the disinfecting station.

2. When a steam disinfector is not available, cotton and linen articles should be boiled for half an hour. Blankets and other woollen articles and coir fibre should be soaked for two hours in Izal solution. Cloth articles should be sprayed with a five per cent. solution of pure carbolic acid in water and exposed to the sun for three or four days. Leather articles should be sponged with one per cent. formalin solution.

3. Feeding and cooking utensils should be boiled for 15 minutes. Immersion in a 20 per cent. *hot* solution of washing soda suffices, however, for most infectious diseases, but it will not serve in cases of infection by the *tubercle bacillus*. Table knives, mounted forks and similar articles which are damaged by high temperatures should be soaked for two hours in a one per cent. solution of formalin.

4. The walls of the rooms occupied by the patient should be scraped and re-limewashed.

5. Furniture, floors and woodwork should be scrubbed with hot water and soap.

6. Earthen floors should be saturated with a disinfectant preparation, either a solution of mercuric chloride, 1 part in 1,000 of water, or kerosene emulsion with cyanide will serve.

7. The woodwork of the bathroom or latrine used by the patient should be scrubbed with mercuric chloride solution and the floor swabbed with the same solution.

If no disinfectants are available, boil everything which can be boiled, for half an hour.

Scrub everything, which can be scrubbed, with hot water and soap, and expose everything else in the sun for a week.

It is often a wise precaution to disinfect any adjacent well by adding two ounces of quicklime or a drachm and a half of permanganate of potassium to each gallon of water which it contains. In adding the solution of permanganate of potassium or emulsion of lime care should be taken to wet each part of the well. The formula for calculating the amount of lime necessary to disinfect a well is :—(Diameter of well in feet) $2 \times$ (Depth of water in well in feet) = Number of pounds of lime required. The answer to the same formula divided by ten will give approximately the number of ounces of permanganate of potassium required.

The Destruction of Insects.

It must be remembered that not only invisible microbes but visible insects, as has been amply demonstrated in the last chapter, are transmitters of disease, and war must therefore be waged against them.

Now, good disinfectants are not necessarily good insecticides as, for example, mercuric chloride, which, although it is one of the most powerful of all disinfectants, has little influence on insect life.

This was conclusively proved at Bombay by placing guinea-pigs from which all fleas had been previously removed in rooms which had been recently disinfected by means of this chemical. After a few hours, the bodies of these guinea-pigs were covered with fleas derived from the rooms. A recent laboratory experiment has also shown that fleas will emerge unscathed from an exposure of ten minutes in an acid solution of corrosive sublimate of such a powerful strength as 1 in 500. Moreover, it has been found by that, that the disinfecting action of this chemical is considerably neutralised by organic matter on floors and walls and specially in the case of the mud floors of native huts and houses which are smeared with cow-dung.

The best insecticides are :—

1. Pesterine.
2. Kerosene Oil Emulsion.
3. Kerosene Oil and Cyanide of Mercury Emulsion.
4. Petrol.
5. Saponified cresols, such as Cyllin, Hycol, Izal, etc.
6. Sulphur Dioxide Gas.
7. Formaldehyde.

The three last mentioned have already been dealt with. The first four require, however, brief special mention.

For general purposes the gaseous disinfectants should be used chiefly as insecticides. For efficient use as disinfectants the rooms to which they are applied should be carefully sealed up, and this is a very difficult procedure with the ordinary Indian room.

In a strength far short of that in which they will destroy bacteria they will, however, act as effective poisons to mosquitoes and other biting flies which survive in nooks and crannies from one year to another.

1. *Pesterine :*—This substance is crude petroleum (fuel oil) and is undoubtedly a powerful insecticide as it instantly kills all fleas, bugs and other insects that come in contact with it. Its method of

application is very simple, as it has only to be brushed on the floors and the walls of rooms to a height of about three feet. It is also a very cheap disinfectant as the cost of treating an averaged-sized room only comes to about ten annas. It is not, however, an elegant preparation, and hence its use in better class houses is open to some objections.

2. *Kerosene Oil Emulsion :*—This emulsion is made according to the following formula :—Common soap three parts ; water 15 parts ; kerosene oil 82 parts.

The soap is dissolved in the water by the aid of heat and the kerosene oil is warmed and gradually stirred into the mixture.

It has been shown that one part in a thousand of this solution will kill fleas in two minutes.

It should ordinarily be used diluted with twenty parts of water.

3. *Kerosene Oil and Cyanide of Mercury :*—This compound consists of two parts of cyanide of mercury added to each hundred parts of kerosene oil emulsion. Cyanide of mercury has already been referred to.

Where cost is not the chief consideration, as is so often the case in the tropics, this compound is an ideal preparation for disinfecting native houses as it is not only an efficient insecticide but a powerful disinfectant.

4. *Petrol :*—This fluid was used with equal parts of cyllin for disinfecting plague-stricken houses in Hongkong. The mixture has to be made up freshly daily as the two ingredients undergo chemical changes producing an inert substance. The emulsion is a powerful insecticide and germicide, but here again the cost is prohibitive.

All things considered, pesterine or kerosene oil emulsion fulfil all requirements.

In concluding this chapter we would insist on the importance of all persons having some knowledge of the why and wherefore of disinfection, so that they may be able to appreciate the importance and difficulty of the procedure.

Large sums of money are annually wasted in this country because municipal authorities, and too often their advisers as well, have failed to understand that the haphazard scattering of expensive chemicals is *not* disinfection but merely a survival of old-world fetishism, whereas *true* disinfection is 'a scientific process with a well-established dogma and elaborate ritual.

CHAPTER XI.

Disposal of the Dead in Hot Countries.

Tombs are the clothes of the dead—a grave but a plain suit, and a rich monument one embroidered.—Fuller.

WHEN it is realised that in India alone the number of deaths annually is over 8,000,000 and that of these over 150,000 die of small-pox, and perhaps another million of infectious diseases, the disposal of the dead is one of the most important matters to be dealt within tropical countries.

Embalming the body was practised in Ancient Egypt, but the process is no longer in favour in Eastern countries.

The ceremonies attending the disposal of the dead in different parts of the world are very curious.

The Wanyamwesis in West Africa carry their dead into the forests to be devoured by beasts of prey and some of the tribes of Guinea cast their deceased relatives and friends into the sea. The Kamtchadales keep dogs to devour their dead as their priests teach that persons consumed by dogs will be masters of fine dogs in the world beyond the grave.

The following methods of the disposal of the dead are adapted by various sects in India :—

1. Burial in its various forms.
2. Cremation.
3. Exposure.

1. *Burial :*—From long established custom, and also for sentimental and religious reasons, both Christians and Mohammedans prefer to bury their dead. Amongst Indian Mussulmans the

practice is more sanitary than amongst Christians, as coffins are not used. Much has been said and written against burial as a method of disposing of the dead, but it has been shown that, if carcases are covered by a foot of suitable earth, the perishable parts disappear inoffensively within twelve months. The efficiency of earth burial varies directly with the depth, and, speaking broadly, it may be said that for every foot of depth below the soil about one year is necessary for resolution. The present practices, however, and even the laws, in temperate climates, are inconsistent with burial sufficiently shallow to permit of the due action of the nitrifying organisms which are found only in the upper layers of the soil. The objects of earth burial are frustrated in Europe by the still prevalent use of metallic or heavy wooden coffins, but this practice happily does not prevail in the tropics.

Cemeteries :—The three chief sanitary considerations to be held in view in the provision of burial-grounds are—(1) Suitable soils and proper elevation of site : (2) suitable position especially with respect to houses and sources of water-supply : (3) sufficient space.

(1) *Soil :*—The objects to be aimed at in burial are—(*a*) Rapid resolution : (*b*) complete oxidation or absorption of the products. Hence the soil of a cemetery should be light, open, porous, and either naturally or artificially drained to a depth of not less than 8 feet, so that air and moisture may pass freely. Loam or sandy mould is about the best soil : clay is difficult to drain, retards decomposition by excluding air and moisture, and either retains the products of decomposition or allows them to escape through fissures. A loose stony soil allows gases to escape too freely.

(2) *Position :*—It is desirable that burial-grounds should not closely adjoin dwellings. While convenient of access, they should, therefore, be placed

outside the limits of probable future buildings. The surface should not be grassed. Cemeteries should not be placed on elevated ground whence the natural drainage may find its way to dwellings below or contaminate a water-supply. For obvious reasons, lands liable to floods, or encroachment by streams or by the sea, are unsuitable.

(3) *Space Required :*—It is usually estimated that an acre of ground is a minimum allowance for a population of a thousand persons for fifty years.

In India bodies should be buried deep enough to prevent jackals, pariah dogs, and other animals, from digging them up and feeding upon them. Heavy flat stones may have to be placed under the surface of the ground to prevent this, or bodies buried in a sort of vault built of stones or bricks. This procedure, of course, delays decomposition, but is much more sanitary and seemly than having the body dug up by these foul animals.

Cemeteries require frequent inspection to prevent such desecration of the dead and the resulting danger to the public health.

There appears to be no doubt that overcrowded cemeteries, such as are very common in the tropics, exercise a bad effect on the health of the communities in the vicinity.

This prejudicial effect is exercised in one of the following ways :—

(1) Contamination of the air by effluvia.

(2) Contamination of neighbouring local water by product of decomposition.

(3) Contamination of wells by specific micro-organisms of disease.

2. *Cremation :*—This method as practised in Western Countries, and in the crematorium for Europeans recently established in Calcutta, is unquestionably the best method of disposal, as in a crematorium of modern construction, a body of average weight is reduced to about 3 pounds of

inorganic ash within two hours.   The fuel employed
is coke, coal, or gas.   In either case a ventilating
shaft with a fire at its base through which the foul
gases and smoke pass from the burning body before
discharge into the air, is necessary.   The chief
objections to cremation are :—(1) That the soil is
deprived of the organic matter that would otherwise
be returned to it : (2) that it involves an unnecessary
waste of the world's limited stock of combined
nitrogen :   and   (3)   that   the   impossibility   of
exhumation may increase the facilities for concealing
homicide.   The first two objections have no great
weight, since little attempt is made to utilize burial-
grounds for cultivation.   The last is, however,
more serious and can only be met by insisting on
the production of a death certificate from a quali-
fied medical practitioner in every case.   The discovery of organic disease, however, does not necessarily exclude the possibility of foul play, and it
must be remembered that only the metallic poisons
such as arsenic and copper can be recovered from
ashes.

As practised by the poorer classes of Hindus,
however, cremation is by no means a good plan of
disposal of the dead.   Fuel is expensive, and very
often the dead Hindu is taken to the burning *ghat*
and his face merely burned with fire : the body is
not burnt thoroughly because of the poverty of
the relatives or the greed or dishonesty of the
people paid to carry out the cremation.

The partially charred body is usually thrown
into a river.   If the deceased has died of a disease
such as cholera, the danger to riparian villages
and towns is obvious.

3.   *Exposure :*—In some parts of the tropical
world bodies are simply exposed to the elements,
and their ultimate disposal left to scavenging birds.
The *Dakhmas*, or towers of silence, of the Parsees
are looked on with something like horror by Western

people ; but they are far from being insanitary, and have never been shown to spread infection.

The platform on which the dead are laid is lined with marble or concrete, and channels are provided for the collection and disposal of fluids which may escape from the bodies.

The corpses are picked clear of flesh in a period ranging from a few hours to a week.

The dry bones are then placed in a large pit, where they gradually undergo resolution into a fine impalpable powder.

This method, though contrary to European and even most Oriental sentiment, is well adapted to the tropics, as it is rapid and effectual.

The favourite method of Eastern criminals of disposing of the bodies of their victims is to throw them down a well—preferably, of course, one not in use. Dead bodies of animals are frequently disposed of in the same way, but more often they are deposited on the village refuse-heap, producing one of the most offensive of many insanitary abominations to be seen in the vicinity of tropical towns.

All dead bodies of animals should be burnt or covered with quicklime and buried.

CHAPTER XII.

THE CLIMATE OF THE TROPICS.

" It is probably much more possible for white men to colonize a tropical country than is imagined, especially if the colony was so organised that sanitary laws could be enforced from the first."—Meridith Townsend's Asia and Europe.

THE question of colonization of the tropics is now being seriously discussed, not only by physicians but by statesmen, in every quarter of the globe, and the present trend of thought is indicated by the above quotation.

The present day distribution of civilization supports the view that tropical or sub-tropical regions are unsuited to the higher developments of civilization. Our most progressive communities are located in temperate regions, and any invasions of the tropical or semi-tropical zones by representatives of northern civilizations have either suffered rapid decline or have been kept vigorous only by constant reinforcements from their source.

However, this superiority of the colder latitudes as a place for human development has not always existed. Almost without exception, the parent sources of human progress have been in tropical, or at least in sub-tropical countries. Mesopotamia, Egypt, and Asia Minor, all represent sites of apparently original civilisation, and are located well within the warmer zones. The mysterious relics of Central America and Mexico on the one hand, and of Peru on the other, are so situated. It is true that in this latter case the altitude is such as to change climatic condition : but there is evidence to show that marked elevation has taken place comparatively recently, and all the more ancient remains in this region actually antedate this elevation.

If, then, the tropics, originally the source of human culture, have been incapable of maintaining it, some change in condition must be responsible. The probable explanation lies in the spreading of the peculiarly tropical diseases ; due to the increased exchange of people and products so characteristic of later years. The decline of Greece and Rome have been ascribed to the introduction of malaria along with African slaves, and in America we have even better-established instances of this sort. Torquemada, speaking of Yucatan, itself a site of pre-historic civilization, says : " Men die of pure old age, for there are none of those infirmities that exist in other lands ; and if there are slight infirmities, the heat destroys them and so there is no need of a physician there." But with the coming of the white man and the negro, and their alien diseases, conditions changed until Southern Mexico and Central America became notorious as hot-beds of tropical fevers.

With progress in sanitary science, this position of the warmer latitudes may undergo another alteration, and already in Cuba and Panama the possibility of mastery over these diseases has been shown.

THE CLIMATES OF THE TROPICS.

The tropical zone, which embraces nearly half the earth's surface, has been bounded—

1. By the Tropics of Cancer and Capricorn, latitude 23° 5' north and south.
2. By the mean annual isotherms of 68°.
3. By the polar margins of the trade winds.

The region has been divided into three belts, *viz.* :

1. The equatorial belt.
2. The trade wind belt.
3. The monsoon belt.

The dominant characteristic of all tropical climates is the regularity in the occurrence of the ordinary weather phenomena.

They lack the proverbial changeableness which characterizes the weather of higher latitudes.

In special regions only, and at special seasons, is the regular sequence of weather temporarily interrupted by an occasional tropical cyclone.

The devastation produced by one of these storms often affects the economic condition of the people in the district of its occurrence for many years.

The following points with reference to tropical climates require consideration :—

1. Temperature.
2. Seasons.
3. Barometric pressure.
4. Winds.
5. Rainfall.
6. Storms.
7. Tropical sunlight.
8. Altitude.
9. Physiological effects of tropical sunlight and heat.

1. *Temperature :*—The sun is always well up in the sky. The length of the day and night varies little. Hence the mean temperature is high, it is very uniform over the whole zone, and there is little variation during the year. The mean annual isotherm of 68° is a rational limit at the polar margins of the zone, and the mean annual isotherm of 80° encloses the greater portion of the land areas, as well as much of the tropical oceans. The isotherms are thus far apart. The warmest latitude for the year is not the equator, but north latitude 10°.

2. *The Seasons :*—In a true tropical climate seasons do not exist. The variations in temperature throughout the year are so slight that

the seasons are not classified according to temperature, but depend on rainfall and the prevailing winds. The life of animals and plants, and of man himself in the tropics, is regulated very largely by the rainfall. Agriculture prospers or fails according to the sufficiency and punctual appearance of the rains. After a long dry season, when the rain comes, there is a remarkable sudden awakening of the parched and dusty vegetation ; but where, as frequently occurs, there is abundant moisture throughout the year, a tree may at the same time be carrying buds, blossoms, and ripe fruit.

3. *Barometric Pressure :*—The annual barometric fluctuations are slight, even on the continents. The diurnal variation of the barometer is so regular and so marked that the time of the day can be told within fifteen minutes if the reading of the barometer be known.

4. *Winds :*—There are two conditions which prevail in the tropics :—

(1) Calms.

(2) Trade winds.

(1) *Calms :*—Where the pressure gradients are weakest—is a belt characterized by long periods of complete calm, called by sailors the " doldrums."

(2) *Trade Winds :*—In striking contrast to the doldrums are the easterly trade winds, blowing between the tropical high-pressure belts and the equatorial belt of low pressure. These supply the first belt with a constant flow of warm air, which already contains a large amount of water vapour, evaporated from the oceans by the trade winds. This saturated air needs only a comparatively high temperature to produce condensation, and thus give abundant rainfall.

These winds blow over nearly half the earth's surface, and add greatly to the uniformity of tropical climates. They have long been favourite sailing routes, because of the infrequency of storms, the brightness of their skies, and the freshness of the air, all of which are in pleasant contrast with the muggy and oppressive calms of the equatorial belt.

These winds, called in the rainy season the " monsoons," control the seasonal change of tropical lands.

5. *Rains :*—The most important climatic phenomena of the year in the tropics is the rainy season. Tropical rains are in the main summer rains—*i.e.*, they follow as a general rule soon after the " vertical sun," the rainy season coming when the normal trade winds give way to the equatorial belt of rains or when the summer monsoon sets in.

The tropical rainy season is by no means a period of continuous rains, falling steadily day and night, week after week. The mornings are often fine and the air comparatively bracing, so that the season is during the " rains " at some fashionable places, such as Poona, etc.

6. *Storms :*—Local thunderstorms are frequent in the humid portions of the tropics. In Northern India hailstorms of great violence occur, and persons have been killed by them.

7. *Tropical Sunlight :*—The intensity of the light from tropical skies is trying to new-comers. The intense sunlight, together with the reflection from the ground, increases the general dazzling glare, and necessitates protection of some sort. The use of blue, smoked, or neutral tinted glasses is recommended to prevent glare and dust affecting the eyes. The use of sun spectacles also keeps the excessive feeling of heat from striking one so forcibly. The far-famed deep blue of the tropical sky is much exaggerated. During much of the time smoke, dust, and water vapour give the sky a pale, whitish appearance. The beauties of the tropical sunrise and sunset and of the tropical night have, however, *not* been over-rated. Twilight within the

tropics is shorter than in higher latitudes, but the
coming on of night is less sudden than is generally
assumed.

It is obvious that sunlight in equatorial and sub-
equatorial regions will be more potent than that of
more temperate zones ; for not only does the perpendicular course of the rays make the intervening
protective layer of the atmosphere relatively
thinner, but it also results in a greater intensity of
illumination for any exposed area. The actual
occurrence of this greater power is readily shown by
measurement of the chemical activity of tropical
sunlight as compared with that of colder latitudes,
and, possibly as a result of such experiments, the
idea has been prevalent that the harmful effect of
sunlight is primarily due to the chemically active
rays. It was because of this idea that orange-
coloured underwear was tried on soldiers in the
Philippines, an experiment which was unsuccessful.
The other view, that it is the infra-red heat rays
that are most powerful for harm, is held by Aron,
and he advances experimental evidence in its
support.

His most interesting experiments were obtained
with apes. In these the superficial temperature is
normally $\frac{1}{2}°$ to $1°$ lower than the deep temperature,
but on exposure, if only for a few minutes, to sunlight, this relation became reversed ; if exposed
long enough to cause death—which takes only a
short time for these animals—the superficial temperature exceeded the deep by $1\frac{1}{2}°$. Shaving the
animals emphasized these differences, and shortened
the fatal period markedly. If a current of air was
kept in circulation over the exposed animal, however, it became capable of resisting the action of
sunlight indefinitely. Conclusive evidence against
the supposed direct action of the chemically active
or actinic rays on the brain was afforded by a
simple experiment. An ape was encased in a

double-walled box in such a way as to expose its head only to sunlight.   Absolutely no harm resulted to the animal, although a superficial scalp temperature of 116·5°F. was attained.

The effect of sunlight on human beings was also studied.   The normal human superficial temperature was found to range from 90° to 92°F., but on exposure to sunlight this rose rapidly to 96° and 97°F. Further exposure resulted, not in a further rise, but in an actual drop of ½° or 1°, coinciding more or less closely with the appearance of perspiration. With muscular exertion this fall was both greater and more rapid.   In general, coloured individuals did not attain as high superficial temperatures as did the white, although, from the greater absorptive powers of pigmented skin, the reverse would be expected.   This is held to be due to the earlier onset of perspiration, possibly occasioned in part by the greater absorption.   The coloured individuals have an advantage in their ability to go uncovered without any danger of the painful irritation of the skin due to the tropical sun to which Europeans are so subject.

We think, however, that the pigment cells form a protective filter screen for the true skin, and protect the tissues underneath.   Although absorption of heat may be greater for coloured skins, it is counterbalanced by the larger and more numerous sweatglands which extract heat by evaporation.

The chief importance of Aron's work lies in its overthrow of the " actinic theory " of solar action. It is obvious that this more correct knowledge of the effect of the sun's rays makes possible the adoption or rational means of protection against them, and so affords an additional step towards increasing the habitability of the tropics for races of northern origin.

8. *Altitude* :—Within the tropics altitude is chiefly important because of its effect in tempering

the heat of the lowlands, especially at night. If tropical mountains are high enough, they carry snow the year round, even on the equator, and the zones of vegetation may range from the densest tropical forest at the base to snow on the summits. The highlands and mountains within the tropics are thus often sharply contrasted with the lowlands, and offer more agreeable and more healthful conditions for European settlement. The climate of many tropical plateaus and mountains has been happily described as a " perpetual spring."

9. *Physiological Effects :*—The continuous moist heat of the tropics renders the tropical resident very sensitive to slight temperature changes, which are readily borne in drier climates. A fall of the thermometer to within a few degrees of 70° seems to some tropical natives almost unbearable cold, and certain African tribes sleep on clay banks heated inside by fires, although the mean temperature of the coldest month is over 70°. The tonic effect of a cold winter is lacking, and after prolonged residence energetic physical and mental action is often difficult, and not infrequently distasteful.

CHAPTER XIII.

The Hygiene of Camps in the Tropics.

*" For the Lord thy God walketh in the midst of thy camp ....
therefore shall thy camp be holy ; that He see no unclean thing in
thee and turn away from thee.—(Book of Deuteronomy, Chapter
XXIII, v. 14).*

NEARLY four thousand years ago there was a
great general and his name was Moses.
He passed many years of his life in the supreme
command of great camps in a tropical country
and it must have soon become apparent to him
that unless strict sanitary legislation was enforced
the troops under his command and their followers
would have been decimated by the various diseases
which dog the footsteps of every great host on the
line of march.

He accordingly published the general order which
has been selected as—so to speak—the text of this
chapter.

His device was successful for we know that his
great following passed through its long years of a
nomadic existence singularly free from epidemic
disease. We cannot copy him by making our
sanitary rules the ritual of a great faith, but we
can adopt the first principle of Moses and start
our camp with clear orders on sanitary subjects
and a definite sanitary *bandobust*.

The following points require consideration with
reference to camps :—

1. Sites.
2. Tents.
3. Water-supply.
4. Cooking arrange-
   ments.
5. Latrines and
   urinals.
6. Disposal of refuse.
7. Camp Incinerators.
8. Sunstroke.

9. Goat's milk and Malta Fever.
10. Flies in Camp.

1. *Sites.*—The site for a camp or bivouac should, if possible, be on a gentle slope to facilitate drainage.

The vicinity of large woods with undergrowth, marshes, paddy fields, or recently ploughed land ought to be avoided as mosquitoes and biting flies are likely to be plentiful in such localities.

Should it, however, become necessary to encamp near ground likely to be infested by mosquitoes the camp should be pitched to the windward of a belt of trees or a screen of some kind with a view to intercepting the mosquito in her flight.

Ravines and water-courses are dangerous sites as a sudden fall of rain may convert them into large streams.

Previously occupied ground should always be avoided, as the soil must have been contaminated and polluted to a greater or less extent, and there is always a possibility that " carriers " of disease may have been present infecting the vicinity with the microbes of enteric or some other disease.

Old camping grounds can be readily recognised by the raised mounds marking the site of the latrines.

An ideal site would be a gentle slope free from any great irregularities of surface, situated near the summit of rising ground on a sandy or gravel soil and adjacent to a mountain stream which has no huts or villages on its banks.

Camping grounds conforming to most of the essential requirements are to be found in most parts of India.

2. *Tents.*—When possible a camp should always be arranged as if for permanent occupation. In regular standing camps it is especially desirable to provide ·sufficient space for the moving of tents so as to cleanse and purify the ground underneath each tent at frequent intervals. All tent flies are to be

looped up the first thing every morning and the tents should be struck periodically, and the ground underneath well swept and left exposed to the sun and air for some hours. The interval between the striking of tents should not exceed fourteen days, and it is desirable that a second site should be available to which the tents can be moved if desired. Tent doors should always face the prevailing wind.

Trenches should always be made round tents to receive rainwater and channels cut to carry off this water and provide surface drainage.

In malarial districts mosquito nets must be used.

The entire contents of the tent should be spread out in the sun frequently. This is a sanitary precaution which should never be omitted.

3. *Water-supply*.—A good water-supply is essential for a camp in any climate, but in the Tropics, it must never be situated at a considerable distance from it, as the native water-carrier thinks one water as good as another and will bring in a polluted supply most light-heartedly if it saves him the least trouble to do so.

All water receptacles should be thoroughly cleaned out daily with a solution of permanganate of potash made by adding one teaspoonful of the crystals to three gallons of water. If after rinsing the solution comes out discoloured it shows that cleansing was necessary. Repeat the process till the water retains its pink colour unaltered.

All vessels for storing water in camp must be kept carefully covered and provided with taps. Drinking direct from taps or direct from storing vessels of any kind, should be dealt with very severely.

Where possible separate intakes for water-supply should be provided for Europeans and camp followers.

Drinking places for animals and wash places should always be allocated lower down stream than these intakes. Horses and animals should be watered from troughs where possible to avoid unnecessary fouling of streams.

The principles affecting water-supplies generally which have been laid down in Chapter IV apply, of course, where practicable to camp supplies.

A simple method of sterilizing any water which it might be dangerous to drink is as follows :—

(a) Take a teaspoonful of bleaching powder (chloride of lime) (containing about $\frac{1}{3}$ available chlorine) and remove the excess of powder by rolling a pencil, etc., along the top of the spoon.

(b) Mix the bleaching powder in a cupful of water, making sure that all lumps are thoroughly broken up, and then add three more cupfuls of water to the solution.

(c) Stir up the mixture, allow it to stand for a few seconds to let any particles settle (this stock solution, if kept tightly stoppered, may be used for 4 or 5 days) and add *one teaspoonful* of this milky solution to 2 gallons of the water to be purified. Stir thoroughly and allow to stand for 10 minutes. This will give $\frac{1}{2}$ part of free chlorine to a million parts of water. 1 lb. chloride is sufficient for 66,000 gallons.

Note.—Bleaching powder (chloride of lime) deteriorates rapidly when kept in cardboard packages or exposed to air. If a weak variety only is obtainable then, two teaspoonfuls of the solution should be added to 2 gallons of water.

4. *Cooking Arrangements.*— Camp kitchens should be situated (a) as far away as possible from the latrines, urinals and refuse receptacles, (b) to the windward of the camp, and (c) as near as possible to the water-supply.

Kitchen waste water contains a large amount of grease, and unless specially treated this substance forms a foul scum in water drains which rapidly becomes offensive and always attracts flies.

The following methods of disposal have been found to be good and easily improvised :—

(1) Two kerosene tins of different sizes or a tin and a basket are taken. The inner and smaller tin or the basket acts as a coarse strainer. When a tin is used it has its bottom perforated all over with a nail. When full it is emptied into a refuse tub. The outer and larger tin directs the water over a small pit which acts as a grease trap, and is filled with dried grass, hay, or brushwood, which is burnt and renewed daily. A narrow and shallow trench runs from the small pit into a large soakage pit. If *large* stones are available, the soakage pit should be filled up with them. The spout of the lower tin is easily made by making an inverted V-shaped incision in its side, turning it down and rounding off.

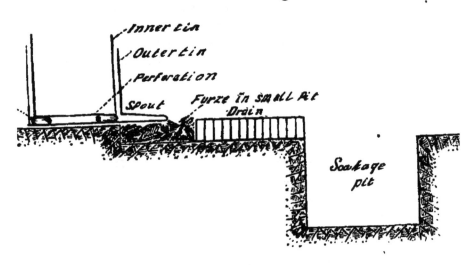

Fig. 45.—METHOD OF DISPOSING OF SULLAGE WATER IN CAMP.

(2) This is simply an adaptation of (1)   When two tins or a tin and a basket are not available, a box is turned upside down over the small pit, a hole is cut out in its bottom, and a piece of perforated tin fitted into the hole.

(3) A grating placed over the soakage pit on which grass, furze or other straining material is placed.   It is not so efficient or cleanly as (1) and (2).

In all the varieties the brushwood or grass used to entangle the grease should be soaked in crude petroleum to keep off flies.   It should be replaced by fresh material and burnt daily.

All food should be kept in covered receptacles and some form of swill tub devised.   Refuse should be sprinkled with petroleum to keep off flies and transported to the camp crematory as soon as possible.   All water for washing up should be boiled and only well baked sand, wood ashes or bathbrick used for cleaning utensils.   The use of *mutti* should be prohibited as it may swarm with microbes.

5.   *Latrines and Urinals.*—These should be placed to the leeward of the camp and one hundred yards from the nearest tent.   They must never be dug in nullahs whence the excreta may be washed into a water-supply by heavy tropical rains.

Each trench should be 3 ft. long 1 ft. wide, and 1 ft. deep, the interspace between each trench being 2½ ft. ; men should use these trenches straddlewise, and at once cover up their deposit with earth. Five trenches will suffice for 100 men for one day ; they should then be filled in with earth.

Trenches required for the second day of occupation will be dug in the spaces between the first row of trenches.

The method of preparing the short trench latrine is shown in Fig. 46.

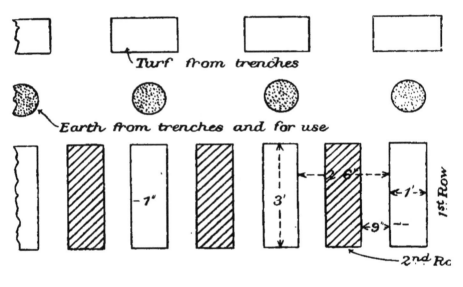

Fig. 46.—SHALLOW TRENCH LATRINE.

If the area of ground be limited the depth of the short trench may be increased to 2 feet ; these deeper trenches should last 2 days.

In exceptional cases deep latrines may be necessary, they should be constructed to seat 5 per cent. of the occupants of the camp one yard per man being allowed.　This type of latrine is shown in Fig. 47.

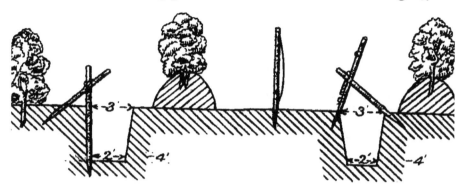

Fig. 47.—DEEP TRENCH LATRINE.

Empty kerosene oil tins are excellent substitutes for trenches and should always be adopted instead of them in a standing camp in the Tropics as they permit of the wet system of conservancy.

Means for preventing paper being blown about the camp must also be devised.　The issue of a little string will generally be all that is necessary for unused paper, but unfortunately it is generally the used paper which is found flying about.

The best type of camp urinal, Fig. 48, consists of shallow trenches leading into pits filled with large stones.　The men urinate into the trenches and the urine flows into the pit and soaks into the ground.

Two trenches about 6 feet long leading to a circular pit 3 feet deep and two feet in diameter are sufficient for a battalion.

The trenches last for a day or two.　When foul it is only necessary to dig fresh trenches leading to the same pit, as the latter will last for about a fortnight.

· The new trenches should move round the pit like the hands of a watch.

Camp Latrines should be marked by white-washed posts and well lighted.　Where camps are likely to be occupied for any length of time the reception of excreta in receptacles and disposal by incineration should be adopted.

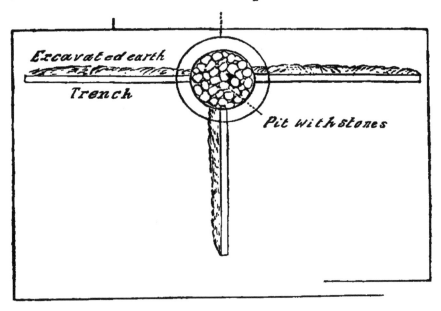

Excavated earth

Trench

Pit with stones

Fig. 48.—SIMPLE FORM OF CAMP URINAL.

Two or three inches of a disinfectant solution are placed in each receptacles.

This plan obviates the plague of flies which is almost unavoidable when trenches are used in hot weather.

6. *Disposal of Refuse.*—All waste food-stuffs, stable litter, and other refuse must be burnt.

An excellent type of destructor is prepared as follows :—

Dig a circular pit, 3 feet deep and 15 feet in diameter. Cover the botom with loose stones to a depth of 14 inches. Build a wall round the pit to the height of one foot above the original ground level, and pack the excavated earth against it so as to form a sloping approach and to prevent surface water gaining access to the pit. Build a pyramid

of large stones 4 to 5 feet high in the centre, to
provide central draught and steady fire. Start a
wood fire and as soon as the stones become hot,
throw in refuse, garbage, &c. The liquid portions
disappear and the solid portions are dried and are
soon reduced to ashes.

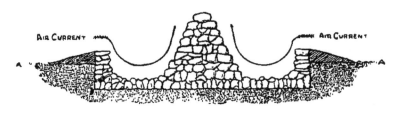

Fig. 49.—AMERICAN INCINERATOR—VERTICAL SECTION.
A. A.—GROUND LEVEL.

Another pattern devised by Lieutenant-Colonel
R. Caldwell, R.A.M.C., has much to recommend it.
It consists of two short trenches about the depth
of those of an ordinary camp kitchen. These
trenches intersect each other at right angles, and a
chimney made of sods of earth is built over the
angles of intersection. A few pieces of iron hooping
support the chimney where it crosses the trenches.

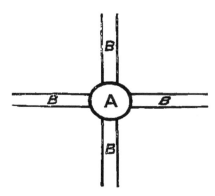

Fig. 50.—CALDWELL'S INCINERATOR.
A—CHIMNEY—BB—TRENCHES.

A fire is lighted at the base of the chimney and
the rubbish thrown down the top. The addition

of a little turpentine or kerosene oil to the rubbish helps matters immensely. There is a fair draught through the trenches and up the chimney, and if the rubbish is put on with ordinary care the fire generally burns itself out.

7. *Camp Incinerator.*—Colonel B. Skinner, M.V.O., has devised a camp incinerator which can be utilised for the disposal of all animal excreta.

This incinerator consists of :—

(1) A clay dome about 2½ to 3 feet in diameter and not more that 3 feet in height.

(2) Iron bars four feet in length to form a grating on which the fuel is placed. About 8 or 9 of these bars are required.

(3) Four ventilators for draught.

The soil adjoining most camps in India can readily be formed into rough clay bricks to form the walls of the dome.

The wall is built in four sections to a height of about nine inches, the bars are then laid on the sections and the dome completed to the prescribed height of not more than three feet.

The bars project from the side so that they can be readily removed to the next camping ground when the camp is vacated.

The construction will be readily understood from Figs. 49—52 and which show the elevation and plan of the incinerator.

Two sweepers should be able to build an incinerator of this type in about one hour.

The incinerator is started working by placing litter, leaves, grass or any combustible material on the bars and setting light to it.

When the furnace is working the dejecta should be placed on the top of the blazing or smouldering material.

ELEVATION.

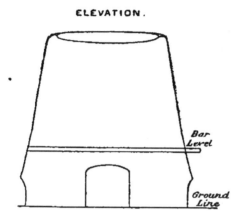

Fig. 51.—CAMP INCINERATOR.

For the adoption of this principle all excreta must be received in pans which may be improvised from kerosene oil tins if necessary.

PLAN

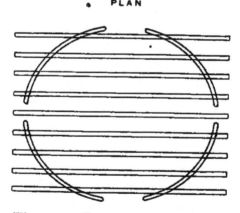

Fig. 52.—CAMP INCINERATOR.

This method of disposal has the advantage of getting rid of not only dangerous human excreta but also stable litter and rubbish which form breeding grounds for flies.

8. *Sunstroke.*—This condition in a mild or severe form has been the cause of much loss of service during hot weather marches in this country. Medical men are not quite agreed as to the cause of the condition. No fewer than four theories as to the cause of sunstroke have their adherents. Some authorities hold that it is due to what are called the actinic rays of the sun which can pierce through anything except a layer of colour which acts as a filter. The colour which keeps out these rays is orange red, and it is recommended that all helmets should be lined with a piece of orange flannel and a pad of the same material worn along the spinal column.

It must be remembered that alcohol is distinctly conducive to sunstroke, and it should therefore never be partaken of when on the march.

The classical symptoms of an acute case are sudden insensibility with flushed face and convulsions, but there are many degrees far short of this in which the man only turns pale and faints or complains of giddiness or dimness of vision.

The treatment of the condition is simply to place the patient on his back in the shade, loosen his clothing, and pour cold water over his head until medical advice can be obtained.

9. *Goats' milk and Malta Fever.*—Whilst in camp, many persons, on account of the difficulty of obtaining cows' milk, are in the habit of taking goats with them and drinking the milk of those animals, especially with their tea. Goats' milk when used for this purpose is almost invariably milked at the time it is required and served fresh. It is practically never boiled, most people being under the impression that the fact of mixing it with hot tea renders boiling unnecessary. This is a fallacy as the mere act of mixing contaminated milk with hot tea is not sufficient to kill all germs that it may contain. Goats' milk very frequently

contains the germs of a serious disease which is known as· Malta fever. This is ordinarily a disease of goats in the same way that plague is ordinarily a disease of rats, and human beings only suffer from it accidentally. In the case of Malta fever, the channel of infection is the milk of the goat. The reason why this disease is called Malta fever is because it was first detected in Malta where it caused great ravages amongst the British troops stationed there, and where its actual causation was carefully worked out by Sir David Bruce, and the Malta Fever Commission. We now know that it exists practically all over the world in tropical and sub-tropical countries, and it has been discovered in the West Indies, Africa, Egypt, India, China, etc. In India, it is chiefly found in the Punjab, but cases have been recorded in· other parts of the country. The main characteristic of Malta fever is its long duration. It is a prolonged fever, in which the febrile attacks alternate with periods when the patient's temperature is normal or sub-normal, and this alternation of febrile and non-febrile periods may last for many months. For this reason it is sometimes called " *Undulant fever.*" Though few patients die of the disease ; it causes grave anæmia and is associated with profuse sweats, and severe pain in the back and lower limbs. So far as we know at present, no remedy has much effect upon the course of the disease, and quinine is absolutely useless. It is most important, therefore, to prevent infection. From what has been said above as regards the way in which the disease is conveyed, it is obvious that the only safe course is either to give up goats' milk altogether or else to see that it is carefully and thoroughly boiled before use. Of the two alternatives, the authors are disposed to recommend the former, because you can never be absolutely certain, as to the actual boiling of the milk. Moreover, nowadays, when it is possible to obtain excellent unsweetened and un-condensed milk in tins, there is no necessity what-ever to run the risk of using goats' milk. If, how-ever, goats' milk is used, then all the precautions noted under the head of cows' milk in Chapter V should be strictly observed ; everything that has been said as regards the importance of boiling cows' milk in order to prevent the risk of tuber-culosis, applies with equal force to goats' milk and Malta fever.

10. *Flies in Camp.*—In a previous chapter we have discussed fully the various methods of dealing with the breeding places of flies. It is obvious, however, that in camps measures of this kind must be useless, partly because one moves about from place to place, but chiefly because, in open country, flies can travel considerable distances up to about 1,000 yards from their breeding places. The only way, therefore, in which we can lessen the " *fly nuisance*" in camp is by taking measures against the adult insects. This may be done in several ways, either by the use of fly papers, of which the non-poisonous varieties (such as " Tanglefoot ") should be preferred, or by the use of balloon or other traps, baited with syrup or stale beer. A far better method, however, is that recommended by Hermes in 1911 which consists in taking ad-vantage of the fact that flies require large quantities of fluid and usually seek something to drink early in the morning. Taking advantage of our know-ledge of this fact, adult flies may be easily destroyed by making a solution of 2 per cent. of formaldehyde in water and placing about the room saucers or shallow dishes filled with this solution. In order to obtain a 2 per cent. solution of formaldehyde, one teaspoonful of formalin, as obtained from the chemist, should be added to one saucer of water. You must remember that if you allow plenty of other fluid material to remain about, then the flies

cannot be expected to drink the formalin solution.
But, if all other fluids are removed or covered up
in the evening, the flies will greedily drink the
formalin solution in the morning. After doing
this they usually die within a short distance of the
vessel. This solution is non-poisonous for human
beings, and therefore, there is no danger in leaving
it about the house or in placing it on tables in the
vicinity of food. Another simple method has
been described by Howard who states that flies
can be effectively destroyed by mixing half a teaspoonful of powdered black pepper, with one teaspoonful each of brown sugar and of cream. This
should be placed in the room or the tent where flies
are troublesome, whereupon they will quickly
disappear.

The " Fly-fighting," Committee of the American
Civic Association recommends the following :—
" Heat a shovel or similar article and drop thereon
20 drops of carbolic acid. The vapour kills flies."
This is a method which might be adopted in the
house, but it is scarcely likely to be of use for the
destruction of flies in a tent. Some authorities
recommend the fumes created by burning pyrethrum powder. So far as the authors' experience
goes, pyrethrum powder, although it is very useful
for the destruction of mosquitoes, as has been described in a previous chapter, cannot be used in
sufficient concentration in living rooms to make it
effective against flies.

CHAPTER XIV.

HYDROPHOBIA IN THE TROPICS.

" Il ne faut pas se moquer des chiens avant qu'on ne soit hors du bois." —French Proverb.

RABIES, or canine madness, is an acute disease of the central nervous system which occurs chiefly in dogs and allied animals such as the jackal and the wolf. It also occurs, but not so frequently, in cattle, sheep, horses, and deer, as well as in the domestic cat. The poison conveying the disease is undoubtedly a living organism, but it has never yet been seen under the microscope or isolated. The disease is communicable to man and the term *Hydrophobia* should only be used when speaking of the disease in this connection, as the fear of water is not seen in the lower animals whereas it is invariably present in human cases. Infection from animal to animal and from animal to man is conveyed usually by means of bites, but human beings may be infected by being licked by mad animals upon the mucous membrane of the nose or the eye, or upon any portion of the skin where there are sores or abrasions. In Europe, rabies is mostly observed in the dog; in Russia, however, epidemics amongst wolves constitute a serious danger both to other animals and to man, whilst in the tropics some of the worst cases of hydrophobia are due to the bites of mad jackals.

In the body of an animal which has died of rabies the poison of the disease is found in the brain, the spinal cord and the large nerves : also in the salivary glands whence it passes into the saliva, which is the active infecting agent both in biting and in licking. For this reason, it is important to know at what stage of the disease the poison enters the saliva of the infected animal. It has been ascertained experimentally that the saliva never contains the poison earlier than 3 days before the appearance of definite symptoms of the disease. Another point to bear in mind in this connection is that, once symptoms have set in, the infected animal rarely lives longer than from 2 to 4 days. From these two facts we may formulate the following proposition :—

If the biting animal remains alive and well for 10 days after biting a human being, the saliva, at the time the bite was inflicted, cannot have contained the poison of rabies and there is no danger that the person bitten will contract hydrophobia.

In such cases, therefore, there is no necessity for proceeding to a Pasteur Institute for treatment.

In England, rabies was stamped out by the introduction in 1894 of a general muzzling order and by the institution of a strict quarantine of three months for all dogs entering the country, together with further police supervision for another three months. Measures of this kind can be adopted in a comparatively small island like England, but it is almost impossible to adopt similar methods in a large continent, like India, where every village is overrun by large numbers of unowned pariah dogs ; we know, however, that of every eighteen dogs bitten by a rabid animal, only one is likely to develop rabies. This demonstrates the importance of endeavouring to reduce the number of ownerless dogs, which are free to roam at large, for it is evident that the more scattered the dog-population, the less are the chances that the rabid animal will be able to bite a sufficient number of dogs to carry on the infection. The importance of jackals, as a means of infection, is demonstrated by the records of the Pasteur Institute at Kasauli, which show that of 17,500 human beings treated there between the years 1902 and 1912, about 15,000 had been bitten by dogs and 2,500 by jackals ; the remaining cases being due to bites by horses, mules, cats, cows, and buffaloes.

INCUBATION PERIOD.

The incubation period of hydrophobia—that is to say, the interval of time that elapses between the bite of a mad animal and the onset of the earlier symptoms of the disease in the bitten person—is extremely variable. It may be as long as 8 months or more, or as short as 15 days, the average being 40 days. It must be remembered that no symptoms of hydrophobia manifest themselves until the poison has reached the brain and the spinal cord, and has set up certain changes therein. The uncertainty as regards the length of incubation is probably due to two factors :—

(1) the inoculation of varying doses of the poison,

(2) the situation of the bite, *i.e.*, its distance from the brain.

Pasteur considered that the poison travelled along the nerves, and that the nearer the wound was to the brain, the shorter was the path to be traversed by the poison, and consequently the shorter the incubation period. We know, as a matter of fact, that bites on the face are especially dangerous, and that in such cases symptoms develop very quickly, but it must be borne in mind that these are always bites on bare skin ; that they are usually very deep ; and that, as they are caused as a rule by some peculiarly ferocious animal, the bites are frequently multiple. It is very probable then that these three factors, namely, the depth of the bite, the bareness of the skin, and the multiplicity of the bites are of greater importance than the actual situation of the bite or its proximity to the brain. Bites on the bare skin are always more dangerous than bites through the clothing, because, in the latter case, much of the saliva is wiped off the dog's teeth before they penetrate the flesh.

The incubation period of rabies in the dog varies from about 16 days as a minimum to a maximum of 90 days, and in the majority of cases symptoms appear between the 25th and 55th day after the bite. This is the reason why a dog which has been bitten by a rabid animal should be segregated for at least three months and kept under careful observation for another three months as is the rule under the Quarantine Regulations in England.

RABIES IN THE DOG.

There are two forms of rabies :—
  (1) Dumb or paralytic rabies.
  (2) Furious rabies.

The disease, however, is essentially the same in both cases. In the dog the furious form is the more common. Sometimes the animal begins by showing furious symptoms, dying later on in a paralysed state. At other times only paralysis is seen. More rarely the animal may be merely restless and off its food, until a few hours before its death, which is preceded by convulsions. It is an interesting fact that the symptoms vary with the kind of dog. Thus, in pariah dogs and in young puppies, furious symptoms are much more common ; hence human beings are often bitten by dogs of this kind. On the other hand, well-bred, full grown dogs practically never bite human beings. In fact, in the earlier stages of the disease they often exhibit an increased affection towards their masters. It is obvious, therefore, that you may fall into fatal error if you await the development of all the classical signs and symptoms, before you admit that your dog is mad. The symptoms of rabies may be classified under two main heads :—
  (1) Those of brain irritation.
  (2) Those of paralysis.

The earliest symptoms of brain irritation are those of restlessness, hallucinations, fury and convulsions. *Restlessness* is shown by the animal straying away from home or aimlessly wandering about the room and every now and then hiding away in dark corners such as under a sofa, a table, or a bed. *Hallucinations* generally take the form of snapping at imaginary objects, and well-bred dogs often show a symptom which is very characteristic of some human lunatics, namely, a tendency to eat filth. *Fury*, as already stated, varies with the type of dog. In well-bred dogs fury is, as a rule, only vented on its own personal belongings, that is to say, it tears up its bedding ; digs up the surrounding ground ; or bites the chain or the post to which it is attached. Such a dog almost invariably quiets down on the approach of his master, but it may viciously attack other animals, even though it rarely bites human beings. With pariah dogs the case is different. They attack every living creature that may cross their path. *Convulsions* are, as a rule, only apparent in the later stages of the disease after paralysis has set in ; except in young animals, in whom they appear very early and may cause death in a few hours. Besides the symptoms mentioned above, other early signs are :—

(1) fever accompanied with rapid pulse,
(2) dribbling of saliva,
(3) wrinkling of the forehead and eye-brows giving rise to a hunted appearance in the dog's expression.

Paralysis generally follows the symptoms of brain irritation and it is first noticed in the hind legs giving the dog a waddling or dragging gait. This may be preceded or followed by paralysis of the throat. The former is shown by difficulty which the animal has in swallowing, and in such cases the owner very often thinks that a bone has stuck in the dog's throat; and he not infrequently puts his fingers into the animal's mouth in order to extract it. Should such a proceeding appear to be necessary, we strongly recommend the employ-ment of a stout pair of gloves to avoid the risk of infection from contact of the saliva with any sore or abrasion on the fingers. The paralysis of the throat may also be shown by a peculiar alteration in the character of the bark, which becomes hoarse, muffled and deeper in tone than normal. The paralysis of the throat finally extends to the jaw-muscles, and the lower jaw droops. The animal then gradually becomes entirely para-lysed, so that it can neither sit, move nor feel, and it is at this stage that convulsions usually appear and bring the disease to a rapid close.

THE DIAGNOSIS OF RABIES.

The following points are those to which attention should be paid when in doubt as to whether a given dog is, or is not, suffering from rabies :—

(1) The short duration of the disease, usually 2 to 4 days.

(2) The invariable termination of the disease in death.

(3) The snapping at imaginary objects and the copious dribbling of saliva.

(4) The paralysis of the throat-muscles and of the hind limbs.

(5) The number of persons or animals bitten at one and the same time ; especially if the attacks have been made without provocation. This applies more parti-cularly to pariah dogs and puppies.

It will be observed that no mention is made of disinclination to drink water, the reason being that in animals there is practically never any difficulty of this kind until the last stage of the disease when paralysis of the throat-muscles set in and the animal is unable to swallow anything. The supposed special fear of water on the part of a rabid dog is a myth. This is a very important point to bear in mind ; because one so frequently hears people say that they were quite sure that the dog could not have been mad because it was able to drink water. This error has probably arisen from the fact that, when the disease occurs amongst human beings, inability to swallow water is invariably present, and it is on that account that the disease in man is called *Hydrophobia.*

There are several diseases in the dog the symptoms of which may be mistaken for those of rabies. The chief of these are distemper and tetanus or lock-jaw. The former is an acute disease affecting the mucous surfaces of the nose, the eyes, and the throat. It occurs in epidemics especially during the months of October to April. The symptoms commence with high fever and running from the eyes and nose, the discharge being at first watery and later on purulent. There may be also diarrhœa and inflammation of the bowels, with black motions and often the passing of blood and slime as in dysentery. The infection may extend up through the nose to the brain, giving rise to inflammation of that organ, or down the throat into the lungs where it starts a form of pneumonia. It will be seen from this description that the symptoms are very different from those of rabies. Dogs suffering from distemper, moreover, live longer, as a rule, than is the case in rabies. Tetanus, or lock-jaw, s characterised by general spasms all over the body and by rigidity of the jaw-muscles. This latter sign is sufficient to differentiate it from rabies, in which there is paralysis and drooping of the lower jaw instead of rigidity.

To obtain an accurate diagnosis in the case of rabies, it is necessary to send to a Pasteur Institute a portion of the brain of the suspected animal, in order that it may be examined in the laboratory attached to the institution. In former days the laboratory test consisted in the inoculation of rabbits with an emulsion of the brain of the suspected animal in order to see whether or no they developed symptoms of rabies. In those days it was only necessary to send a small portion of the brain in a phial which had been filled with glycerine. Now-a-days, however, the inoculation test has been practically abandoned, and, instead of it, a special microscopical examination is made of the brain with a view to detect the presence of the so-called *Negri bodies*.

The reasons for abandoning the inoculation test were fourfold :—

(1) The incubation period in an inoculated rabbit is very variable. It may be as short as ten days or as long as two months. It fails, therefore, to give the immediate information which is required in order to decide whether or no the bitten person requires the Pasteur treatment.

(2) The poison of rabies is extremely sensitive to heat and when brains have been sent by post over long distances in the plains of India during the hot months, it has frequently been found that the poison has been destroyed before the sample reached the Pasteur Institute, with the result that the inoculation experiment has been negative, though all the symptoms pointed to the fact that the dog had suffered from rabies.

(3) If the brain should become decomposed during transit, the inoculated animal is liable to develop blood-poisoning and die before rabies can show itself. In this way the test is vitiated.

(4) The adoption of the microscopic test renders unnecessary the inoculation of rabbits with the emulsion of the brain of the suspected animal.

The adoption of the microscopical test for the *Negri bodies* has rendered it necessary that very great care should be taken in the packing of the brain which is sent to the Pasteur Institute for examination.

Three points require careful attention in connection with the despatch of the brain, namely, how to remove, how to preserve and how to pack it.

In order to remove the brain from the skull, the first thing to do is to wash the head of the dog with an antiseptic such as carbolic acid, phenyle or some similar disinfectant. Then take a hammer and with a few sharp blows fracture the vault of the skull through the intact skin. The skin is then slit up and turned back ; the pieces of fractured bone removed with a pair of forceps ; the membranes covering the brain incised ; and the brain *divided down the centre into two equal longitudinal halves,* one of which can easily be lifted out by the aid of a knife and a pair of forceps. In performing this operation, the greatest care must be taken to prevent the brain substance or any saliva from coming into contact with the hands, and it is advisable always to wear a pair of leather gloves. It is important to remember that *you must send one longitudinal half of the brain,* and not merely a small portion, as in the case of the old inoculation test. After the brain has been lifted out, it should be placed in a large wide-mouthed bottle, having a capacity of at least two pints, the bottom of which has been covered by a layer of cotton wool. The bottle is then filled with a mixture consisting of one part of commercial formalin to 3 parts of water ; a salt-spoonful of common salt being added to each pint of the fluid. If formalin be not obtainable, then the brain may be packed in rectified spirit or methylated spirit, but the formalin solution is the best. The lid of the jar is now sealed and it is carefully placed in a box with saw-dust. *Inside the box should be placed the name and address of the sender, together with full particulars of the case.* In connection with the test for the discovery of *Negri bodies*, it is important to bear in mind that this is only of value if a positive result is obtained. That is to say, if *Negri bodies* exist in large quantities in the brain, then the animal is certainly suffering from rabies ; but it is not justifiable to conclude that it is not suffering from rabies merely because the *Negri bodies* have not been found. It is on this account that you should never kill a suspected dog unless it is absolutely necessary to do so. Instead of killing it and sending its brain to a Pasteur Institute, it is far better to tie it up and see whether it lives for ten days after the infliction of the bite.

Measures to be Adopted for Animals Bitten by a Rabid Animal.

When the attacking animal develops symptoms of rabies and either dies or is killed, all the animals which it has bitten must be treated on the assumption that they are liable to develop rabies within three months, and even possibly within six months. They must, therefore, be carefully isolated and tied up in the way already recommended. If the bitten animals are not valuable, and especially if there are children in the house, it is better not to run any risk, and to destroy all the animals bitten. As, however, every animal bitten by a rabid dog does not necessarily develop rabies, the owner of a valuable animal may decide to run the risk of keeping it alive. If he does so, it must be remembered that he does so at his own risk and he should bear in mind that he is—morally, if not legally—responsible for any damage done by that animal should it develop rabies at a later date. In this connection it is important to bear in mind that *it is useless to tie up a suspected animal, unless it is carefully watched* and other animals are prevented from approaching it. *Measures which merely prevent the biting of human beings, though of great importance, have no effect in controlling the spread of the disease.*

MEASURES TO BE ADOPTED FOR PERSONS BITTEN BY MAD OR SUSPECTED ANIMALS.

(a) *Treatment of the wound.*—As soon as possible the wound should be well washed, dried, and then thoroughly cauterised. The best agent to employ is pure carbolic acid, but if this cannot be obtained, either permanganate of potash, lunar caustic, or pure nitric acid will do quite well. To thoroughly cauterise a bite, each separate tooth mark must be dealt with in turn, and care must be taken that the caustic actually comes into contact with the sides and penetrates to the very bottom of the wound. It is not necessary to rub the caustic over the skin, or to destroy large areas of the skin round the wound. Cauterisation, however, cannot be absolutely depended upon to remove all chances of infection ; all it does is to destroy a considerable portion of the poison and thereby diminish the quantity left in the wound, thus giving the Pasteur treatment a better chance of success later on.

(b) *The Pasteur treatment for the prevention of hydrophobia.*—After having cauterised the wound, the next point to decide is " Should the bitten person be sent up to a Pasteur Institute ?" If a medical man is available, he should always be consulted and his decision acted upon with promptitude. It not infrequently happens, however, that a person is bitten whilst camping in the jungle or residing in some place where no medical aid or advice is available. For this reason, we give here a few hints which may help you to arrive at a decision in such a case. Here you are face to face with three alternatives :—

(1) The dog is dead.
(2) The dog is unknown.
(3) The dog is still alive and is under observation.

(1) If there be reason for suspecting that the dog was mad, all persons bitten and all persons

licked on definite cuts or abrasions should proceed
at once for treatment to a Pasteur Institute.

(2) If the attack has been unprovoked, it is
better to assume that the dog was mad and to send
up the patient for treatment at once.

(3) Under no circumstances should the dog be
destroyed; it should be tied up and watched. If
the animal remains alive at the end of 10 days,
the saliva cannot have been infective at the time
the bite was inflicted and the bitten person need
have no further fear. If the rabid animal, on the
other hand, dies within ten days, it may be surmised
that it was mad and that the Pasteur treatment
is necessary. In any cases of doubt or difficulty a
detailed telegram should be sent to the Director
of the nearest Pasteur Institute, stating all the
circumstances of the case and asking for advice. In
cases where treatment is not necessary, this may
often save you from the expense and trouble of a
long journey. At the present moment Pasteur
Institutes exist in India at Kasauli, Coonoor, and
Rangoon, and two others will shortly be opened
at Shillong and Bombay.

The Pasteur Treatment.

The object of this treatment is to confer immunity
upon patients by daily doses of an attenuated poison
so that they may be fully protected before the
virulent poison, contained in the wound caused by
the bite, has reached the central nervous system.
Treatment is necessary for a period of 14 days before
full protection is secured. No time, therefore, should
be lost in sending to a Pasteur Institute any person
who has been badly bitten, especially upon the face.
*Once symptoms of hydrophobia have declared themselves,
it is useless to attempt the Pasteur treatment.* Formerly
attenuation was secured by drying or by dilution of
the living poison, but nowadays, thanks to the
experiments of Sir David Semple, we know that it

is unnecessary to use any form of living poison and the treatment consists of the injection of a carbolised emulsion of dead poison which has been killed by heat. During the treatment the patients are not in any way inconvenienced, and not the slightest danger to health need be apprehended. The inoculations do not cause fever and there is no necessity for confinement to the house. During the treatment, however, patients should avoid the use of alcohol, though no restriction is placed on diet. They should also be careful to avoid excessive exercise such as tennis, dancing, etc., and should keep themselves warmly clad in order to avoid chills.

Should any readers require further information as regards the arrangements, etc., at Kasauli, they are recommended to apply to the Director of the Pasteur Institute for a copy of an admirable pamphlet by Captains Acton and Knowles, I.M.S., of which we have made free use in compiling this chapter, and for which we wish to express our acknowledgments to the authors.

INDEX.

A

B

C

U

Underfeeding, 125.

V

Ventilation and air, 48.
,,   of dwelling-houses, 144.
Ventilators, 61.

W

Water and water-supplies in the tropics, 69.
,,   qualities according to source, 71.
,,   pollution of, 79.
,,   purification of, 83.
,,   quantity required in health, 91.
Waterproof fabrics, 130.
Water-supply, 6.
Woollen clothing, 129.

Y

Yellow fever, 35.
,,   ,,   carriers of, 37.

ImTheStory.com

Personalized Classic Books in many genre's

Unique gift for kids, partners, friends, colleagues

Customize:

- Character Names
- Upload your own front/back cover images (optional)
- Inscribe a personal message/dedication on the
  inside page (optional)

Customize many titles Including
- Alice in Wonderland
- Romeo and Juliet
- The Wizard of Oz
- A Christmas Carol
- Dracula
- Dr. Jekyll & Mr. Hyde
- And more...